The Original Constitution
Fourth Edition

THE ORIGINAL CONSTITUTION
Fourth Edition

©2010, 2011, 2015, 2025 by Robert G. Natelson. All rights reserved.

Cover is public domain painting "Signing of the U.S. Constitution" by Junius Brutus Stearns, 1856. Photo restoration by Fiverr user Alpi123.

ISBN: 979-8-9879929-0-6

Printed in the United States of America.

Without limiting the rights under copyright reserved above, no part of this publication may be reproduced, stored in or introduced into a retrieval system, or transmitted, in any form, or by any means (electronic, mechanical, photocopying, recording, or otherwise), without the prior written permission of the copyright owner.

THE ORIGINAL CONSTITUTION
Fourth Edition

Robert G. Natelson

APIS BOOKS

Filiabus Carissimis

CONTENTS

PREFACE
A Tavern in 1791 i
   Evidence for the Original Constitution iii
   Definitions: Framers, Ratifiers, Federalists, Anti-Federalists, Founders, and Congresses iv
   The Structure and Approach of this Book vi
   Additional Details vii
   Acknowledgments viii

CHAPTER ONE
History, Structure, and Preamble 1
   1.1 The Founders' Common Heritage 1
   1.2 Framing, Ratification, and Bill of Rights 3
   1.3 The Founders' Core Political Values 7
   1.4 The Common Legal and Governmental Background 17
   1.5 The Constitution's Structure 19
   1.6 The Preamble 20

CHAPTER TWO
Interpreting the Constitution 23
   2.1 The Founders' Guide: the "Intent of the Makers" 23
   2.2 Finding the "Intent of the Makers": 18th-Century Dictionaries 25
   2.3 Finding the "Intent of the Makers": Reading What the Founders Read 26
   2.4 Finding the "Intent of the Makers"—Learning Latin 26
   2.5 Finding the "Intent of the Makers"—Sharing Their History 27
   2.6 Finding the "Intent of the Makers"—the Rules of Construction 27

2.7 Finding the "Intent of the Makers"—Equitable Construction 30
2.8 Common Errors of Interpretation 31

CHAPTER THREE
The States 35
3.1 The States in the Constitutional System: Compact or Popular Grant? 35
3.2 The States in the Constitutional System: Implied Sovereign Authority? 38
3.3 Differences from the Articles of Confederation 39
3.4 State Powers 40
3.5 State Immunity from Lawsuits and the Eleventh Amendment 42
3.6 Qualifications on State Sovereignty: In General 45
3.7 Qualifications on State Sovereignty: War, Immigration, and Foreign Affairs 45
3.8 Qualifications on State Sovereignty: Foreign Commerce 48
3.9 Qualifications on State Sovereignty: Internal Commerce 50
3.10 Qualifications on State Sovereignty: Promoting Interstate Comity 51
3.11 Qualifications on State Sovereignty: The Ban on Bills of Attainder .. 54
3.12 Qualifications on State Sovereignty: The Ban on Ex Post Facto Laws 55
3.13 Qualifications on State Sovereignty: the Ban on Laws Impairing the Obligation of Contracts 56
3.14 Qualifications on State Sovereignty: The Supremacy Clause 57

CHAPTER FOUR
The House, the Senate, and the Vice President 59
4.1 Organization of Article I 59
4.2 The Two Houses of Congress Were Not Interchangeable 60
4.3 The House of Representatives—In General 61
4.4 The Constitution's Gender Neutrality 64
4.5 "Emoluments" 64
4.6 Special Prerogatives of the House of Representatives 66
4.7 The Senate—In General 70
4.8 Special Prerogatives of the Senate 72
4.9 The Senate's Executive Powers 73
4.10 The Vice President 75

CHAPTER FIVE
About the Grants of Powers to Congress 79
- 5.1 The Enumerated Powers 79
- 5.2 Limitations on Powers 80
- 5.3 Construing Congressional Powers 82
- 5.4 The Fiduciary Nature of Congressional Powers 83
- 5.5 The Necessary and Proper Clause(s) and Congressional Discretion .. 84

CHAPTER SIX
The Authority of Congress 89
- 6.1 Revenue-Raising 89
- 6.2 Borrowing and Spending 93
- 6.3 Congressional Economic Powers: Commerce across Political Lines, Bankruptcy, the Postal Clause, Patents, Copyrights, and Money and Other Weights and Measures 97
- 6.4 Congressional Military Powers 105
- 6.5 Congressional Judicial, Criminal, and Immigration Powers ... 109
- 6.6 Congressional Powers over Federal Land—the Enclave Clause and the Territories and Property Clause 110
- 6.7 Congressional Powers to Promote Concord among the States 115
- 6.8 Congressional Administrative Powers 116

CHAPTER SEVEN
The Executive 121
- 7.1 Introduction 121
- 7.2 Executive Designation Clause or Executive Vesting Clause? ... 122
- 7.3 The Term of the President and Vice President and the Presidential Election Procedure 126
- 7.4 The President's Qualifications, Compensation, and Oath 131
- 7.5 The Enumerated Powers of the President—In General 133
- 7.6 Presidential Powers—Arguably Legislative or Judicial 135
- 7.7 Domestic Executive Powers 138
- 7.8 Military Powers 140
- 7.9 Foreign Affairs and Treaties 141
- 7.10 Limitations on the President 147
- 7.11 The Meaning of "Officers" 148

CHAPTER EIGHT
The Judicial Branch 151
 8.1 Judicial Powers 151
 8.2 Judicial Review 156
 8.3 Limitations on the Judicial Power 157

CHAPTER NINE
The Bill of Rights and Other External Limitations on Federal Powers 161
 9.1 The Unamended Constitution's Protections for Liberty, and the Adoption of the Bill of Rights 161
 9.2 "Good Government" Restrictions... 165
 9.3 Restrictions on Federal Retroactivity: The Article I, Section 9 Ex Post Facto and Attainder Clauses and the Fifth Amendment Takings and Due Process Clauses... 170
 9.4 Protecting "Property" in Slaves 179
 9.5 The First Amendment: Preliminary Comments 180
 9.6 The First Amendment Religion Clauses 181
 9.7 The First Amendment Speech and Press Clauses 182
 9.8 The First Amendment Assembly and Petition Clauses 190
 9.9 The Second and Third Amendments: Health, Hearth, and Home... 192
 9.10 Protections for the Accused—Treason, Habeas Corpus, and the Fourth, Fifth, Sixth and Eighth Amendments 194
 9.11 The Seventh Amendment: Protecting the Common Law Jury 202
 9.12 Application of the Bill of Rights to Military Personnel 203
 9.13 What About Unenumerated Rights?.. 208

CHAPTER TEN
The Ninth and Tenth Amendments 211
 10.1 Review of Some Founding-era Concepts 211
 10.2 The Ninth Amendment 213
 10.3 The Tenth Amendment 217

CHAPTER ELEVEN
Removal from Office 221
 11.1 Removal Following Impeachment and Trial............................ 222
 11.2 Removal of Executive Officers by the President 224

CHAPTER TWELVE
Ratification and Amendment 229
   12.1 Ratification 229
   12.2 Amendment 231

CHAPTER THIRTEEN
Conclusion 237

BIBLIOGRAPHY 245
   General Sources 245
   Chapter One: History, Structure, and Preamble 247
   Chapter Two: Interpreting the Constitution 249
   Chapter Three: The States 250
   Chapter Four: The House, the Senate, and the Vice President 251
   Chapter Five: About the Grants of Powers to Congress 252
   Chapter Six: The Authority of Congress 252
   Chapter Seven: The Executive 253
   Chapter Eight: The Judicial Branch 254
   Chapter Nine: The Bill of Rights and other External Limitations on Federal Powers 254
   Chapter Ten: The Ninth and Tenth Amendments 257
   Chapter Eleven: Removal from Office 257
   Chapter Twelve: Ratification and Amendment 258
   Chapter Thirteen: Conclusion 259

APPENDIX
The Constitution of the United States as of December 15, 1791 261
Articles in Addition to, and in Amendment of, the Constitution of the United States 274

INDEX 279

ABOUT THE AUTHOR 291

The Original Constitution
Fourth Edition

PREFACE

A Tavern in 1791

It is Thursday, December 22, 1791. You live in Philadelphia, then the temporary capital of the newly created United States of America. It has been only fifteen years since Independence was declared, and less than three years since the federal government began functioning under the United States Constitution.

For a long time, it was doubtful whether the Constitution would be ratified at all. Five states approved the document only after the Constitution's supporters and moderate opponents cut a political deal for a Bill of Rights. Two other states, North Carolina and Rhode Island, initially refused to ratify.

Moreover, two of the most important states, Virginia and New York, sought substantial changes in the document and therefore formally applied for a convention for proposing amendments. Only after Congress approved the Bill of Rights did Virginia and New York abandon their applications, and only then did North Carolina and Rhode Island join the Union. The fourteenth state, Vermont, joined early in 1791.

Earlier today, you learned that the Bill of Rights had been ratified a week earlier—on December 15. So now, you reflect, the union seems reasonably secure, evening has come, your work day is done. And you are on a Philadelphia street corner with nothing particular to do. The weather is chilly and blustery, but there is a cure for that: a warm punch in a cozy tavern.

You enter the tavern and look around for a seat. The place is nearly full, but there is bench space at a long wooden table on one side of the room. Sitting around the table are men you recognize, eminently respectable men—some of Philadelphia's leading judges and lawyers. They are deep in debate about an abstruse point of real property law. Not being a lawyer yourself, you do not think that topic is the key to a good time. But there are no other seats.

You slip onto the bench and order your punch while the talk swirls around your head. Eventually, you decide to turn the conversation elsewhere. You give a little cough.

The lawyers had barely noticed you, but now they turn their heads and break off the debate. "I regret that I feel unqualified to comment on your subject," you say. "But, gentlemen, you know I am not a lawyer. May I suggest another topic?"

They seem interested. The prior discussion had been wearing thin anyway. "You no doubt have observed," you continue, "that ten new constitutional amendments were proclaimed last week."

"Yes," responds one of your listeners. (You know him to be a distinguished judge.) "They should work some change upon the system."

"That is exactly what I wished to pursue," you say. "What is that system? And what change does the Bill of Rights effect upon it?"

The lawyers look at one another. One of them—an expert in wills and fiduciary trusts—smiles. "Well, my friend, that is an expansive inquiry whose response might consume some time. Are you otherwise engaged for the next few hours?"

The others laugh, but you press your question. It is only seven o'clock, your spouse has gone to Carlyle to visit relatives, and you have no other plans. Neither are you particularly eager to leave the warm tavern.

"I am at complete leisure," you respond. "Please, say on."

The lawyers glance at each other. "Well, why not?" asks one. "As it happens, we are not engaged either. The courts are closed tomorrow, and our wives are enjoying the comfort of each other's society. I dare say they have no present need of us!" More laughter.

"I think I can speak for my learned colleagues here," the trust attorney interjects, "when I tell you that there is no topic on which we would rather discourse than our new Constitution. We have exchanged views on this subject before, and we differ on the small points. But I flatter myself that we are in accord on the great ones."

You are amused at how easy it is to induce lawyers to talk. You draw deep from the warm punch and sit back and listen.

* * *

What would those lawyers have told you that evening? How would they interpret the scope of the new federal government and its powers? What would they say of the role of the states or of the people? What, in other words, was the legal effect of our Constitution as lawyers and informed lay people understood it in 1791?

This book answers those questions.

Evidence for the Original Constitution

A common mistake about the Constitution is that it is a simple document, and that to understand it you need only read it. But that's not true. It's just not.

The Constitution is written in 18th-century English, which was somewhat different from modern English. Some apparently ordinary words in the document have changed meaning. Furthermore, the Constitution contains many technical legal terms—some of which you might not recognize as technical legal terms (such "Office under the United States" and "necessary and proper"). It is true that the Framers tried to make the Constitution understandable to the American public. But that public spoke 18th-century English and was unusually knowledgeable about 18th-century law.

For this reason, those interested in the Constitution frequently consult outside sources. Traditionally, most people have limited themselves to scholars call the "standard sources." These include the notes of the 1787 federal convention, the debates in the state ratifying conventions, *The Federalist*, William Blackstone's legal commentaries, and a few other items.

For resolving some questions, however, the standard sources are not sufficient. So professionals also consult a range of other sources:

- Histories, sermons, literature and other written materials popular among the founding generation.
- 18th-century law books, dictionaries, and other reference works.
- Collections specifically relevant to the Constitution, especially the Documentary History of the Ratification of the Constitution and the Bill of Rights, the Documentary History of the First Federal Congress, and Herbert Storing's The Complete Anti-Federalist.
- Computer databases such as Google Books, the National Archives' *Founders Online*, and Gale's *Eighteenth Century Collections Online*.

In composing this book, I have used all these materials and many more, and I am grateful to the people who made them available. Readers who would like to know more about such materials may consult my essay, *A Bibliography for Researching the Original Understanding*, https://i2i.org/wp-content/uploads/Originalist-Bibliography-2016-0930.pdf.

Definitions: Framers, Ratifiers, Federalists, Anti-Federalists, Founders, and Congresses

This book refers frequently to the views, goals, methods, and comments of the people who wrote, debated, and adopted the Constitution and the Bill of Rights. The *Framers* were the fifty-five men who drafted the Constitution at the federal convention in Philadelphia between May 25 and September 17, 1787. The *Ratifiers* were the approximately 1641 delegates at the state ratifying conventions held between late 1787 and May 29, 1790.[1] The *Federalists* were participants in the public ratification debates who argued for adopting the Constitution. History

---

[1] The figure is based on the number of votes cast for or against ratification. The actual number was somewhat higher for two reasons: (1) Some delegates did not vote, either by choice or because of ill-health or death and (2) the figure excludes those delegates who attended the first North Carolina convention (held at Hillsboro) but not the second convention (held at Fayetteville) where the ratification vote was taken.

In addition, there were 109 delegates to the Vermont ratifying convention. Vermont was not initially part of the United States but joined the Union with its ratification of the Constitution on January 10, 1791

has (unfairly) labeled their opponents *Anti-Federalists*. The *Founders* were all those who played significant roles in the constitutional process, whether they were Framers, Ratifiers, Federalists, or Anti-Federalists. Although the Framers and Ratifiers were all male, the Founders were not. Women such as Mercy Otis Warren, an important Anti-Federalist writer (and later a leading historian), helped shape public opinion about the Constitution.

Also among the Founders were the members of the Confederation Congress (1781–89) and the members of the initial session of the first Federal Congress (1789). That session drafted the Bill of Rights and debated and resolved several constitutional issues while North Carolina and Rhode Island were still weighing whether to join the Union, and while Virginia and New York were pushing for constitutional amendments.

Many Founders fit into more than one category. For example, James Madison and Alexander Hamilton were Framers, Ratifiers, and leading Federalists. John Jay, who served the Confederation as Secretary for Foreign Affairs, did not attend the constitutional convention, so he was not a Framer. But he did serve as a delegate to the New York State ratifying convention, and he wrote some of the essays in *The Federalist* (also called *The Federalist Papers*) urging that the Constitution be approved. Jay was therefore a Ratifier and a Federalist as well as a Founder. Elbridge Gerry of Massachusetts actively participated in the federal convention, but publicly opposed the final result, so he was a Framer and an Anti-Federalist. He was not a Ratifier, but he did play a prominent role in the first Federal Congress. Like Gerry, George Mason was a Framer and an Anti-Federalist. He also was a delegate at the Virginia ratifying convention, and therefore a Ratifier.

In this book, the phrase *founding generation* means the entire involved populace—Framers, Ratifiers, Federalists, Anti-Federalists, Founders, and anyone else participating formally or informally in the great national debate over ratification.

The word *Congress* originally denoted a gathering of diplomats from separate sovereignties. During the 18th century, conventions of representatives from different colonies or states were frequently denoted "congresses." Thus, in 1765, commissioners from nine colonies met in the *Stamp Act Congress* to deliberate on how to respond to Parliament's adoption of the Stamp Act. British pressure was further resisted by the *First Continental Congress*, a gathering of 12 colonies that met from September 5 to October 26, 1774. Continued resistance to Great Britain was coordinated by the 13-member *Second Continental Congress*, which convened on May 10, 1775 and continued to hold sessions until March 1, 1781.

The only authority for any of these three gatherings came from the commissions the individual colonies or states gave their delegates.

The Second Continental Congress issued the Declaration of Independence, and drafted a treaty for the 13 new states called the Articles of Confederation. (The status of the Articles as a mere treaty rather than a constitution is explained in Section 3.3.) The Articles became effective on March 1, 1781, and the Second Continental Congress dissolved into the *Confederation Congress*.[2] The latter continued until it permanently lost its quorum after October 10, 1788. A hiatus followed in which full sovereignty presumably returned to the states. It was not until April, 1789 that the legislature authorized by the Constitution convened with a quorum. It is known as the *First Federal Congress*.

The Structure and Approach of this Book

Our lawyer friends in the Philadelphia tavern probably would not explain the Constitution clause by clause. It is more efficient to approach the subject by general topic. We shall begin by surveying history and values shared by the founding generation—material everyone knew about in 1791 but unfamiliar to most modern readers—and then will proceed by theme.

For example, one chapter examines the role of the states in the federal system. Another addresses Congress's enumerated (listed) powers, no matter where in the Constitution they appear. Still another discusses the executive branch. Because we are speaking of the Constitution as it stood in late 1791, the book generally uses the past tense. This also reminds you that the content does not necessarily reflect constitutional law as the courts apply it today.

I recognize that some claim it is impossible to reconstruct the original Constitution. However, competent Founding-era scholars largely agree on the meaning of most of the document's terms. Where there are areas of uncertainty, I have flagged them.

---

[2] Some writers incorrectly label the Confederation Congress as the Continental Congress.

Unlike most constitutional writing these days, this book is not a work of advocacy. In reconstructing the meaning of the original Constitution, I have tried to be as objective as possible, whether I liked the results or not.

Additional Details

Identifying the Constitution's Clauses: Lawyers tag particular phrases in the Constitution as named "clauses," whether or not they qualify as clauses grammatically. For example, the General Welfare Clause is a part of the larger formal Taxation Clause (Article I, Section 8, Clause 1) and the Indian Commerce Clause is just a few words in the larger Commerce Clause (Article I, Section 8, Clause 3).

Some clause names (such as the Commerce Clause) are standardized. Others are not. For example, Article I, Section 8, Clause 15 has been called both the "Militia Clause" and the "Calling Forth Clause." In cases of doubt, I generally conform to the *Heritage Guide to the Constitution*, to which I am a contributor.

About footnotes: This book is primarily for the layperson, so I've avoided the dense footnoting typical of scholarly publications. Many of the footnotes are either cross-references to other sections of the book or references to the part of the Constitution being discussed. Fully-footnoted academic studies supporting the text are in the chapter-by-chapter bibliography.

Abbreviations. Following are abbreviations of reference works cited throughout this book:

Documentary History: The Documentary History of the Ratification of the Constitution and the Bill of Rights (Merrill Jensen et al. eds., 1976-present).

DeLolme: Jean Louis (J.L.) DeLolme, The Constitution of England (4th ed. 1784) (re-issued, David Lieberman, ed., 2007).

Farrand: The Records of the Federal Convention of 1787 (Max Farrand ed., 1937).

Farrand-Supp.: Supplement to Max Farrand's The Records of the Federal Convention of 1787 (James H. Hutson, ed. 1987).

Maclay: The Diary of William Maclay, in 9 Documentary History of the First Federal Congress of the United States (Johns Hopkins Univ. Press 1988).

<u>Vattel</u>: Emer de Vattel, The Law of Nations (Knud Haakonssen ed., 2008) (originally published, 1758) (the author's first name sometimes is reported mistakenly as "Emmerich").

Acknowledgments

I'd like to thank my wife, Elizabeth J. Natelson, and my late parents, Sydney and Florence A. Natelson, for their unbounded assistance. I also I owe much to the clients who supported me when I was in law practice and to the citizens and taxpayers who supported me, both financially and politically, during my subsequent academic career.

Also of great help were many conscientious and intelligent librarians, particularly at the University of Montana and the University of Colorado, at the Bodleian Law Library and the Codrington Library at the University of Oxford, at London's Middle Temple, and at the Library of Virginia. Since leaving academia in 2010, I also have benefited from support from the Independence Institute and Citizens for Self-Governance, both of which provided me with untrammeled academic freedom.

CHAPTER ONE

History, Structure, and Preamble

1.1 The Founders' Common Heritage

The Founders shared a common heritage. In 1787, a plurality of Americans were of British extraction, although there were notable minorities, including Germans, Dutch, American Indians and African-Americans. Most of the Framers had been born in the thirteen colonies, and all had been born under the British flag. Nearly all the other Founders had been British subjects before 1776, and a significant number had been educated in Britain.

British history—especially its English[1] and American branches—included a long tradition of crafting documents of constitutional importance. The tradition began with a charter issued by King Henry I in 1100. It continued with Magna Carta (1215),[2] the Petition of Right (1628),

---

[1] England, Scotland, and Wales occupy the island of Great Britain. The United Kingdom consists of those three plus the province of Northern Ireland.

[2] Magna Carta (Medieval Latin for "Great Charter") is the most important of all Anglo-American constitutional documents. It was extracted from King John by English barons under the guidance of Stephen Langton, Archbishop of Canterbury. Magna Carta guaranteed a range of civic benefits—not just for barons, but for freemen, women, and unfree agricultural laborers. Its provisions fore-

a short-lived constitution called the Instrument of Government (1653), a second short-lived constitution called the Humble Petition and Advice (1657), the Habeas Corpus Act (1679), and the English Bill of Rights (1689). In America, the mileposts included the colonial charters, the commissions and other instructions from the Crown to colonial governors, the Mayflower Compact (1620), the Fundamental Orders of Connecticut (1639), the Massachusetts Charter of Rights and Liberties (1641), the constitutions of eleven newly independent states[3] (plus Vermont), the Virginia Declaration of Rights (1776), and the Articles of Confederation (1781).

As the Founders recognized, this constitutional tradition was unique. While many civilized peoples had committed law to writing, the Anglo-American constitutional tradition imposed law not merely on ordinary people, but also on government. Constitutional documents obliged political actors to follow rules that protected individual liberty and produced better social results.

Throughout the Founding era, American leaders repeatedly mined the British legal and constitutional tradition. For example, the structure of the Declaration of Independence owed much to the English Bill of Rights.

The Anglo-American tradition included education in the classical writings of ancient Greece and Rome. It also encompassed the theory of "mixed" government reflected to a greater or lesser extent in the governments of all 14 states (the 13 United States plus Vermont). When writing and discussing the Constitution, the Founders operated within the context of Anglo-American law.

The Founders also were influenced by certain beliefs and values[4] held

---

shadowed trial by jury, due process, compensation for takings, and freedom to travel. As explained by the 17th-century legal scholar Edward Coke, it greatly influenced the Founders. Parts of Magna Carta are still law in England today.

[3] Two states, Rhode Island and Connecticut, continued to operate under modified versions of their colonial charters.

[4] But the Founders were not cookie-cutter people, and some were outside the mainstream. One example was Noah Webster, who later compiled Webster's dictionary. Unlike most members of the founding generation, Webster believed that:

by those Britons known as "radical Whigs."[5] Among those beliefs was that God had established a natural law for mankind as laid out by John Locke and similar philosophers—the theory incorporated into the Declaration of Independence. From natural law theory, the Founders deduced the principles that should control government, and the values government should serve. Section 1.3 further discusses those principles and values.

The most recent part of the Founders' common heritage was their participation in the political contest that led to the American Revolution, the Revolution itself, and the unsettled period between Revolution and ratification.

1.2 Framing, Ratification, and Bill of Rights

When English political leaders deemed major changes necessary, they sometimes called *conventions* through which delegates acting in the name of the people retook political power and arranged ("constituted") affairs anew. Under the influence of these precedents,[6] American colonial

---

- Government was based on necessity and utility rather than compact, Noah Webster, A Collection of Essays and Fugitiv [sic] Writings 56 & 66 (1790);
- An elected legislature had absolute power, including power to change a constitution, (*id.* 38, 45, 49–58, 61);
- The federal Constitution was a mere pact among states (*id.* 58); and
- "Liberty of the press" protected obscene and blasphemous writings (*id.* 145).

On other important points, Webster agreed with most of the other Founders.

[5] In the 18th century, British political life was defined in part by the division between Whigs and Tories. In general (there were many exceptions), Tories defended the prerogatives of the Crown while Whigs defended the prerogatives of the House of Commons. Whigs and Tories were split into factions. The term "radical Whigs" referred to the most democratic and egalitarian Whigs. Almost all American political leaders were Whigs; Americans branded as "Tories" usually were really conservative Whigs. In the 19th century, the Whig and Tory factions became the British Liberal and Conservative Parties.

[6] James Wilson, a member of the Continental Congress, listed three English conventions: the assembly of barons that forced King John to adopt Magna Carta (1215), the "convention parliament" that recalled Charles II (1660), and the "convention parliament" that awarded the crown to William and Mary and

leaders occasionally held conventions within individual colonies. Colonial governments also sent representatives (called "delegates," "deputies," or, more formally, "commissioners") to inter-colonial conventions to discuss common problems. In the years before 1776, over 20 inter-colonial conventions were held; and in the years 1777–87, another 11 interstate ones.

One of these gatherings was the Annapolis Convention of 1786, a meeting of five states to consider granting Congress more power over commerce. The Annapolis commissioners adopted a resolution asking their home states to call yet another convention to address more generally the deficiencies in the American political system. This led to a call from Virginia later that year and a positive response from seven states. In February, 1787, the Confederation Congress issued a tepid endorsement (which some writers mistake for the convention call), after which five more states agreed to participate.

Accordingly, between May 25 and September 17, 1787, 55 commissioners from 12 states met in Philadelphia and drafted a new Constitution. As explained below, nearly all the commissioners had full authority to do this; the common claim that they exceeded their powers is not accurate.

Most of the commissioners were present for substantially the entire time. Some, such as Alexander Hamilton, were absent for extended periods, but still contributed significantly. Others, such as Hamilton's New York colleague Robert Yates, participated for several weeks, but then went home when they saw that the final product would not be one they could support. George Wythe of Virginia, a leading legal scholar, law professor, and judge, remained only for a few productive days. Notified of his wife's fatal illness, Wythe returned home to be with her. He later chaired the committee of the whole at the Virginia ratifying convention.

George Washington, also of Virginia, was convention president. However, much of the debate took place in the Committee of the Whole, where Nathaniel Gorham of Massachusetts, a former president of Congress, presided. The proceedings were kept secret, but there was an official journal and several commissioners took notes. The most copious notes were those of Virginia's James Madison.

---

secured the English Bill of Rights (1688–1689). 4 J. Cont. Cong. 137 (Feb. 13, 1776).

On the day of adjournment (September 17), 41 commissioners were still present. John Dickinson of Delaware had just left because of illness, but he had his colleague George Reed sign the Constitution for him. Only three of the commissioners still present refused to sign: Elbridge Gerry of Massachusetts (who, unlike most delegates, could plead lack of authority) and Virginia's George Mason and Edmund Randolph.

Although the commissioners were acting under their states' reserved powers and not under the Articles of Confederation, as a courtesy they transmitted the Constitution to the Confederation Congress. Congress decided it had no authority to endorse the document, but submitted it to the states for ratification. At least some members of Congress interpreted this as a tacit endorsement.[7]

Once the Constitution's terms became known, a storm of opposition arose. There were many reasons for this opposition, but by far the most important was the fear that the Constitution would create a central authority too powerful to be consistent with federalism or liberty.

Nevertheless, the Delaware legislature quickly called an in-state ratifying convention, which by a unanimous vote on December 7, 1797, became the first to endorse the Constitution. The next convention to ratify was that of Pennsylvania, but the majority endorsed the Constitution only after Federalists explained the meaning of crucial words and phrases. These explanations served to reassure listeners that the document would erect only a limited and relatively democratic government rather than the all-powerful oligarchy the Anti-Federalists feared. Federalist explanations in Pennsylvania and in other states remain highly useful for constitutional interpretation.

Next, conventions in New Jersey and Georgia ratified unanimously. But in Connecticut, ratification came only after Federalists made further representations as to the Constitution's meaning. The Connecticut representations were broadly consistent with those in Pennsylvania.

In Massachusetts, the vote was close. The Federalists prevailed only after issuing representations similar to those made earlier and promising to support a Bill of Rights once the Constitution was adopted.

Next, Maryland ratified by a wide margin. But all subsequent ratifi-

---

[7] Robert G. Natelson, *Did Congress Approve the Constitution? A Member's Letter Says "Yes,"* https://i2i.org/did-congress-approve-the-constitution-a-members-letter-says-yes/ (2016).

cations—South Carolina, New Hampshire, Virginia, New York, North Carolina, and Rhode Island—came only after further Federalist representations of constitutional meaning and the promise of a Bill of Rights.[8]

After 11 states had ratified, the Confederation Congress set the agenda for establishing the new government. Congress fixed January 7, 1789 for appointment of presidential electors, February 4 as the day the electors would vote for President, and March 4 as the day the government would begin operations in New York City.[9] The government remained in New York until December, 1790, when it relocated to Philadelphia. It moved to Washington, D.C. in 1800.

In accordance with Federalist promises, on June 8, 1789, Congressman James Madison introduced his proposed bill of rights in the House of Representatives. Variations of most of Madison's proposals eventually passed both houses in the form of twelve proposed amendments. The requisite number of states ratified ten of the twelve.[10]

Like other constitutional instruments in the Anglo-American tradition, the federal Constitution consisted largely of rules to bind politicians. Forrest McDonald, a leading 20th-century constitutional historian, observed that, "The main body of the Constitution, more than two-thirds of it, addresses the task of making government act in accordance with law."[11] Thus, the Constitution denied officeholders the power to alter it as they could alter other law. As Elbridge Gerry—former federal convention commissioner and later Vice President—explained to his colleagues in the First Federal Congress: "The people of America can never be safe,

---

[8] Vermont was not part of the United States until after its convention ratified the Constitution on January 10, 1791. By then, Congress already had proposed a Bill of Rights, so there was no need for the convention to demand one.

[9] 34 J. Cont. Cong. 522–23 (Sep. 13, 1788). The source of Congress's authority to fix these dates is not clear. However, decisions necessary to jumpstart a newly authorized entity often are made informally, as when a new legislature or convention chooses temporary officers. The Federal House of Representatives obtained a quorum on April 1, 1789, and the Senate on April 6.

[10] One of the other two proposed amendments was finally ratified, as the Twenty-Seventh, in 1992.

[11] Forrest McDonald, *Preface*, in M.E. Bradford, Original Intentions on the Making and Ratification of the United States Constitution, xii (U. Ga. Press 1993).

if Congress have a right to exercise the power of giving constructions to the constitution different from the original instrument."

1.3 The Founders' Core Political Values

With rare exceptions, the Founders—Federalists and Anti-Federalists alike—accepted certain common political values. The Federalists and Anti-Federalists differed primarily in the weight they gave to each value and how well they thought the Constitution would preserve and promote them. Those who thought the Constitution would further common values tended to be Federalists. Those who thought the Constitution would subvert them tended to be Anti-Federalists. But all agreed that the nation's basic law should be structured to further those common values.

They can be summarized as follows:

- Liberty, in the sense of Lockean natural rights
- Effective government
- Republican government
- Decentralization
- Fiduciary government

We shall consider each in turn.

1.3.1 Natural Rights: Liberty and Locke

The Constitution, unlike the Declaration of Independence, did not discuss natural rights explicitly. Nevertheless, the Constitution was influenced heavily by the theory of natural rights propounded by John Locke and repeated endlessly in Whig political writings. The first step to understanding this theory is to understand that Locke and the founding generation gave a broader scope to word "right" than we do today. When we think of an individual right, we usually think of immunity from government interference with some activity we choose to undertake. Thus, when we refer to the right of free speech, we usually mean we are immune from punishment for speaking our minds. When we refer to our right to property, we usually mean that government may not take our property from us.

During the Founding era, however, the term "right" also could mean a power or prerogative.[12] This usage paralleled closely the Latin equivalent—*jus*—a word with an array of meanings, including power or prerogative. Such parallel English/Latin uses were common at a time when learned men regularly read, thought, and composed in both languages.

According to Locke (at least as interpreted by the founding generation), God bestowed certain powers upon individuals, which Locke and the Founders usually called "rights."[13] In a primitive state of nature, a person's rights or powers included all those actions of which he or she was capable. These included self-defense, providing for oneself and one's family, and being able to affect others for good or for ill. They also included the more mundane choices of daily life, such as whether to wear a hat and what time to get up in the morning. The number of rights/powers was limitless.

Early in human development (Locke wrote), people left the state of nature and entered into society. When doing so, they voluntarily conveyed to a central authority some of their natural rights/powers for the better preservation of the remainder. In particular, they "alienated" (transferred) to government rights/powers to initiate force against others and otherwise to harm others. The government thereby amassed a pool of power that enabled it to keep the peace and protect the rights remain-

---

[12] For example, the 1786 edition of Samuel Johnson's English dictionary included among the definition of "right" the following: "just claim," "that which justly belongs to one," "property, interest," "power, prerogative," and "immunity, privilege."

[13] Theophilus Parsons, a prominent Massachusetts ratifier and later his state's chief justice, explained the usage this way:

> The rights [people] possess at their birth are equal, and of the same kind. Some of those rights are alienable, and may be parted with for an equivalent. Others are inalienable and inherent, and of that importance, that no equivalent can be received in exchange. Sometimes we shall mention the surrendering of a power to controul [*sic*] our natural rights, which perhaps is speaking with more precision, than when we use the express parting with natural rights—but the same thing is intended.

Theophilus Parsons, *The Essex Result,* in 1 American Political Writing During the Founding Era 1760–1805, p. 487 (Charles S. Hyneman & Donald S. Lutz, eds., 1983).

ing in the people.

Although the exact powers/rights given to government varied with the society, there were some that were so central to liberty that they could not justifiably be given away. These were rights that were inalienable or unalienable, which means "not transferable." It was particularly important that government protect individuals' enjoyment of inalienable rights. These rights included such things as the preservation of one's life; locomotion; freedom to pursue a vocation; freedom to acquire, use, and transfer property; and freedom to engage in expressive activities, such as speech, art, and the free exercise of religion—so long as doing so did not impair others in the exercise of their own rights.

Among the people's reserved rights was the *censorial power*. In the language of the time, to "censure" was to judge or express an opinion on something, not necessarily in a negative way. Jean Louis DeLolme, a Swiss attorney who wrote an influential book on the English constitution, described the censorial power as "the province [domain] of openly canvassing and arraigning the conduct of those who are invested with any branch of public authority"[14] and of exposing their actions to public view.

Some governments lodged the censorial power partly in magistrates. The ancient Roman censor was an official elected every five years, whose duties included correcting problems that impeded the proper operation of the government. The constitutions of Pennsylvania and Vermont adopted in the 1770s each provided for a council of censors to be elected every seven years to inquire as to whether the state constitution was being followed, to order impeachments, and to recommend reforms.

However, DeLolme recommended that the people reserve the entire censorial power. This left the people with freedom to petition, freedom of speech, and freedom of the press.[15] By exercising these powers, the people and press could motivate electors and shame erring public officials

---

[14] DeLolme, p. 201.

[15] James Madison also referred to freedom of the press as a branch of the censorial power. DeLolme did not mention freedom of speech explicitly, but it is clear that he viewed it as part of the censorial power. *Cf.* John Trenchard & Thomas Gordon, Cato's Letters 110–11 (Liberty Fund 1995) (describing the censorial power in an essay on freedom of speech).

into doing the right thing.[16]

The upshot of the Founders' philosophy was that in a proper society, the people retained at least their inalienable rights, and their government protected them in the enjoyment of those rights. This system secured an expansive field of personal liberty for individuals and private associations.

1.3.2 Effective Government

Nearly everyone participating in the constitutional debates of 1787–91—irrespective of whether he or she supported the Constitution—believed government under the Articles of Confederation had been insufficiently effective. There was a wide consensus that the central authority needed to be strengthened. In Founding-era discourse, effectiveness in government usually was called "energy in government." A central feature of the Constitution's plan for promoting effective government was the power to tax and regulate individuals directly. The new government would not have to rely on the states for revenue or for enforcement of federal laws.

1.3.3 Republican Government

Although the Founders had grown up under a monarchy, by the end of the Revolutionary War, nearly all agreed that American governments should be republican. However, it is difficult to fix a firm Founding-era definition of "republican." Dictionary definitions differed somewhat, and the Founders did not always agree on the precise contours of the term. For example, most of the participants in the constitutional debates who addressed the subject thought a republic could include an aristocracy (as did the Roman and Dutch republics), but some believed aristocracy was inconsistent with republicanism. That may be why the Constitution resolved the question by forbidding states from awarding titles of nobility as well as from adopting non-republican forms of government.

On the other hand, there were some clear points of agreement about what republicanism meant. Nearly everyone agreed that a government

---

[16] The First Continental Congress closely followed DeLolme when it stated that, through freedom of the press "oppressive officers are shamed or intimidated, into more honorable and just modes of conducting affairs." 1 J. Cont. Cong. 108 (Oct. 25, 1774).

was not a republic if it included a king.[17] Everyone agreed that to be republican, a government must follow the rule of law and be ultimately responsible to the electorate for its decisions. However, ultimate responsibility to the electorate did not mean that a republic was necessarily a democracy in the modern sense—that is, with a widely enfranchised populace that can sacrifice minority interests readily in the pursuit of the perceived common good. The Founders believed that their state and federal republics should limit short-run democratic governance to promote wise decision making, individual liberty, and democratic governance in the long run. For this reason, the Constitution took certain decisions out of the hands of the majority, at least until the document was duly amended.

Some of the Founders believed that republics could survive only if the citizenry was virtuous. They argued that government should ban immoral practices and promote religion. The Constitution reflected this view to the extent that it forbade the states from enacting some laws, such as tender laws,[18] which were seen as inconsistent with republican virtue. However, the Founders left most issues of religion and morality to the states.

1.3.4 Decentralized Government (Federalism)

Some of the Framers would have preferred a constitution that rendered the states largely subordinate to the central authority, much as counties are subordinate to state government. Throughout May, June, and early July of 1787, the federal convention was headed in that direction.

But for reasons not entirely clear, the tide turned in mid-July. The convention began to defeat proposals that strengthened the central government and to adopt proposals that retained strong states. The final result was a decentralized system in which the central authority would enjoy only limited powers. Perhaps the Framers changed course because they recognized that the public would reject the Constitution if the document did not protect the coordinate authority of the states. Indeed,

---

[17] John Adams was alone in maintaining that England qualified as a "republic" because of popular representation in the House of Commons.

[18] Section 3.9.

even with the changes incorporated during the convention's final weeks, the public almost rejected the Constitution as too centralizing. To secure ratification, the Constitution's advocates had to agree to amendments further limiting federal prerogatives.

Some have argued that the Constitution's provisions for decentralization should receive little respect because they resulted not from the Framers' will, but from concessions to political reality. However, the Framers did not convert the document into law; the Ratifiers chosen by the people in each state did. The political reality, in other words, was the choice of the founding generation as a whole: Americans wanted, to the extent possible, to be governed close to home if they were to be governed at all.

This decision made sense. Decentralization offered greater access to government for the average citizen, and rendered government by a national aristocracy much less likely. Decentralization enabled different states to respond to the preferences and cultures of local majorities. It enabled states to experiment with different policies and to compete for citizens and businesses. Because state government was closer to the people, it usually enjoyed better information about the people's abilities and needs, and its officers identified more closely with them.

1.3.5   Fiduciary Government—"Public Trust"

On July 28, 1788 in Hillsborough, North Carolina, the state's ratifying convention was in session. James Iredell, North Carolina's most respected lawyer (destined to serve on the U.S. Supreme Court), rose to answer claims that the Constitution would grant the federal government powers beyond those enumerated:

> [The Constitution] is a declaration of particular powers by the people to their representatives, for particular purposes. It may be considered as a great power of attorney, under which no power can be exercised but what is expressly[19] given. Did any man ever hear, before, that at the end of a power of attorney it was said that the attorney should not exercise more power than was there

---

[19] The word "expressly" in this context probably meant "clearly," and did not necessarily exclude implied powers. See Section 10.3.

given him? Suppose, for instance, a man had lands in the counties of Anson and Caswell, and he should give another a power of attorney to sell his lands in Anson, would the other have any authority to sell the lands in Caswell?—or could he, without absurdity, say, "'Tis true you have not expressly authorized me to sell the lands in Caswell; but as you had lands there, and did not say I should not, I thought I might as well sell those lands as the other."[20]

A *power of attorney*—or, as it was often known then, a letter of attorney—was (and is) a legal document, usually notarized, by which a person entrusts all or some of his affairs to another. The word "attorney" in this context does not mean an attorney at law, but an "attorney in fact"—a kind of agent.[21]

The power of attorney was only one of many kinds of legal documents by which persons granted authority to others. Additional power-granting documents included corporate charters, trusts, and real-estate-management agreements. In the 18th century, power-granting documents probably were more familiar to the average person than they are today.

As Iredell pointed out, the Constitution was largely a power-granting document by which "We the People" bestowed authority. They bestowed authority on Congress, the President, and the judiciary. They assigned specific tasks and powers to state legislatures and state governors. They granted authority to persons who were not part of any government at all: presidential electors, convention delegates, federal jurors, and voters in congressional elections. (Modern courts refer to constitutional powers granted to persons and entities outside the U.S. government as "federal functions.")[22] Finally, the Constitution granted a few powers to "the

---

[20] 30 Documentary History, p. 360. Other Federalists also used the power of attorney analogy. William Cushing, Undelivered Speech in the Massachusetts Convention, c. Feb. 4, 1788, in 38 *id.*, pp. 288, 289; "Giles Hickory" (Noah Webster), N.Y. Mag. Mar. 1, 1788, in *id.*, pp. 345, 356

[21] To *attorn* is an old word for turning over some business to someone. The person who turns it over is, therefore, an attornor, and the person to whom it is attorned is an attornee (attorney).

[22] See bibliography to this chapter.

United States," meaning the government as a whole.[23]

These grants took several forms. The most common was a straightforward formula, such as "The Congress shall have Power to . . ." Other grants took the form of obligations, such as the Article II mandate that the President "shall take care that the Laws be faithfully executed," the Article IV mandate that the United States guarantee each state a republican form of government, and the Article VI requirement that Confederation-era debts and other obligations be honored. These are power grants because when a principal lays an obligation on an agent, the principal authorizes the agent to fulfill the obligation.

In private life, when one person delegates power to another, the two are said to be in a *fiduciary* relationship. The word "fiduciary" is related to "faith" and "fidelity." It is a legal term that refers to the special obligations one assumes when one manages the property and affairs of another. An agent is a fiduciary. So are trustees, corporate directors, guardians, property managers, the executors of wills, and administrators of the estates of persons not leaving a will. The person for whom a fiduciary acts often is called the *principal*.

For many years before the Constitution was adopted, the idea prevailed both in Britain and America that government should be a fiduciary enterprise.[24] Participants in the constitutional debates often referred to government officials as the people's "agents," "trustees," "servants," or "guardians." The Founders believed that public officials were, or should be, fiduciaries and bound by the standards traditionally imposed on fiduciaries.

Those standards were fairly similar to those prevailing today. They were, and still are, considerably stricter than the legal standards otherwise applied to daily life. Some obligations of fiduciaries were:

---

[23] *Id.*

[24] The concept of public office as a fiduciary enterprise is traceable to Socrates. Aristotle and Roman Stoic writers such as Cicero and Seneca developed the concept further. It passed through medieval and early modern writers on religion, such as John Calvin, to the 16th-century Scottish Presbyterian humanist, George Buchanan. Calvin's and Buchanan's co-religionists—the Puritans—popularized the concept and brought it to America.

- To obey any instructions given them, and therefore to honor any limits imposed on their power;
- To act in a manner loyal to the interests of those they work for, and therefore to avoid (or at least disclose) conflicts of interest;
- To act in good faith—that is, to be honest;
- To exercise independent judgment;
- Not to delegate that judgment without authorization by the government documents or by the principal;[25]
- To exercise an appropriate level of care;
- If a fiduciary managed property for more than one person (e.g., several family members), to treat each of them impartially; and
- To provide regular accountings (reports) explaining how funds and other property were managed.

Today, relatively few people are conversant with fiduciary standards, but this was not true of the founding generation. A much higher portion of the public served as fiduciaries. Small farmers hired larger farmers as commissioned factors (brokers) for the sale of produce. Larger farmers employed factors overseas. The higher death rate created a great need for guardians, trustees, executors, and administrators. Fiduciaries very often served in teams, so a minor who has only one guardian today might have three or more during the Founding era. Since there were virtually no institutional fiduciaries (such as trust departments in banks), individuals had to serve. Hence, when a ratification-era writer labeled a public official as a guardian or trustee of the people, most of his or her readers understood what that implied.

Several principles followed from the notion that public office was a public trust:

- Like private fiduciaries, government decision makers had to follow "instructions"—i.e. the terms of the Constitution and the laws.
- Public officials had to be loyal to the people they represented. They ought to have an identity of interest with the people. The

---

[25] In accordance with the maxim, *Delegata potestas non potest delegari* ("Delegated power cannot be delegated").

Founders called this identity of interest *sympathy*.
- Public officials should be honest.
- Decision makers—whether public officials or voters—should be able to exercise independent judgment. They should not be in positions in which their best judgment might be overridden by others. For this reason, most Founders believed that only self-sufficient people of independent judgment should vote or hold office.
- Independent judgment required that agencies of government remain independent of each other. State officials should be reasonably free of federal influence and federal officials reasonably free of state control. Within the federal government, the legislative, executive, and judicial branches ought to be independent of each other. This independence should not be confused with "separation of powers," which was a subordinate (and less consistently followed) principle derived from the need for independence.
- Public officials had a duty to treat citizens as impartially as possible—a duty the Founders stressed perhaps more often than any other fiduciary obligation.
- Government officials had to account to the public for their actions.
- Just as an agent could not delegate decision making without the consent of his employer, so the people's legislative agents could not delegate their decision making. This is why proxy voting was prohibited in the British House of Commons.[26]

The Constitution provides that "[a]ll legislative Powers herein granted shall be vested in a Congress of the United States . . . ."[27] Notwithstanding this statement, during the modern era, Congress has delegated vast powers to the President and to independent agencies.

Whether an agent (such as Congress) may delegate a function generally depends on whether the principal has authorized the delegation. Simi-

---

[26] Members of the House of Lords could delegate, because peers represented only their personal interests.

[27] Article I, Section 1, Clause 1.

larly, whether a delegation by Congress is constitutional depends on whether the people, acting through the Constitution, have authorized it. We can best answer that question by examining the Founding-era background behind the power being delegated. For example, there is little chance the Constitution's Ratifiers consented to Congress delegating the taxation power to the President: the Anglo-American tradition jealously guarded legislative control over taxation. By contrast, there was no firm tradition of legislative control over post office procedures, which often were treated as an executive function.

Thus far, legal scholars have not done sufficient research to determine how far each congressional power can be delegated.

***

To a great extent, the Constitution reflects the founding generation's acceptance of the values of liberty, effective government, republicanism, decentralization, and fiduciary government. In some instances, the Framers had to make compromises, such as when they provided that state legislatures would elect U.S. Senators—a decision that furthered the cause of federalism at the expense of the principle of independence.

1.4 The Common Legal and Governmental Background

The education of the leading Founders was supplemented by practical experience in business, agriculture, politics, diplomacy, and war. As a group, they were especially experienced in the law.

During the 18th century, talented men who today might enter business or engineering often turned to law and government. All gentlemen, even those who did not choose legal careers, were expected to have some knowledge of the law. Next to works of theology, law books were the most common kind of book in American libraries.

Most of the leading Founders were, or had been, lawyers at the top of their profession. Illustrative are four key Framers: John Rutledge of South Carolina, Edmund Randolph of Virginia, John Dickinson of Delaware, and Oliver Ellsworth of Connecticut. Each was the leading attorney in his respective state—although Randolph shared honors with Edmund Pendleton and George Wythe. Rutledge, Dickinson, and other leading Founders had been trained at London's Inns of Court, which were (and are) institutions for educating English barristers.[28] Others, such as James Wilson of Pennsylvania who clerked for John Dickinson, had been apprenticed to lawyers who had attended the Inns. The Constitution was the product of the best legal learning of the time.

The basic structure of the Constitution would have been familiar to any lawyer. So also would the Constitution's many terms with specialized legal meanings. To the modern reader, some these terms (such as "habeas corpus") are obviously legal, but it is easy to overlook others (such as "necessary and proper"). We can decipher them by consulting Founding-era law books.[29]

Unfortunately, most writers on the Constitution have no background in 18th-century law. Disputes over meaning fester for years because none of the participants examined the Founders' law books. Pertinent examples include the long and needless arguments over the meaning of "direct taxes"[30] and "high Misdemeanor."[31]

At the Virginia ratifying convention, Madison pointed out that "where a technical word was used [in the Constitution], all the incidents belonging to it necessarily attended it."[32] What he meant was that a legal term both had a core meaning and carried with it other customary aspects. Thus, when the Constitution required that criminal trials be conducted "by Jury," it further mandated the customary incidents of trial by jury: twelve jurors, unanimous verdict, the right to challenge jurors, and so forth.

Some the Constitution's terms can be clarified by leading court cases familiar to the Founders. For example: When the document assigns decisions to a legislature or convention but doesn't specify a particular vote margin (such as two thirds), then what vote margin is required? *Oldknow v.*

---

[28] The Inns trained six signers of the Declaration of Independence, seven commissioners to the constitutional convention, three key Virginia ratification figures, and Peyton Randolph, who served as the first president of the Continental Congress.

[29] John Worrell's bibliography of English law (1788) is nearly 300 pages long. Many of the works listed were common in the colonies.

[30] Section 9.2.2

[31] Section 11.1.

[32] 10 Documentary History, p. 1409.

Wainright,[33] announced in 1760 by Lord Mansfield, England's greatest chief justice, answers that question: Unless the governing document requires some other standard, assemblies decide by a majority of those voting (assuming a quorum is present). Similarly, another then-famous English decision, *Calvin's Case*,[34] offers guidance as to what the Constitution means when it uses the word "citizen."

Most of the leading Founders had not only practiced law but served extensively in government. Again, Rutledge, Randolph, Dickinson, and Ellsworth are examples. Rutledge had been the long-time governor of South Carolina. Randolph was then governor of Virginia. Dickinson had been president of both Delaware and Pennsylvania. Ellsworth had served for years in the upper house of the Connecticut's legislature and as a state judge. All four had logged time in Congress. Because the state governments grew out of British institutions, the Founders' political backgrounds consisted of broadly similar political practices and vocabulary.

1.5 The Constitution's Structure

Much of the Constitution was organized like a British royal charter. A royal charter was a formal document in which the king granted property or powers to named grantees. In royal charters, the name of the grantor (e.g., Georgius R.")[35] was placed first in majestic letters. In the Constitution, the name of the grantor—"We the People"—also was placed first in majestic letters. Then, continuing the charter form,[36] Article I described a grantee (Congress), listed its powers, and then limited its powers. Articles II (executive branch) and III (judicial branch) followed the pattern more loosely.

The tripartite structure of government outlined in Articles I, II, and III tracked the tripartite governmental structure in Britain: Parliament, Crown, and courts.

Article IV contained provisions defining the connection between the central government and the states. Article V outlined the amendment

---

[33] [K.B. 1760] 2 Burr. 1017, 97 Eng. Rep. 683.

[34] [1608] 77 Eng. Rep. 377, 406; 7 Co. Rep. 1, 24b (K.B.)

[35] Georgius Rex—that is, King George.

[36] Section 7.2.

process. Article VI established some general rules for reading the document. Article VII provided for ratification.

Articles I–IV were divided into sections. Articles V, VI, and VII were much shorter, and therefore not so divided.

Following Anglo-American legal practice, the paragraphs within sections and the paragraphs in Article VI were called "clauses." Thus, a specific provision in the Constitution is cited in the form, "Article I, Section 8, Clause 2" or "Article VI, Clause 3."

The Amendments in the Bill of Rights were labeled in the order in which Congress listed them when sending them to the states. Because the first two proposed amendments were not ratified at that time, the third in order became what we know as the First Amendment, the fourth became the Second Amendment, and so on through the twelfth (Tenth).

In accordance with a practice common in 1787 (and still prevailing in the German language), nouns in the original Constitution were capitalized—except for a few oversights.[37] That practice was not followed as closely in the Bill of Rights.

1.6 The Preamble

In common with many contemporaneous legal documents, the Constitution began with a preamble, from the Latin *praeambulare*, meaning "to walk before." The preamble to a legal instrument identifies the parties, recites crucial facts, explains the purpose of the instrument, or does a combination of those things.

A preamble is not a source of controlling rules, but its statement of assumptions and purposes can serve as a "key to open the mind of the makers,"[38] and thus shed light on the meaning of the main body of the document. The Constitution's preamble read as follows:

---

[37] They are as follows: "defence" in the Preamble; "credit" in Article I, Section 8, Clause 2 (the congressional borrowing power); "discipline" in Article I, Section 8, Clause 16 (training the militia); "duty" in Article I, Section 9, Clause 1; and "present" in Article I, Section 9, Clause 8.

[38] The expression was popularized by Sir Edward Coke (pronounced "Cook"), the 17th-century jurist whose Institutes of the Lawes [*sic*] of England was for many years the most widely used book of English law and served as a training manual for law students.

We the People of the United States, in Order to form a more perfect Union, establish Justice, insure domestic Tranquility, provide for the common defence, promote the general Welfare, and secure the Blessings of Liberty to ourselves and our Posterity, do ordain and establish this Constitution for the United States of America.[39]

The preamble began with the phrase "We the People"[40] to communicate that the people were deputizing the new government.[41] It listed six goals for the Constitution, which in turn reflected the core values and principles explained earlier:

- To make a union already existing more "perfect"—a word that in the 18th century usually meant "complete." This goal was to tighten a union already formed by the Articles. The value behind it was effective government.
- To establish justice. By playing favorites among citizens, some states had acted unjustly. The Founders' interest in justice reflected their fiduciary principle of impartiality.
- To insure domestic tranquility, which was then threatened by contention among states and social classes. This furthered the cause of effective government.
- To provide for the "common defence," which the drafters believed had been insufficiently secured because of the weakness of Congress under the Articles. This goal obviously was connected to the principle of effective government, but it also reflected the principle of impartiality: During the Revolutionary War, some officeholders notoriously had favored the defense of their own states over the common defence.

---

[39] Gouverneur Morris drafted the Preamble. His words followed an identifiable pattern of poetic meter and semi-rhyme. Robert G. Natelson, *Understanding the Constitution: The Style of the Preamble*, https://i2i.org/understanding-the-constitution-the-style-of-the-preamble/.

[40] The expression may have come from DeLolme, p. 315.

[41] Nevertheless, over the years, many have argued that the states rather than the people created the federal government. Section 3.1.

- To promote the "general Welfare"—as opposed to the welfare of particular individuals, regions or interests. This impartiality was a central element of the fiduciary ideal.
- To "secure the Blessings of Liberty"—a direct statement of another of the Founders' core values.

Because all of these recitals shed light on the meaning of the Constitution, none should be read exclusively. For example, the intent to create a "more perfect [complete] Union" did not mean that every law centralizing power in the federal government was constitutional, because forming a more complete union was only one of the six purposes listed. Too much centralization might well conflict with other goals, such as furthering the general welfare or securing liberty. That is why the Preamble called for a more perfect (complete) union, not a totally perfect one.

CHAPTER TWO

Interpreting the Constitution

2.1 The Founders' Guide: the "Intent of the Makers"[1]

The Framers deliberately wrote the Constitution for the ages. "We are not forming plans for a Day Month Year or Age, but for Eternity," John Dickinson wrote.[2]

Everyone understood, however, that the text could not answer all questions in advance. New circumstances would arise that would bring to light uncertainties and omissions. Future generations would have to interpret or construe the text to apply it to new problems.[3]

People sometimes make either of two opposite errors about the Constitution. One error (common among lay people) is that the document needs no interpretation—that you can "just read it." The previous

---

[1] See Bibliography for this chapter.

[2] 28 Farrand-Supp., p. 129 (notes for a speech). Other Founders also hoped the Constitution would last well into the future. See, *e.g.*, *id.* 280 (Rufus King and Nathaniel Gorham projecting 1600 members of the House of Representatives in a century).

[3] Some modern writers distinguish between interpretation and construction, but as far as I can tell Founding-era lawyers did not.

chapter explained why this is not accurate. The opposite error (common among commentators) is that you can read the Constitution using rules different from those applied to other kinds of legal documents.[4]

However, the Founders wrote and ratified the Constitution with the understanding that, with a few accommodations, it would be interpreted according to established rules. If they thought the document would be interpreted by other rules, they would have written it differently.

When the Constitution was written (and, for the most part, today as well), the fundamental guideline for interpreting a legal document[5] was to find and apply "the intent of the makers."

Who the "makers" of a document were depended on the kind of document it was. If a contract, the makers were the contracting parties. If a will, the testator; if a statute, the legislators. And if a constitution, the makers were the Ratifiers. Thus, the goal for interpreting a constitution was to reconstruct what the Ratifiers understood it to mean or likely understood it to mean. In this book, the understanding of the Ratifiers is called the *original understanding*.

Of course, you cannot look into the head of each maker to find his intent or understanding. You have to deduce it from outside evidence. During the 18th century (as today), lawyers and judges had established procedures for doing so.

Unfortunately, we cannot reconstruct a coherent original understanding for every single phrase in the Constitution. For some phrases, there is a lack of evidence. For others, pieces of evidence conflict irreconcilably. In such cases, Founding-era lawyers construed the document as a reasonable, informed person would have read it when it became effective. Modern writers call this the *original meaning* or *original public meaning*.

---

[4] When people change the rules of interpretation, they almost invariably are promoting a political agenda. For example, during the Supreme Court's liberal activist career in the mid-20th century, many liberal law professors cheered when the court overturned precedent. Those same professors began to preach about the value of preserving (liberal) precedent once the court became more traditional.

[5] Land conveyances partly excepted.

Consider this illustration:

The Constitution's Privileges and Immunities Clause[6] prohibits each state from discriminating against out-of-state visitors in the exercise of the "Privileges and Immunities" of citizenship. Suppose a state discriminates against out-of-state visitors who practice a disfavored religion. Is this a violation of the Privileges and Immunities Clause?

The answer depends on whether freedom of religion is a privilege or immunity as the Constitution uses those words.

The records of the constitutional debates contain little discussion of the Privileges and Immunities Clause. So there is not much proof of how the Ratifiers understood it. But we do know that the founding generation applied the words "privileges" and "immunities" to benefits created by government,[7] but classified freedom of religion as a natural right existing *before* government. Hence, according to the original public meaning, freedom of religion is not a privilege or immunity of citizenship within the scope of the Privileges and Immunities Clause.

Distinct from original understanding and original meaning is *original intent*. This refers to the intention of the Constitution's Framers (drafters). The original intent is not authoritative, since the Framers were not the Constitution's "makers"—they merely drafted the document for others to approve, much as a legislative lawyer drafts a bill for the legislature to consider. However, the original intent can serve as evidence of the original understanding or original meaning.[8]

2.2 Finding the "Intent of the Makers": 18th-Century Dictionaries

A person formally interpreting the Constitution should read it as a member of the founding generation would have read it. But the English language has changed in important respects since the Constitution was adopted. For this reason, specialists often consult 18th-century diction-

---

[6] Article IV, Section 2, Clause 1.

[7] Section 3.10.2.

[8] The relevant legal maxim was "Intention secret must give way to the legal intent."

aries, including law dictionaries. These are now available in downloadable form from the Internet.

2.3 Finding the "Intent of the Makers": Reading What the Founders Read

People studying the constitutional debates sometimes come across comments that are inscrutable unless they are familiar with what the founding generation studied during and after their school years. Their most-read book was, of course, the Bible. Also, collections of sermons on religious issues were popular to an extent it is hard for most of us modern Americans to understand.

Boys (and some girls) aspiring to be educated began to study classical Greek and Roman authors at an early age: Plato, Aristotle, and Cicero; the historians Herodotus, Thucydides, Livy, Sullust, and Tacitus; the biographer Plutarch; and the poets Homer, Virgil, Ovid, and Horace. The founding generation also read books on the history of Britain and Western Europe and on economics, science, politics, agriculture, and philosophy. Favored authors included John Locke, Baron Montesquieu, Niccolò Machiavelli, and David Hume.

The 18th-century American public also was unusually literate in law. Many examined the works of Edward Coke and William Blackstone, and the more erudiate studied other legal authors as well. This legal literacy proved to be highly useful in public debates over the Constitution.

For lighter fare, members of the founding generation enjoyed almanacs and newspapers.

2.4 Finding the "Intent of the Makers"—Learning Latin

Latin was the language of learning all through the Medieval and early modern period, and its study was central to a boy's education from age eight through college. (Girls customarily focused on modern languages, such as French and Italian.) It was the second language for all educated men. It also was necessary for the study of law: Some English legal materials were written in Latin and have not been translated to this day.[9]

Even when speaking or writing English, the Founders often used

---

[9] See the bibliography to this chapter.

words in a Latinate manner. (Recall the word "perfect," meaning "complete," discussed in Chapter One.)

Unfortunately, most modern writers on the Constitution have not studied Latin. This sometimes results in embarrassing mistakes.

2.5 Finding the "Intent of the Makers"—Sharing Their History

The dedicated constitutional scholar also needs to be familiar with the history of the founding generation (see Section 1.1). That history helps answer such questions as, "What problems did the Founders wish to solve?" "What drafting customs did they follow?" "What assumptions did they have?" "What did they say about the subject at the time?" "If there was no specific agreement on a point, what would they have understood to if they had considered the issue?" And so forth.

This history encompasses the struggle with Great Britain, the Continental and Confederation Congresses, and the constitutional debates.

The record of the constitutional debates includes the journal of the Federal Convention of 1787; notes taken at the convention; speeches, articles, and pamphlets about the Constitution; the proceedings in the state ratifying conventions (1789-1790); and the constitutional debates in the first (1789) session of the First Federal Congress—the same session that proposed the Bill of Rights.

Also helpful are the debates in the Vermont ratifying convention (January 7–10, 1791), mostly in confirming what had been said earlier.

2.6 Finding the "Intent of the Makers"—the Rules of Construction

The Constitution's text carried along with it a well-recognized set of rules about how to interpret a document. As we have seen, the basic principle of interpretation was to apply the "intent of the makers." The rules of construction—often referred to as "canons of construction" or "maxims"—were guidelines to help the reader find the intent of the makers.[10] Perhaps 90 percent of them were expressed in Latin.

---

[10] Several rules of construction referred expressly to the need to find the intent behind a document: *Animus hominis est anima scripti* ("The mind of the person is the spirit of the writing"); *Charta est legatus mentis* ("The writing is the envoy of the

The rules of construction helped fill in gaps in available evidence by instructing readers on how the parties to legal documents usually act—and therefore what they probably meant. For example, when people prepare a document, they might insert words of explanation and they might repeat a point. But they generally avoid throwing in large chunks of useless text. So the courts developed the rule *Verba aliquid operari debent—debent intellegi ut aliquid operantur.* That means, "Words should signify something—they should be understood to have effect." If there were two possible interpretations of a phrase, but one possible interpretation results in large chunks of meaningless text while the other gives effect to all or most portions, then the interpreter should favor the latter.[11] Although some surplus is acceptable,[12] the more excess wording created by a suggested meaning, the less likely that suggested meaning is correct.

Here is an example from the ratification debates: The Constitution grants Congress to "lay and collect Taxes . . . to pay the Debts and provide for the . . . general Welfare."[13] Some opponents claimed this phrase would enable Congress to pass any law it believed would "provide for the general Welfare." In response, Federalists explained that this phrase was merely a limit on the taxing power. They pointed out that if it had meant Congress could do anything it wished, then by adding over thirty additional congressional powers, the Framers would have inserted gobs of useless surplage[14] One reason the Federalists carried the day was

---

mind"); and *Verba intentioni non e contra debent inservire* ("Words should faithfully serve the intention, not the contrary").

[11] At the North Carolina ratifying convention, Federalist John Steele expressed the rule this way:

> Is it not a maxim of universal jurisprudence, of reason and common sense, that an instrument or deed of writing shall be so construed as to give validity to all parts of it, if it can be done without involving any absurdity?

30 Documentary History, pp. 290–91.

[12] In accordance with the maxim *Abundans cautela non nocet* ("Overflowing caution doesn't harm").

[13] Article I, Section 8, Clause 1.

[14] Seventeen of these additional powers were in Article I, Section 8; the remainder were scattered throughout the document. See Chapter Five.

that the public knew that legal documents were interpreted to minmize surplus verbiage.

Another rule of construction stated that, in case of doubt about the meaning of a provision, you should consult the document's preamble (if any), because the preamble was a "key to open the Mind of the Makers."[15] Still another was, *Inclusio unius est exclusio alterius*—the naming of one thing implies the exclusion of the other.[16] This meant that if a document lists a number of items, then you presume that similar, but unnamed, items are not included. Thus, if your spouse tells you to pick up lettuce, tomatoes, peppers, and onions at the supermarket, this implies (absent family custom to the contrary) that you need not buy celery. Chief Justice John Marshall applied the *Inclusio unius* canon just a few years after the Founding in the famous case of *Marbury v. Madison*,[17] the first time the Supreme Court declared a federal law unconstitutional.

Some modern writers dismiss the rules of construction as meaningless, but during the 18th-century, they enjoyed great authority.[18]

The Founders recognized that the rules of construction must be used with discretion. They are useful only insofar as they cast light on the makers' intent. A maxim can be overruled by evidence to the contrary, and the weight of maxims differ with different kinds of documents.

Sometimes, a document contained its own rules of construction, to be applied specifically to that document. The Constitution contained several: the Necessary and Proper Clause, the Supremacy Clause, and the Ninth and Tenth Amendments.[19]

---

[15] This was an oft-repeated rule. See, *e.g.*, 19 Viner's Abridgment 521 (1746).

[16] This canon was very popular, and had a number of different versions: *Affirmativum negativum implicat* ("The affirmative implies the negative"); *Expressio unius personae est exclusio alterius* ("The expression of one person [or character] is the exclusion of another").

[17] 5 U.S. (1 Cranch) 137 (1803).

[18] 1 Wood's Institutes, p. 6 ("[Maxims] are of the same Strength as Acts of Parliament when once the Judges have determined what is a Maxim"). An early American court accepted this view in State v.—, 2 N.C. 28, 1 Hayw. 29 (1794) ("And maxims being foundations of the common law, when they are once declared by the Judges, are held equal in point of authority and force to acts of Parliament").

[19] The Necessary and Proper Clause is Article I, Section 8, Clause 18; see Section 5.5. The Supremacy Clause is Article VI, Clause 2; see Section 3.14. The Ninth and Tenth Amendments are discussed in Chapter Ten.

2.7 Finding the "Intent of the Makers"—Equitable Construction

On rare occasions, Founding-era legal interpreters resorted to a procedure called *equitable construction*. This procedure was used when the literal wording in a documented clearly conflicted with the makers' intent. This may have been due to oversight or error during the drafting process, or to conditions the makers had not foreseen. In equitable construction case, the courts enforced the proven intent over the literal words.

English courts applied equitable construction to statutes, because parliamentary intent, not parliamentary words, was the supreme law. English judges affirmed that they applied equitable construction only to further the intention of the makers, never to promote other views.[20]

The document's words might conflict with the intent by being impossible to apply, or simply too narrow or too broad. If the enactment was so internally inconsistent or illogical that the lawmakers themselves would have repudiated it, it was impossible to apply and the court could void it—although this was exceedingly rare.

If the wording was too narrow, the court might adjust the underlying common law to comply with the rule of the statute. If the wording of a statute was too broad—that is, covered more than the legislature intended—the courts cut it down to comply with the lawmakers' intent. Sir Edward Coke, one of the greatest English legal commentators, justified it this way:

> Although a law speaks in general terms, it should be cut back so as to follow the rule that when the purpose [reason] for the law ceases the law itself ceases: For since the purpose is the soul and power of the law itself, it does not seem that the legislator would have agreed to what is outside the purpose even if the generality of the words would seem, on first impression, to suggest otherwise.[21]

---

[20] Courts today have a similar procedure called *reformation* whereby they correct defective private documents (such as contracts and real property deeds) to reflect the understanding of those who made them.

[21] 4 Institutes 330–31. Coke wrote the original in Latin:

Some Founding-era American judges applied equitable construction to state statutes. A South Carolina court, for example, held that the legislature could not have intended to apply a change in a law to people who had no way of knowing of the change. So the court inserted an exception not in the text.[22] Shortly after the Founding, a few American judges suggested in dicta (unbinding side comments) that, when determining whether a law was constitutional, equitable construction might be applied even to a written constitution[23]—but, again, only to effectuate the constitution makers' intent.

Fortunately, there is little need for equitable construction in interpreting the original Constitution, because very few phrases in the Constitution clearly contradict the Founders' understanding. I believe there are only two issues of this kind: The Fifth Amendment grand jury guarantee probably did not apply to hostile alien combatants accused of war crimes, and congressional resolutions in the Article V amendment process probably were not subject to presidential veto.[24]

2.8 Common Errors of Interpretation

Much has been written about the original Constitution that is just not so. The following pages will describe many examples. Here are some of the reasons for common mistakes:

Sometimes, a writer isn't seeking the truth, but is instead arguing a case. A person with an agenda may emphasize the evidence he or she likes and underplay the rest. Professor Henry Monaghan, himself a distinguished law professor, once charged that law professors are among the worst offenders.[25] They frequently generate novel, and often ingen-

---

Quamvis lex generaliter loquitur, restringenda tamen est, ut cessante ratione et ipsa cessat: cum enim ratio sit anima vigorque ipsius legis, non videtur legislator id sensisse quod ratione careat etiamsi verborum generalitas prima facie aliter suadeant.

[22] *Ham v. McClaws*, 1 Bay 93 (S.C. 1789) (holding that the legislature did not intend to impose a statute on parties retroactively).

[23] Notably in *Kamper v. Hawkins*, 3 Va. 20 (1793) (Roane, J.).

[24] Sections 9.11.2 and 12.2.

[25] Henry P. Monaghan, *Our Perfect Constitution*, 56 NYU L. Rev. 353, 377–78 (1981).

ious, "interpretive theories" to force the Constitution to mean what they want it to mean. A degree from a top law school is no proof against this error.[26]

Another kind of error arises from guesswork—failing to examine the Constitution's text or what the Founders said about that text. This may be due to pursuing an agenda, or from laziness, or from misconceptions about the historical record. During the 19th century, for example, some judges and lawyers argued that the Commerce Clause vests the power over foreign, interstate, and Indian commerce *exclusively* in Congress. This means that if Congress has not acted, the states may not either. But if they had dug deeper, they would have found that this is inconsistent both with the clear language of the Constitution and with what the Founders said about it.[27]

Still another sort of mistake comes from misunderstanding 18th-century English. A prominent legal historian once concluded that the President was to be subservient to the Senate in foreign affairs because several Founders referred to the President as an "agent." But in the 18th century, the term "agent" could mean merely "one who acts." In this context, it did not imply subservience.[28]

Some mistakes derive from unfamiliarity with 18th-century legal terminology. In a famous 1985 speech at Georgetown University, the late Supreme Court Justice William Brennan said of the Constitution that, "The phrasing is broad and the limitations of its provisions are not clearly marked. Its majestic generalities and ennobling pronouncements are both luminous and obscure."[29] This shows that Justice Brennan was not familiar with 18th-century law and governmental practice, because when you take them into account, very little in the Constitution is obscure.

On occasion a writer has done some homework, but not quite enough. Former Supreme Court Justice Stephen Breyer, once a Harvard

---

[26] One reason is that legal interpretation, including constitutional interpretation, is essentially a prosaic endeavor. Unrestrained intellectual brilliance is the enemy of the prosaic.

[27] Sections 3.7 and 6.3.2.

[28] Section 7.9.1.

[29] Justice William J. Brennan, Jr., *Speech to the Text and Teaching Symposium*, Georgetown University, Oct. 12, 1985.

law professor, understands fully that you should interpret the Constitution in light of its underlying principles. But he erroneously believes that "democracy" was the basic constitutional principle. Democracy (or rather, self-government) was important to the Founders, but ranked lower on their list than several other values, including liberty and fiduciary government. If you start in the wrong place, you usually end up in the wrong place.

Finally: There are mistakes that arise from bad historical methods. It is easy to write bad history, and very many people have done so, and in very many ways. Here are two ways: (1) using too little historical material and (2) using too much.

You are using too little historical material if you think the Constitution can be "just read" without any background in 18th-century history, law, and word usage. You are using too little historical material if you rely exclusively on statements by just a few Founders, such as James Madison and Alexander Hamilton.

The following claim also is based on too little evidence: "We can't recover the Constitution's original force because ratification records from Delaware, New Jersey, and Georgia contain little information about their conventions' understandings."

It is true that the ratification records from those states are scanty: All three states ratified early and unanimously, without a great deal of discussion. But the claim overlooks the conduct of those states' opinion molders immediately *after* their conventions. During later debates they expressed no dissatisfaction with how the Constitution was being represented. They did not join with Virginia and New York in seeking a new federal convention. They did not differ appreciably from other Americans in their attitude toward a Bill of Rights.

The opposite error in historical method is to use too much historical material. A common example is relying on events, documents, and practices dating from months or years after the completion of the 1787-91 constitutional settlement. Historians call this error "anachronism"—more colloquially, "reading history backwards."[30]

---

[30] Several Supreme Court justices have expressed concern about the use of "evidence" of constitutional meaning arising after, or long before, the American Founding. See *New York State Rifle & Pistol Association Inc. v. Bruen*, 142 S.Ct. 2111 (2022).

The most obvious problem with reading history backwards is that events, documents, and practices arising after the constitutional settlement could not have been part of that settlement because they hadn't happened yet.

Even the Founders' own later statements about what they had understood "back in the day" are of dubious reliability. A Founder writing in 1820, or even in 1798, was living under different conditions from those prevailing in 1787-91. Between the first and second sessions of the First Federal Congress, there had been a dramatic change in political alliances. Founders who faced one set of incentives as Framers or Ratifiers might later face very different incentives later. And, of course, with the passage of years, memories fade.

Therefore: When interpreting the unamended Constitution, this book generally restricts the inquiry to evidence arising before the thirteenth state, Rhode Island, ratified on May 29, 1790. For interpreting the Bill of Rights, the cut-off time is the day the bill was declared ratified: December 15, 1791.

There are only minor exceptions to these cut-off times. For reasons discussed in Chapter Three, the history of the Eleventh Amendment (ratified in 1795) offers an important clue to the original meaning of the language it clarified. Another exception consists of uncontroversial materials dating from soon after the ratification that confirm earlier uncontradicted evidence. In this category are the records of the Vermont ratifying convention and a few 1790s court decisions.

* * *

The Founders understood that legal interpretation is not always easy. But they would not have wanted us to invent our own theories of how to proceed, and they certainly did not expect us to simply give up the process as hopeless. They gave us a carefully constructed legal document to serve as the basis for popular government under the rule of law. They expected us to rise to the challenge of applying it correctly.

CHAPTER THREE

The States

3.1 The States in the Constitutional System: Compact or Popular Grant?

One of the great accomplishments of the Founding was *dual sovereignty*. Previously, people conceived sovereignty as an indivisible attribute, always located in one person or institution. However, the Constitution divided sovereignty between the states and the federal government—that is, between the American people as a whole and subsets of the American people operating through their state governments.

Much debated has been question of whether in 1787 there was a single American people or only peoples of separate states. Some writers contend that the Constitution created merely a compact (contract) among the separate peoples of thirteen states. They point out that the Constitution was ratified state by state. This *compact theory* has been used to contend that if the federal government breaks the terms of the federal contract, the states may void ("nullify") the offending federal actions or even secede from the Union.

Others argue that the Constitution was less an interstate compact than a grant of powers from the American people as a whole. More precisely, the Constitution reallocated authority, granting a long list of powers to the new central government and its officers and departments, granting a few to the states or legislatures and conventions, and reserving the rest in the states. Advocates of this *popular grant theory* contend that ratification by state conventions was simply a concession to practicality, and did not imply that states were the parties (or at least not the only parties) to the Constitution.[1] Advocates of both theories support their views with Founding-era evidence.

The compact/grant dispute reached a peak just before the Civil War, when southern states used the compact theory to justify secession. Even today, the debate stirs passions in some quarters.

I have studied the evidence offered by both sides over the course of many years. After holding the compact theory for a while, I eventually came to believe that the grant theorists have the better of the argument. Here are my reasons:

First: One basis of the compact-theory is that in 1787 there was no single American people—just thirteen different societies. But the Declaration of Independence—the formal justification of American independence under international law—directly contradicts this. It identifies Americans as "one people," although grouped into "free and independent states." Indeed, there have been many cases in which a discrete people, as defined by language, ethnicity, values and culture, have been grouped into multiple sovereign units.[2]

Second: The dominant view expressed during the ratification debates, by both Federalists and Anti-Federalists, was that the Constitution would

---

[1] In *McCulloch v. Maryland*, Chief Justice John Marshall argued the point this way:

> [T]he people voted for the Constitution in the only manner in which they can act safely, effectively and wisely, on such a subject, by assembling in convention. It is true, they assembled in their several states—and where else should they have assembled? No political dreamer was ever wild enough to think of breaking down the lines which separate the states, and of compounding the American people into one common mass. Of consequence, when they act, they act in their states. But the measures they adopt do not, on that account, cease to be the measures of the people themselves, or become the measures of the state governments.

17 U.S. (4 Wheat.) 316, 403 (1819).

[2] Examples include the Greeks before the Roman conquest, Italians and Germans from the collapse of Rome until 1870, Germans during the Cold War, and Arabs and Koreans today.

be a grant from the people rather than from the states. Noah Webster of Connecticut held the compact view, and you can argue that John Dickinson did as well. But nearly everyone else who spoke on the issue—whatever they may have said in later political battles—either assumed or argued outright that the people, not the states, were creating the federal government.

Advocates of the compact theory point to the common use of the word "compact" at the Virginia ratifying convention. But nearly all those usages referred the Constitution as a social compact among *individuals*.[3] In fact, Virginia's instrument of ratification recited specifically that "the powers granted under the Constitution" were "derived from the people of the United States."

Third: In stark contrast to the treaty/compact structure of the Articles of Confederation, the Constitution was patterned on 18th-century grants. For example, "We the People," appeared in the same location and in the same kind of script as the grantor in a British royal charter. Many Anti-Federalists understood this and were upset by the implications. Patrick Henry demanded to know of the Framers, "Who authorized them to speak the language of, *We, the people*, instead of, *We, the states?*"[4]

In other places also, the Constitution referred to "the people" in a manner showing that it meant the American people as a whole rather than as peoples of individual states. Thus, the First, Second, Fourth, Ninth, and Tenth Amendments all referred to the people generally. The only reference to the division of the American people was to clarify that citizens could not vote for Congress in states other than their own.

It is certainly true that ratification was by state. But the Constitution provided that it became effective only if nine states ratified it. Nine happened to be the minimum number necessary to assure that the ratifying states represented a majority of the American people.[5]

By the more accurate theory, therefore, the Constitution was an act

---

[3] For example, Edmund Pendleton, the Virginia convention chairman, in arguing for the Constitution, said, "This is the only government founded in real compact . . . Where is the cause of alarm? We, the people, possessing all power, form a government, such as we think will secure happiness." 9 Documentary History, p. 945.

[4] 9 *Id.*, p. 930.

[5] Section 12.1.

by which "one people" of America granted and distributed enumerated powers.

3.2 The States in the Constitutional System: Implied Sovereign Authority?

Complementing those (usually on the political right) who argue that the Constitution is a mere compact among states are those (usually on the political left) who contend that the states did not become independent sovereignties upon Independence, but were always subject to central governance. According to this hypothesis, in 1775 the Second Continental Congress assumed national powers over foreign and military affairs, and perhaps other subjects as well. When the Articles of Confederation became effective in 1781, national authority passed to the Confederation Congress, and in 1789 it passed to the new federal government. Thus, from the time the Constitution was adopted until the present day (the argument goes), the federal government has been endowed with certain powers received not from the Constitution but by inheritance and need.

This is the doctrine of "inherent sovereign authority." Just as the compact theory became popular in the 19th century, the doctrine of inherent sovereign authority became popular in the 20th. The Supreme Court adopted it in a 1936 case,[6] and apologists for central power have cited it to justify extra-constitutional federal authority in a range of areas, particularly foreign affairs and relationships with American Indians.

The case for inherent sovereign authority is a good deal weaker than the case for the compact theory. The theory literally contradicts historical fact, the wording of the Declaration of Independence and of the 1783 Treaty of Paris, and even the rules of logic.[7] Its continued life[8] demonstrates, however, that influential people find it useful.

---

[6] *United States v. Curtiss-Wright Export Corp.*, 299 U.S. 304 (1936).

[7] For a complete explanation, see Robert G. Natelson, *The False Doctrine of Inherent Sovereign Authority*, 24 Federalist Soc'y Rev. 346 (2023).

[8] *E.g.*, *Haalan v. Brackeen*, 599 U.S. 255 (2023).

3.3 Differences from the Articles of Confederation

Some refer to the Articles of Confederation as "our first constitution," but this is not quite right. In 18th-century English, the word "confederation" meant a treaty, alliance or league. Accordingly, the Articles describes themselves only as "a firm league of friendship" for defense and other purposes.

In other words, the Articles erected a treaty organization rather than a government.[9] A fairly close modern analogue is the North Atlantic Treaty Organization (NATO), with the North Atlantic Council playing a role somewhat comparable to that of the Confederation Congress: In NATO, as in the Confederation, the member states remain sovereign, the central assembly has not power to tax, but must request money, and it has no power to pass laws within the member states. Moreover, in NATO, as in the Confederation, states sometimes deal with one another outside the treaty framework. The American states did this when meeting in convention repeatedly from 1777 through 1787.[10]

Unlike the Articles, the Constitution created a true government, although for limited purposes. The new government was largely independent of the states: Members of the House of Representatives were elected directly by the people, and, within its proper sphere, the federal government could tax and regulate citizens without state intervention. The federal government was, however, not entirely independent of the states. As explained in the next section, it depended on them to exercise some functions the Constitution had assigned to them.

---

[9] John Adams, 1 Defence of the Constitutions of Government of the United States, (1787), pp. 362-63 ("[C]ongress is not a legislative assembly, nor a representative assembly, but only a diplomatic assembly"). Adams added that "the deputies are responsible to the states." *Id.* at 363. See also *A Citizen of Pennsylvania*, Pa. Packet, Oct. 12, 1787, in 32 Documentary History, pp. 299, 304:

> When the several states were thus formed into thirteen separate and independent sovereignties, Congress . . . and their respective legislatures thought it proper . . . that a confederation should be prepared and executed. . . . [T]his was *a compact among thirteen independent states* of the nature of a perpetual treaty. It was acceded to by the several states as sovereign.

[10] Section 1.2.

3.4 State Powers

The Constitution bestowed only a limited list of powers on the central government, with all else reserved to the states. State authority was not restricted to any list. Each state enjoyed wide powers to tax and regulate for the public safety, health, and morals. In addition, the Constitution bestowed some enumerated powers on state governments or on branches of state governments (now called "federal functions").

During the ratification debates, Federalists repeatedly assured the public that the Constitution would leave the states as the sole government regulators of the vast majority of human activities. Federalists represented that the central government would have almost no role in agriculture or other forms of land use, real estate titles or conveyancing, use of personal property outside of commerce, wills or inheritance, business regulation or licensing, manufacturing, local government, marriage or family, religion, education, criminal law (other than treason, commercial crimes, and crimes against international law or on the high seas), civil disputes between citizens of the same state, or social services. The central government would have more extensive powers only in (1) federal territories outside state lines, (2) in the capital district and in other enclaves created by the consent of individual states, and (3) on land titled to the federal government, most of which the government was expected to sell.

The Founders' decision to retain state jurisdiction over most human activities did not reflect a view that those activities were isolated from the wider world. On the contrary, they repeatedly emphasized the close interrelationship between state-regulated conduct, such as agriculture, and federally regulated conduct, such as foreign commerce. But they believed that whatever inconveniences might arise from dividing responsibility between different levels of government would be outweighed by the benefits of decentralization. If in a particular instance the inconvenience proved very great, states could coordinate by interstate compact, subject to congressional approval.[11]

If the Constitution granted the federal government authority to regulate a particular subject, in most cases the states could regulate it, too. In other words, the states enjoyed *concurrent jurisdiction* with the federal government. The example most often cited during the constitutional

---

[11] Article I, Section 10, Clause 3.

debates was that both federal government and states would have power to tax. Congress and the states also would have concurrent jurisdiction over defensive warfare and over foreign, interstate, and Indian commerce.[12] Within the area of concurrent jurisdiction, if federal and state law conflicted, then federal law prevailed. As explained later in this chapter, there were a few subjects on which the Constitution limited the scope of concurrent jurisdiction.

In addition to conferring enumerated powers on federal officials, the Constitution granted what modern courts call "federal functions" to state governments or branches of state governments. The Constitution granted the states (subject to congressional override) power over the times and manner of holding elections for members of Congress.[13] States retained control over election campaigns, but this was by virtue of their reserved authority under the Ninth and Tenth amendments, not by virtue of constitutional grant.[14]

The Constitution gave some powers to each state legislature acting as an independent assembly and other powers to each general state legislative authority (including the representative assembly and the governor's veto, if any, and judicial review). Powers in the "independent assembly" category included electing U.S. Senators,[15] acting in the amendment process,[16] and applying for federal troops in event of an insurrection or other widespread violence.[17] Powers exercised by the entire state legislative authority included passing election laws to designate the places for choosing Senators and (subject to congressional override) the places for choosing Representatives.[18] Also in this category was the indirect authority to fix the property, age, and other qualifications of electors voting for

---

[12] That the states had some concurrent jurisdiction over defensive warfare and foreign commerce is not widely understood. See Section 3.7. The states also retained minor concurrent jurisdiction over foreign affairs. See Section 3.6.

[13] Article I, Section 4, Clause 1.

[14] Robert G. Natelson, *The Original Scope of the Congressional Power to Regulate Elections*, 13 U. Pa. J. Const. L. 1 (2010).

[15] Article I, Section 3, Clause 1.

[16] Article V.

[17] Article IV, Section 4.

[18] Article I, Section 4, Clause 1.

the House of Representatives, because these were same as those for voting for the lower house of the state legislature.[19]

It is uncertain whether other "federal functions" the Constitution assigns to state legislatures were to be exercised by the representative assembly acting alone or by the state's general legislative authority. The areas of doubt include choosing the method of electing presidential electors[20] and exercising a veto over creation of federal enclaves within state boundaries[21] and exercising a veto over the division of a state or its combination with other states.[22]

3.5 State Immunity from Lawsuits and the Eleventh Amendment

In traditional Anglo-American law, private parties were not permitted to sue a sovereign government unless the government had allowed itself to be sued—that is, had "waived sovereign immunity." In England, sovereign immunity applied to the Crown,[23] and the Crown had waived it for certain cases.

After Independence, the American states became the legal successors to the Crown, and generally claimed the privilege of sovereign immunity. However, the Constitution granted the federal courts jurisdiction over "Cases, in Law and Equity . . . between a State and Citizens of another State" and "between a State . . . and foreign . . . Citizens or Subjects."[24] Some argued that this grant of jurisdiction abolished state sovereign immunity, because it seemed to permit out-of-staters to sue a state in federal court. Naturally, many state officials were unhappy with this prospect.

The issue first arose during the ratification debates. John Winthrop of Massachusetts, one of the best of the Anti-Federalist writers,

---

[19] Article I, Section 2, Clause 2.

[20] Article II, Section 1, Clause 1.

[21] Article I, Section 8, Clause 17.

[22] Article IV, Section 3, Clause 1.

[23] In accordance with the legal maxims, "The King can do no wrong"; *Rex non potest fallere nec falli* ("The King can neither cheat nor be cheated"); and *Rex quid injustum est facere non potest* ("The King cannot do anything unjust").

[24] Article III, Section 2, Clause 1.

addressed it, concluding that the Constitution would not change the sovereign immunity rule. On the other hand, the author of the thoughtful Federal Farmer essays contended that the Constitution would abolish sovereign immunity. Most other Anti-Federalist writers agreed with the Farmer.

A number of important Federalists also spoke to the issue, including Alexander Hamilton, John Marshall, James Madison, Rufus King, and Edmund Randolph.[25] They said the Constitution would preserve sovereign immunity against lawsuits brought by private parties.[26] They explained that the grant of jurisdiction to the federal courts over states would apply only if the state itself was the plaintiff or had agreed to the court's jurisdiction. Federalist representations are, of course, particularly persuasive of the original understanding, for the Ratifiers approved the Constitution on the basis of such representations. Both the New York and Rhode Island ratifying conventions incorporated these specific representations in their formal resolutions of ratification.[27]

There is additional evidence for the conclusion that state sovereign immunity survived the ratification—in other words, that a private party could not haul a state into federal court without the state's consent. The Constitution conferred on federal courts power only over "Cases" and "Controversies." But courts never had exercised jurisdiction over suits by individuals against unwilling states. Those suits were not cases or contro-

---

[25] In addition, during the Massachusetts convention, Federalists reportedly represented that sovereign immunity would survive. Caleb Nelson, *Sovereign Immunity as a Doctrine of Personal Jurisdiction*, 115 Harvard L. Rev. 1559, 1593 (2002).

[26] Writers arguing the contrary cite a comment by Edmund Pendleton at the Virginia ratifying convention, which was at least arguably ambiguous; an ambiguous statement by Alexander Hamilton in *Federalist* No. 80, which he clarified against federal jurisdiction in *Federalist* No. 81; a remark by Edmund Randolph irrelevant to the subject, since it addressed Article I, Section 10, not the judicial power; another Randolph remark, also ambiguous; and a comment by James Wilson at the Pennsylvania ratifying convention that actually addressed only the fairness of federal courts in a "controversy" between state and citizen, not whether a citizen could be a plaintiff.

[27] The resolutions were worded similarly. New York's provided, "That the Judicial Power of the United States in cases in which a State may be a party, does not . . . authorize any Suit by any Person against a State." This sweeping language contradicts the hypothesis, advanced by some, that sovereign immunity applied only when a plaintiff's suit was based on state rather than federal law.

versies as the terms were then used.

Post-ratification developments generally are poor indications of original understanding. However, the public response to the Supreme Court's decision in *Chisholm v. Georgia*,[28] decided three years after Rhode Island ratified the Constitution, was so overwhelming and bipartisan that it has some value as confirmatory of earlier evidence.

In *Chisholm*, the court, over the dissent of Justice Iredell (a leading Ratifier), held that citizens of South Carolina could bring an unwilling State of Georgia into federal court. Outrage was so strong that within a few months Congress had proposed a constitutional amendment to overturn *Chisholm*. The amendment provided:

> The Judicial power of the United States shall not be construed to extend to any suit in law or equity, commenced or prosecuted against one of the United States by Citizens of another State, or by Citizens or Subjects of any Foreign State.

As first introduced in the Senate, the words "be construed" were absent, but they soon were added. The addition makes sense only as a signal that the amendment was clarifying, not changing, the original understanding. A few in Congress tried to weaken the amendment, but they were defeated, and on the final vote the proposal passed both chambers by overwhelming margins.

Also instructive is who voted for the amendment. At the time there were sixteen Founders in Congress: ten Framers and another six Founders who had played significant roles in the ratification debates.[29] Of these sixteen, every single one—Federalists and Anti-Federalists alike—voted for the amendment. Since people tend to be protective of their own handiwork, this certainly implies that these Founders thought the amendment reflected their original understanding.

Despite the slowness of 18th century, communications and transportation, the requisite number of states ratified the Eleventh Amendment in less than a year.

---

[28] 2 U.S. 419 (1793).

[29] This is an approximation, which depends on one's definition of "significant role."

3.6 Qualifications on State Sovereignty: In General

The Constitution qualified state sovereignty in three ways:

- In areas of life where both the federal government and the states could act—that is, where state and federal governments had concurrent jurisdiction—Congress could override state laws.
- Article I, Section 10, Clauses 2 and 3 listed several instances in which state action, even if otherwise consistent with federal law, required explicit congressional approval.[30]
- Article I, Section 10, Clause 1 and a few other provisions listed areas in which states could not act even with congressional consent. In those areas, federal regulation was exclusive rather than concurrent.

3.7 Qualifications on State Sovereignty: War, Immigration, and Foreign Affairs

The Declaration of Independence proclaimed the creation of thirteen "free and independent states" with "full power to levy war, conclude peace, contract alliances, establish commerce, and do all other acts and things which independent states may of right do." Thus, the states claimed power to wage war, conduct foreign affairs, and control their borders.

The power to wage war included both offensive and defensive war. During the Founding-era, a just offensive war was conflict waged for compensation or to deter or punish. A nation generally commenced offensive hostilities with a declaration of war. Defensive war was a military response to insurrection, invasion, or imminent invasion. "Invasion" might be an organized incursion by a foreign army, but the term also included attacks by international criminal gangs and unauthorized immigration, even if peaceful.[31] Defensive war might

---

[30] This was a vestige of a provision in the "Virginia Plan," an outline for a constitution advanced by the Virginia delegates early in the federal convention. Under the Virginia Plan, Congress could have vetoed any state legislation, much as the British Crown previously could veto colonial legislation.

[31] Robert G. Natelson & Andrew T. Hyman, *The Constitution, Invasion, Immigration, and the War Powers of States*, 13 Brit. J. Am. L. Stud. 1 (2024).

include necessary and temporary incursions into other countries. Taking defensive action did not require a declaration of war.

Also included in state sovereignty was the conduct of foreign affairs and control of immigration and emigration across state borders.

Until 1781, the states conducted foreign and military affairs informally though the Second Continental Congress. That assembly derived all its authority from specific commissions given by each state to its congressional delegates. On March 1, 1781, the Articles of Confederation became effective. Under this treaty arrangement, the states agreed to cooperate in foreign policy. They divided military responsibilities in a complex way, but it can be summarized by saying that Confederation Congress received almost exclusive authority to wage offensive war, while the Confederation Congress and the states had concurrent authority to wage defensive war.

The Articles did not alter the states' plenary control over immigration and emigration. Late in the Confederation period, when Congress became concerned about European nations sending its "malefactors" to America, all it could do was to ask the states to enact laws addressing the problem.

The Constitution altered these arrangements somewhat. The new federal government was given primary responsibility over foreign affairs, war, and immigration, and emigration. These federal powers are discussed in subsequent chapters.

In the area of foreign affairs, the Constitution unconditionally prohibited states from entering "into any Treaty, Alliance, or Confederation."[32] However, states could enter into an "Agreement or Compact with another State, or with a foreign Power" if they had congressional permission.[33]

A *compact* was any contract, agreement, or bargain among several parties. A *treaty* was a special kind of compact.[34] It was a compact in

---

[32] Article I, Section 10, Clause 1.

[33] Article I, Section 10, Clause 3. In *U.S. Steel Corp. v. Multistate Tax Comm'n*, 434 U.S. 452 (1978) the Supreme Court held that certain kinds of interstate compacts did not require congressional approval. This seems to contradict the plain words of the Constitution.

[34] Emer Vattel is the source for these definitions. He is supported by Georg Friedrich von Martens, Summary of the Law of Nations 53 (William Cobbett trans. 1795) (first published in German in 1789). Martens distinguished

which (1) the parties were sovereign over their international relations and (2) there would be mutual performance over a very extended period of time. Thus, a one-time prisoner exchange or a short-term loan was a mere compact (or contract or agreement), but an agreement setting the terms of future commerce among nations was a treaty. An agreement of peace was a treaty, for besides such one-time terms as transfers of territory, it laid down rules to govern the parties' relationship over an extended and indefinite period.

The Constitution grouped alliances and confederations (also called "leagues") with treaties and subjected them all to the same rules. Alliances and confederations were also long-term agreements among sovereigns—and, indeed, generally took the form of treaties.

The third clause of Article I, Section 10 addressed agreements and compacts. Since treaties, alliances, and confederations were types of agreements or compacts, it might seem at first reading that the third clause also governed treaties, alliances, and confederations. But established rules of construction provided that specific terms usually override general terms.[35] Because treaties, alliances, and confederations were specific kinds of compacts, the first clause of Article I Section 10, not the third clause, governed them.

Under the Constitution, states could wage war if invaded or about to be invaded. No permission from Congress was necessary, as it had been under the Confederation.[36] However, permission was required for raising armies or navies in peacetime and for issuing letters of marque and reprisal—documents authorizing ship captains to privateer on behalf of the state.[37]

States retained general control of their militias, which were traditionally employed only in defensive war. The Constitution provided that Congress could nationalize the militia only for three specific defensive

---

"treaties," which required performance over an extended period of time from "transitory pacts"). However, nineteen years apparently was insufficient for an agreement to be called a treaty, since a nineteen-year loan agreement between France and the Confederation Congress was labeled a "contract."25 J. Cont. Cong. 773–78 (Oct. 31, 1783).

[35] In Latin: *Generalibus specialia derogant* and *Generalia sunt praeponenda singularibus*.

[36] Article I, Section 10, Clause 3.

[37] Article I, Section 10, Clauses 1 and 3.

war purposes: "to execute the Laws of the Union, suppress Insurrections and repel Invasions."[38] In the event of nationalization, the President would assume command. At other times, the states would regulate their militias and appoint their officers, but the training regimen would be prescribed by Congress.[39]

The Constitution contained no provision for the kind of broad federal control of the militia now exercised under federal "national guard" laws.

Finally, states retained concurrent power with Congress over immigration and emigration, but Congress could override their laws on those subjects. The power to override immigration laws was limited as to the original thirteen states until the year 1808.[40]

3.8   Qualifications on State Sovereignty: Foreign Commerce

The Constitution limited state concurrent jurisdiction over commerce with foreign nations, although it did not wholly displace state power in the area.

Tariffs and import-export duties were considered a form of regulating commerce.[41] The Constitution banned states from imposing duties on imports or exports without the consent of Congress.[42] Included

---

[38] Article I, Section 8, Clause 15,

[39] Article I, Section 8, Clause 16:

> To provide for organizing, arming, and disciplining, the Militia, and for governing such Part of them as may be employed in the Service of the United States, reserving to the States respectively, the Appointment of the Officers, and the Authority of training the Militia according to the discipline prescribed by Congress.

Notice the 18th-century meaning of the word "discipline": a body of learning.

[40] Article I, Section 9, Clause 1 ("The Migration or Importation of such Persons as any of the States now existing shall think proper to admit, shall not be prohibited by the Congress prior to the Year one thousand eight hundred and eight, but a Tax or duty may be imposed on such Importation, not exceeding ten dollars for each Person."). "Migration" refers to voluntary immigration; "Importation" refers to the slave trade. The latter was classified as a form of "commerce."

[41] Sections 6.3.1 & 6.3.2.

[42] Article I, Section 9, Clause 2 & 3.

explicitly in this ban was the kind of import duty known as *tonnage*,[43] an exaction laid on the cargoes of ships. Even if Congress granted consent to state duties, any money raised from those duties would inure to the benefit of the U.S. Treasury, and Congress could revise them at any time. The Constitution exempted from congressional pre-approval any duties imposed, other than tonnage,[44] for the sole purpose of funding state inspection laws.[45]

The exemption of state inspection laws reflected their importance: For many years, Maryland, Virginia, and North Carolina had required tobacco growers to send their product to state warehouses, where it was held and inspected for quality before export. The purpose of the program was to ensure maintenance of the high international reputation of American tobacco.[46] But tonnage was not exempt from congressional pre-approval, because it was imposed for purposes irrelevant to inspection laws.

During the 19th century, some claimed that the Constitution forbade states from regulating any sort of commerce the federal government was empowered to regulate. This would forbid state governance of foreign, interstate, or Indian commerce even in areas in which Congress had not acted. The idea survives in the modern Supreme Court's "dormant

---

[43] For definitions of tonnage and other Founding-era financial impositions, see Robert G. Natelson, *What the Constitution Means by "Duties, Imposts, and Excises"—and Taxes (Direct or Otherwise)*, 66 Case Western Res. L. Rev. 297 (2015).

[44] That this was an exception is clear from the Constitution's separate treatment of tonnage in Article I, Section 9, Clause 3, and from the various rules of construction to the effect that specific terms override general ones: *Generalia specialibus non derogant, Generalibus specialia derogant*, and *Generalia sunt praeponenda singularibus*. The "specific" term here is "tonnage," a subset of the general word "duties."

[45] At the federal convention, James Madison and George Mason described such programs as those providing for "inspecting packing storing & indemnifying the losses in such produce while in the custody of public officers." 2 Farrand, pp. 597 & 607.

[46] A detailed description of the Virginia Tobacco Law, which became effective in 1732–33, appears in George Webb, The Office and Authority of a Justice of the Peace 326–42 (1736) (1969 reprint, Wm. W. Gaunt & Sons, Inc., Holmes Beach, FL).

commerce clause doctrine,"[47] in some modern Indian Commerce Clause cases, and in judicial claims that Congress's power over foreign commerce is exclusive.

Yet this claim is clearly inaccurate. Although there are areas in which the Constitution does grant exclusive authority to federal officials (the Enclave Clause is one example),[48] the document nowhere suggests that congressional regulation of foreign, interstate, or Indian commerce is exclusive. On the contrary, the historical record demonstrates that the Constitution left the states free to govern foreign, interstate, and Indian commerce,[49] subject only to preemption by federal laws and treaties.

3.9 Qualifications on State Sovereignty: Internal Commerce

Another set of restrictions on the states applied to internal American commerce.[50] States could not "coin Money"—a term that, properly construed, forbade the states from issuing paper as well as metallic currency.[51] Nor could states issue bills of credit, which were paper evidences of state debt intended to circulate as money. States were barred from passing tender laws—laws that required creditors to accept particular items as payment—except when the tendered item was gold or silver coin.

The ratification record discloses several reasons for these rules. One was to forestall interstate commercial disputes, such as those arising under the Articles of Confederation. Another was to restore public credit,

---

[47] The Supreme Court uses its fictitious "dormant commerce clause" doctrine to invalidate state laws that Congress has not superseded, but the Court deems unduly restrictive of interstate commerce.

[48] Article I, Section 8, Clause 17.

[49] *E.g.*, 2 Farrand, pp. 440–41 (noting that the states would remain free to impose foreign embargoes). A similar disposition had been proposed in a congressional committee's recommendation the previous year. 31 J. Cont. Cong. 495 (Aug. 7, 1786). See also Robert. G. Natelson, *The Original Meaning of the Indian Commerce Clause*, 85 Denver U. L. Rev. 201 (2007) (explaining that states regulated Indian commerce both before and after the Constitution's adoption); Robert G. Natelson, *The Original Understanding of the Indian Commerce Clause: An Update*, 23 Federalist Soc'y. Rev. 209 (2022).

[50] Article I, Section 10.

[51] The term "coin" in this context included paper money. Sections 5.3 & 6.3.2.

which had been badly damaged by state laws allowing debtors to shirk their obligations. Still another was to improve public morality: Most of the Founders thought paper money and tender laws had encouraged fraud by creditors, cheating by debtors, and worthless speculation. Tender laws in particular were seen as violations of the public trust, because they discriminated in favor of one part of the community (debtors) and against another (creditors).

As was true of foreign commerce, the states were free to regulate interstate commerce, although federal law could overrule state action. In other words, congressional control over interstate commerce was not exclusive.[52]

3.10 Qualifications on State Sovereignty: Promoting Interstate Comity

3.10.1 Comity Rules in General

Several non-commercial qualifications on state power were designed to promote interstate respect ("comity"):

- The law of the states in which the capital district and other federal enclaves were located was to have no effect.[53] This prevented a federal installation from being held hostage to the demands of the host state.
- Each state was required to give "Full Faith and Credit" to public acts, records, and court judgments of other states,[54] and Congress could adopt rules by which state official acts were to be proven to officials in other states.[55]
- States had to respect extradition requests from other states, and runaway slaves had to be returned to their home states.[56]

---

[52] Section 3.8 & 3.9.

[53] Article I, Section 8, Clause 17.

[54] This was in accordance with the maxim, *Judicium semper pro veritate accipitur* ("A judgment is always taken [accepted] as the truth").

[55] Article IV, Section 1.

[56] Article IV, Section 2, Clauses 2 & 3.

- States could enter into compacts with each other to address multi-jurisdictional problems, but such compacts were subject to congressional approval.[57]

3.10.2   The Privileges and Immunities Clause

The Privileges and Immunities Clause of Article IV provided, "The Citizens of each State shall be entitled to all Privileges and Immunities of Citizens in the several states."[58] It sometimes is called the Comity Clause.[59]

In 18th-century law, a privilege was a benefit bestowed, contrary to the usual course of law, on one or more people.[60] (A modern synonym is "entitlement"). A privilege generally created a corresponding immunity. For example, the privilege of a tax exemption was an immunity from paying taxes. The privilege of a business license was an immunity from being prosecuted for not having one. While it probably would have been sufficient to draft this clause using the word "privileges" alone, the phrase "privileges and immunities" was very common, and may have rendered the language of the Clause more familiar to 18th-century readers.

Privileges and immunities did not include natural rights existing prior to government, such as free speech or property. On the other hand, the term "right" could be used to refer to a privilege. An illustration appears in the Constitution's grant of power to Congress to authorize patents and copyrights to secure "to Authors and Inventors the exclusive Right to

---

[57] Article I, Section 10, Clause 3.

[58] Article IV, Section 2, Clause 1.

[59] The Privileges and Immunities Clause (Comity Clause) sometimes is confused with the Privileges or Immunities Clause of the Fourteenth Amendment. The Comity Clause protected visitors from other states in the enjoyment of privileges granted by a host state to its own citizens. The Privileges or Immunities Clause protected U.S. citizens from state efforts to infringe privileges they had by virtue of their United States citizenship. There is dispute about what the privileges or immunities of United States citizenship were intended to be.

[60] A relevant maxim was *Privilegium est quasi privata lex* ("A privilege is like a private law"). Blackstone indicated that a privilege might represent a *disadvantage* imposed by law on a person, but this use of "privilege" seems to have appeared in Roman, not English, law.

their respective Writings and Discoveries."[61]

Although privileges and immunities did not include natural rights, privileges and immunities could be important vehicles for protecting natural rights. The privilege of a patent protected the natural right of property and the privilege of the writ of habeas corpus protected the natural right to liberty.

Each state conferred particular privileges on identified persons or groups. The privilege of voting was granted to those citizens who met specified qualifications. States bestowed some other privileges on citizens merely by virtue of the fact that they were citizens. Massachusetts, for instance, bestowed the privilege of habeas corpus on all citizens. The Comity Clause meant that if a state government provided a privilege to its own citizens merely by virtue of their being citizens, that state had to provide the same benefits to visiting citizens of other states. This required states to grant visitors such entitlements as access to the courts and the ability to acquire land according to procedures fixed by law.

On the other hand, the exclusion of natural rights from the definition of "privileges and immunities" had some surprising implications. The Comity Clause did not protect visitors who wished to speak out on local political issues, because free speech was a natural right, not a privilege. And contrary to widespread modern belief, the Comity Clause did not protect a right to interstate travel, because travel was a natural right, not a privilege. The Founders respected the right to travel, but they left its protection to Congress.[62]

3.10.3   The Guarantee Clause

The Guarantee Clause (Article IV, Section 4) provided that the United States would guarantee to every state a republican form of government. That meant that the federal government was obligated to intervene if the rule of law broke down within a state, or if a state erected a monarchy or a government immune from citizen control. The Founders were particularly anxious to prevent any of the states from becoming

---

[61] Article I, Section 8, Clause 8.

[62] The Comity Clause in the Articles of Confederation had protected the right to travel, but this was removed from the Constitution's version, presumably because of the grant to Congress to regulate interstate commerce.

monarchies, because the history of federations had shown that member-states governed by kings sometimes undermined their republican neighbors. Otherwise, the states had broad power to choose their own style of governance.

Over the years, many writers have claimed the Guarantee Clause bans state institutions with which those writers disagree. One of the most persistent claims of this kind is that allowing voters to pass laws directly through citizen initiatives and referenda is inconsistent with the "Republican Form of Government."[63]

This contention has no basis in the original Constitution. Although most Founders were not devotees of direct democracy, they believed that it was consistent with the republican form for the people to exercise legislative power directly. The republican form was infringed only when the state surrendered the rule of law entirely to the mob by eliminating executive and judicial magistracies.

Most of the Founders also believed that a republic could include a hereditary aristocracy, as did the ancient Roman republic and the contemporaneous Dutch republic. However, the Constitution forestalled aristocratic republics by forbidding grants of any title of nobility.[64]

3.11 Qualifications on State Sovereignty: The Ban on Bills of Attainder

At common law, *attainder* was the passing of sentence on a person convicted or outlawed for treason or other felony. Such a person was attainted (i.e., "tainted" or out of grace) in the eyes of the law. Originally, an attainted person was punished by the permanent forfeiture of all his lands, by a sentence of death, and by "corruption of blood." Corruption of blood meant that the person could not inherit land from another, nor transmit it to his heirs or his spouse.

However, these were not necessary punishments for attainders,[65] for by the time of the Founding, Parliament had abolished corruption of

---

[63] The argument originated in the first half of the 19th century.

[64] Article I, Section 10, Clause 1.

[65] *Compare* Raoul Berger, *Bills of Attainder: A Study of Amendment by the Court*, 63 Cornell L. Rev. 355, 357 (1978) (erroneously stating that corruption of blood and death were necessary incidents of attainders).

blood for many attainted persons. An attainted person lost a life estate in his land rather than a fee simple—meaning that when he died, his family would acquire his property.

Enacting a law declaring a person to be guilty of a crime and imposing punishment traditionally was not seen has as an invasion of the judicial power. A legislature might adopt a bill of attainder to outlaw and attaint a person for treason or other felony, or adopt a bill of pains and penalties for other purposes.[66] However, the Constitution barred both Congress and the states from passing bills of attainder.[67]

The Fifth Amendment's Due Process Clause subsequently prohibited Congress, although not the states, from passing bills of pains and penalties.[68] Neither Congress nor the states were prevented from imposing attainder as part of a general criminal code applicable to everyone. Indeed, the Constitution explicitly recognized attainder as a permissible punishment for treason, so long as it did not include corruption of blood or forfeiture for longer than the "Life of the Person attainted."[69] The clear inference was that Congress and the states could adopt general statutes mandating attainder, even with corruption of blood, as the punishment for other felonies.

3.12 Qualifications on State Sovereignty: The Ban on Ex Post Facto Laws

The Constitution banned the states as well as Congress from passing ex post facto laws.[70] The Founders understood that if the legislature

---

[66] Blackstone spoke of "acts of parliament to attaint particular persons of treason or felony, or to inflict pains and penalties, beyond or contrary to the common law..." 4 William Blackstone, Commentaries, *256.

[67] Article I, Section 9, Clause 3 (Congress); Article I, Section 10, Clause 1 (states). These Clauses were much more limited than commonly thought today. See, *e.g.*, *United States v. Brown*, 381 U.S. 437 (1965) (construing "bills of attainder" much more broadly).

[68] Section 9.3.4. This power was taken from the states by the Due Process Clause of the Fourteenth Amendment.

[69] Article III, Section 3, Clause 2.

[70] Article I, Section 9, Clause 3 (Congress) Article I, Section 10, Clause 1 (state). This policy against retroactivity was in accordance with the common law dictum (borrowed from the Roman law) that *Nova constitutio futuris formam imponere debet,*

adopted a measure declaring an act to be a crime that had been legal when committed, the measure would be an ex post facto law. But when the Constitution became public, there was an initial dispute about whether a retroactive *civil* law, such as a retroactive tax or a statute curing technical errors, also was ex post facto. During the ratification debates, the Federalists repeatedly represented ex post facto laws as criminal only, suggesting that legislatures still would be free to adopt retroactive civil legislation. The New York ratifying convention approved the Constitution on that explicit understanding.[71]

However, the Fifth Amendment Due Process Clause curbed somewhat Congress's power to pass retroactive civil laws.[72]

3.13 Qualifications on State Sovereignty: the Ban on Laws Impairing the Obligation of Contracts

The Contracts Clause forestalled somewhat state tendencies to adopt retroactive civil laws. It prohibited states from passing "Laws impairing the Obligation of Contracts."[73] Specifically, it prohibited states from altering the terms of a contract between the contacting parties after the pact was made. It was targeted at state laws shielding debtors from their obligations.

There were at least three reasons behind the Contracts Clause. First, the Founders generally believed that, except in unusual circumstances, evading lawful debts was immoral. Second, legally countenanced debt evasion discouraged creditors from lending money. This resulted in very high interest rates, a shortage of capital, or both. Third, to the extent creditors were citizens of other countries, such laws might breach American treaty commitments: In 1786, Confederation Foreign Secretary John Jay issued a lengthy report showing ways in which many states' anti-creditor laws had caused the Confederation to violate its recent peace treaty

---

non praeteritis ("A new ruling should impose structure on things to come, not those already past"). This dictum had other forms also.

[71] Several years later, the Supreme Court confirmed this understanding. *Calder v. Bull*, 3 U.S. (3 Dall.) 386 (1798).

[72] Sections 9.3.2 and 9.3.4.

[73] Article I, Section 10, Clause 1.

with Great Britain.[74]

The Contracts Clause did not bar courts from applying the traditional body of law known as *equity*, by which the judges could relieve a contracting party who was the victim of fraudulent or other reprehensible conduct by the other contracting party.[75] This was fair, because for centuries, all contracts had been made in the context of a legal system that recognized this role for equity.

3.14 Qualifications on State Sovereignty: The Supremacy Clause

The Supremacy Clause imposed the following rule on all state courts:

> This Constitution, and the Laws of the United States which shall be made in Pursuance thereof; and all Treaties made, or which shall be made, under the Authority of the United States, shall be the supreme Law of the Land; and the Judges in every State shall be bound thereby, any Thing in the Constitution or Laws of any State to the Contrary notwithstanding.[76]

The Supremacy Clause thereby defined a hierarchy for legally prioritizing federal and state enactments. Technically, the Supremacy Clause was a mere rule of construction, spelled out to minimize future disputes.[77]

The Supremacy Clause clarified that the Constitution and duly enacted federal laws and treaties were superior to state constitutions and state laws. It also suggested the relative rank of different kinds of federal

---

[74] *31* J. Cont. Cong. 797–874 (Oct. 13, 1786). See also 33 *id.* 522–26 (Sep. 27, 1787) (dealing with a Virginia law that violated a treaty with the Netherlands).

[75] *Cf. The Federalist* No. 80 (Hamilton):

> It is the peculiar province ... of a court of equity to relieve against what are called hard bargains: these are contracts in which, though there may have been no direct fraud or deceit sufficient to invalidate them in a court of law, yet there may have been some undue and unconscionable advantage taken of the necessities or misfortunes of one of the parties, which a court of equity would not tolerate.

[76] Article VI, Clause 2.

[77] In accordance with the maxim, *Abundans cautela non nocet* ("Overflowing caution does not harm").

enactments. The U.S. Constitution was mentioned first—before "Laws ... made in Pursuance thereof"—to indicate that the Constitution was superior to statutes. Statutes were listed second and treaties third. However, the Founding-era understanding was that treaties and statutes were of equal force.[78] As was true of successive inconsistent statutes, a later enactment (whether treaty or statute) could repeal an earlier one (whether treaty or statute).

Under the Supremacy Clause, a federal statute was the supreme law of the land only if Congress passed it "in Pursuance" of the Constitution. Thus, the statute had to both conform to the Constitution and be adopted *after* the Constitution was ratified. But a treaty was the supreme law if made "under the Authority of the United States." Thus, a treaty was the supreme law even if the Continental or Confederation Congress adopted it before the Constitution was ratified.

In sum, state and federal courts were to apply sources of law in the following hierarchy:

Highest:	U.S. Constitution
Second:	U.S. laws and treaties, duly made within the scope of federal power
Third:	State constitutions
Lowest:	State laws

Federal actions taken outside the scope of federal power were not, of course, to be law at all.

---

[78] *E.g.*, 33 J. Cont. Cong. 727 (congressional notes of James Madison for Mar. 21, 1787).

CHAPTER FOUR

The House, the Senate, and the Vice President

4.1 Organization of Article I

Article I was devoted mostly to the organization and powers of the two Houses of Congress: the Senate and the House of Representatives. Article I also assigned to the Vice President the job of serving as president of the Senate.

Most of Article I followed a four-step pattern common in 18th-century documents granting enumerated powers: First, it designated the recipient of the powers to be granted—in this case, the new federal Congress.[1] Second, it set forth details of organization and procedure, including the Vice President's responsibility.[2] Third, it enumerated the powers granted.[3] And fourth, it listed restrictions on those powers.[4] After

---

[1] Article I, Section 1.

[2] Article I, Sections 2–7.

[3] Article I, Section 8.

[4] Article I, Section 9.

this four-part organizational scheme, Article I listed restrictions on the states.[5]

4.2 The Two Houses of Congress Were Not Interchangeable

Since the Founding, the two chambers in bicameral legislatures generally have become more similar to each other. At the federal level, the Seventeenth Amendment (1913) provided that the Senate, like the House, would be elected by the people. At the state level, pursuant to a 20th-century Supreme Court decision, both chambers of state legislatures are apportioned by population. In most states today there is little difference between upper and lower houses other than their sizes and the lengths of their terms.

But in the Founders' tradition, the upper and lower chambers differed greatly. Great Britain's House of Lords was mostly a hereditary body and its members served for life. By contrast, members of the House of Commons were elected for seven-year terms, subject to earlier dissolution by the Crown. Lords represented only themselves, and could vote by proxy. The Commons were agents of the people, and fiduciary principles forbade proxy voting.[6] Each chamber sometimes acted alone, exercising distinct responsibilities. The House of Lords was England's supreme court. The Commons initiated all "money bills" (taxes, other financial exactions, and appropriations) and controlled the executive ministry.

The legislative chambers in the American colonies were similarly diverse. In most colonies, members of the upper house were appointed by the Crown and served at the pleasure of the king. Members of the lower house were elected for a fixed term. The upper chamber usually served as a court. The lower controlled the purse strings.

After Independence, eleven states retained bicameral legislatures.[7] The chambers in those legislatures were more similar than they had been

---

[5] Article I, Section 10.

[6] *DeLolme*, p. 158.

[7] The bicameral states were New Hampshire, Massachusetts, Connecticut, Rhode Island, New York, New Jersey, Delaware, Maryland, Virginia, North Carolina, and South Carolina. The new Pennsylvania, Vermont, and Georgia state constitutions provided for unicameral legislatures.

during the colonial era, but important distinctions still remained. A citizen often had to own more property to vote for members of the upper house or to serve in it. The lower chamber usually had greater authority over finance, while the upper (or some of its members) exercised executive or judicial functions.[8]

The terms of office of the upper and lower chambers also varied widely. In Maryland, New York, Virginia, and Delaware, members of the lower chamber served for only a year. But members of the upper house were elected for five years in Maryland, four in New York and Virginia, and three in Delaware.

Today we think of bicameralism primarily as a way to prevent hasty legislation. But in the Founders' view, bicameralism also brought diverse perspectives to government and created distinct agencies for distinct functions.

The original Constitution continued the tradition of diversity between two legislative chambers. When acting together, the Senate and House of Representatives composed Congress. However, each chamber was marked by unique characteristics and exercised different functions..

4.3 The House of Representatives—In General

In the republics of the ancient world and of 18th century Switzerland, a magistrate or council initiated legislation, which was then approved or disapproved by a popular assembly composed of all, or a large portion of, the citizen body. In America's wide spaces, it was impractical to gather large numbers of citizens in one place. So when drafting the state and federal constitutions, the founding generation opted for elected lower houses to substitute for citizen assemblies.

The Founders used the word *sympathy* to denote similarily in feelings and interest between the people and those they elected. This was particularly important in the legislature's lower house because it was supposed to be representative of public opinion.

State constitutions promoted sympathy in the lower house by limiting

---

[8] See Robert G. Natelson, *The Founders' Origination Clause*, 38 Harvard J.L. & Pub. Policy 629 (2015) (surveying special functions of Founding-era state legislative chambers). For example, the New Jersey legislative council served as the state supreme court, N.J. Const. (1776), Art. IX, and tried impeachments forwarded by the lower house. *Id.* Art. XII.

terms of office to short periods. The longest term in any state was South Carolina's two years. In Rhode Island and Connecticut the term was six months, and elsewhere it was a year. For the federal House of Representatives, the Framers decided on a two-year term[9]—a compromise between the annual elections prevailing in most states and the three-year period favored by some Framers.

To further encourage sympathy between people and members of the federal House of Representatives, the Framers distributed membership among the states in rough proportion to their ability to produce tax revenue. (Think of the Revolutionary slogan, "No taxation without representation.") For the most part, they chose state population as a proxy for tax revenue, and they provided for a decennial census to ensure frequent readjustment.[10] The only qualifications on apportionment by population were that (1) each state was to have at least one Representative, and (2) a state's slave population was counted as 60 percent of free persons.[11] The latter qualification is called the *three-fifths compromise*.

The three-fifths compromise always has been controversial. Slave states, of course, would have preferred representation based on their entire populations, slave and free. Opponents of slavery portrayed the three-fifths compromise as a victory for the slave states, and most modern writers take that view.

The truth, however, is more nuanced.

As just noted, the Framers believed that tax contributions rather than population, should be the primary basis for representation. Population was merely a proxy for revenue production. But slavery violated the rule that tax revenue was related to population because slavery was an inefficient economic system. Slaves (of any race) were less productive than free people and therefore generated less tax revenue: A study previously commissioned by the Confederation Congress concluded that they were only about 60 percent as productive. This figure was the basis for the three-fifths compromise.

Thus, the compromise was a statement about the economic failures

---

[9] Article I, Section 2, Clause 1.

[10] Article I, Section 2, Clause 3.

[11] Article I, Section 2, Clause 3.

of slavery, not an expression of support. From the Framers' viewpoint, it was a penalty on the slave states, not a reward. Moreover, reducing congressional representation for slaves was consistent with the Founders' principle of independence: slaves were less entitled to representation because they were dependent on their masters.[12]

Another way of promoting sympathy between a lower house and the general public was to make the lower house relatively numerous. A small chamber required large election districts, and large election districts favored wealthy candidates and powerful special interests. Smaller districts offered more opportunity to candidates of modest means and more representation for localities and for weaker voices that otherwise might never be heard.

On the other hand, the Framers also understood that a very large chamber could display mob-like characteristics. Accordingly, they fixed the initial House of Representatives at 65 members and limited its growth by prohibiting more than one Representative for every 30,000 people.[13]

When the Constitution became public, many argued that the House was not large enough. The first amendment in Congress's twelve-amendment Bill of Rights would have expanded it. Shortly thereafter, the results of the first census showed that even without this change, population growth would enlarge the House more quickly than expected. Accordingly, the requisite number of states never ratified the original first amendment.

Still another way to promote sympathy was establish minimal qualifications for serving in the House. A Representative was required to be only twenty-five years old, an inhabitant of the state he was to represent, and a citizen of the United States for the previous seven years.[14] The Constitution imposed no property qualifications for the House or for any other federal office. This not only promoted sympathy, but recognized that the economies of the states were so different that uniform property qualifications were impractical.

---

[12] Section 1.3.5.

[13] This was originally one Representative for every 40,000 persons, but on the last day of the federal convention, George Washington requested that the House be enlarged to one for every 30,000, and the convention agreed.

[14] Article I, Section 2, Clause 2.

4.4 The Constitution's Gender Neutrality

The Constitution did not impose a gender qualification for the House of Representatives or for any other federal office. This apparently was a conscious decision rather than an oversight. Some early drafts contained the arguably male words "man" and "freeman" but the Framers changed them to the unarguably neutral word "person."[15] They did retain the pronoun "he" and its variants, but everyone understood that "he" and its variants designated both genders. The Framers also removed the phrase "He or She" from a draft of the Fugitive Slave Clause[16]—not because the Clause didn't apply to female slaves, but presumably because its presence in the Constitution might imply that "he" and its variants were used in a purely masculine sense.

In an age in which only men held elective office, why would the Framers decide to make the Constitution gender neutral? The Framers were conscious that they were writing for the ages, and the status of American women was rising. American women enjoyed a significantly higher status than those in Europe. In some states, such as Massachusetts, women voted without explicit legal permission. Moreover, the constitution of one state, New Jersey, granted suffrage to female heads of households who met a unisex property requirement, and New Jersey women voted in considerable numbers. Thus, the Framers may well have anticipated a time when women would be elected to political office. Indeed, this possibility was a point of Anti-Federalist attack: Some assailed the Constitution precisely because it would permit a woman to become President.

4.5 "Emoluments"

Also furthering the principle of sympathy was the Constitution's ban on members of Congress serving in executive office. In Britain, the king had acquired great influence in Parliament by doling out offices and benefits to members—a practice Whigs called "corruption."[17] Although Par-

---

[15] For example, a proposed definition of treason employing the word "man" was rejected. 2 Farrand, pp. 347–48.

[16] 2 *Id.*, p. 577.

[17] It also violated the legal rule, *Nemo utatur duobus officiis* ("No one should exercise two offices").

liament had imposed some limits on dual officeholding,[18] commentators such as Catherine Macaulay Graham (a historian popular in America) urged that members of Parliament be banned from the executive branch entirely. In 1779, the Continental Congress adopted a policy stating that,

> Congress will not appoint any member thereof during the time of his sitting, or within six months after he shall have been in Congress, to any office ... for which he ... may receive any salary, fees or other emolument.[19]

Article I, Section 6, Clause 2 (the Congressional Emoluments Clause) provided that, "no Person holding any Office under the United States, shall be a Member of either House during his Continuance in Office." The same provision stated that a member of Congress could not (even by resigning) accept an office that had been created during his present term or "the Emoluments whereof shall have been encreased" during that term."

In addition to the Congressional Emoluments Clause, the Constitution uses the word "emoluments" in two other places. The Foreign Emoluments Clause[20] bans federal officers from receiving emoluments from foreign kings and governments. The Presidential Emoluments Clause[21] bars the President from supplementing his formal compensation with emoluments from the United States or any state.

During the Founding era, the word "emoluments" could have any of four distinct meanings—all commonly used: (1) fringe benefits accompanying one's salary, (2) fringe benefits plus salary, (3) fringe benefits, salary, and profits or revenue from one's business, and (4) any benefit whatsoever—such as the "emolument" of fresh air.

The scope of these clauses depended on which of the four definitions the constitution-makers intended. For example, does the Foreign Emoluments Clause permit an officer to retain an interest in a business

---

[18] DeLolme, pp. 78–79. Several bills for more thorough reform had been rejected. *Id.* 263.

[19] 15 J. Cont. Cong. 1269 (Nov. 15, 1779).

[20] Art. I, § 9, cl. 8.

[21] Art. II, § 2, cl. 7.

that sells goods to foreign governments? If definition (3) or (4) applies, then (in the absence of Congressional consent), the answer is "no." If definition (1) or (2) applies, the answer is "yes."

My own research demonstrates that the Constitution clearly did not use the word "emoluments" to mean either definition (3) or (4). As between the first and second meaning, the second (fringe benefits plus salary) is much more likely.[22]

To return to the Congressional Emoluments Clause: If a Senator was elected in 1792 for a six-year term, and the members of the President's cabinet all received raises in 1793, the fact that the raise occurred during his term disqualified the Senator from appointment to the cabinet until his six-year term had expired.

An officer receiving merely a cost-of-living raise seems to have enjoyed an "encrease" in emoluments. This is because a person who receives a cost-of-living increase on December 1 receives a wage hike over what he earned on November 30. Some of the Founders' comments support this conclusion.[23]

4.6 Special Prerogatives of the House of Representatives

The Constitution granted the House of Representatives, as a chamber, some specific prerogatives and powers that it could exercise separately from the Senate. Most of these were suggested by British parliamentary experience. These prerogatives and powers preserved

---

[22] Robert G. Natelson, *The Original Meaning of "Emoluments" in the Constitution*, 52 Ga. L. Rev. 1 (2017).

[23] James Madison argued against fixing salaries in the Constitution in these words:

> The various vicissitudes, or rather the gradual diminution, of the value of all coins and circulating medium, is one reason against ascertaining them immutably; as what may be now an adequate compensation, might, by the progressive reduction of the value of our circulating medium, be extremely inadequate at a period not far distant.

10 Documentary History, p. 1262. See also *id.* 1264. Obviously, Madison did not think of mere cost-of-living adjustments as consistent with "fixing [compensation] immutably." He must, therefore, have thought of them as "encreases" [*sic*].

House independence from other branches of government,[24] thereby better enabling it to reflect popular sentiment.[25]

Thus, the Constitution gave the House of Representatives power to choose its own speaker and officers and establish its own rules.[26] It granted the House authority to judge the elections, returns, and qualifications of its own members; to punish and expel members; and to compel the attendance of absent members.[27] The Constitution required the House to keep a journal, but granted that chamber sole discretion to delete parts the members thought required secrecy.[28] The Constitution granted Representatives a certain immunity from arrest in the course of their duties.[29] The Speech and Debate Clause[30] bestowed absolute immunity from retribution from the other branches for comments on the floor. For example, Representatives were not subject to defamation suits for floor speeches. However, the House could punish its own members for statements—on or off the floor—that were untrue, defamatory, or that revealed secret information.[31]

Many Founders believed the legislative privilege of speech and debate empowered the legislature to punish citizens for serious insults—particularly defamation and challenges to duels—directed at lawmakers because

---

[24] The offsetting powers in the two chambers of Parliament kept debate quite civil. DeLolme, p. 337.

[25] See, *e.g.*, Thomas Tudor Tucker, *Philodemus* (1784), in 1 American Political Writing During the Founding Era *1760–1805*, 606, 611 (Charles S. Hyneman & Donald S. Lutz, eds., 1983) (stating that legislative privileges ought to be defined by the Constitution and set at the minimum necessary to protect the votes of the citizens).

[26] Article I, Section 2, Clause 5; Article I, Section 5, Clause 2.

[27] Article I, Section 5, Clauses 1 & 2.

[28] Article I, Section 5, Clause 3.

[29] Article I, Section 6.

[30] Article I, Section 6 ("... for any Speech or Debate in either House, they shall not be questioned in any other Place").

[31] In 1782, the Confederation Congress had severely condemned David Howell, a delegate from Rhode Island, for communicating untrue information and diplomatic secrets to his constituents. 23 J. Cont. Cong. 791–93, 812–14, 818–19 (the affair in the official journal); 863–64 & 868 (James Madison's description).

of statements or acts during the lawmakers' legislative duties.[32] This legislative privilege probably did not survive the adoption of the Fifth Amendment's Due Process Clause.

In the absence of a constitutional provision or House rule to the contrary, the rule of decision in the House was the one prevailing throughout the Anglo-American world: a majority of those voting.[33]

The Constitution granted the House power to veto any effort by the Senate to adjourn for more than three days.[34] This enabled the House to prevent the Senate from blocking measures merely by adjourning. The Constitution also followed British practice in granting the House the right to impeach[35]—that is, to indict a person for misconduct in office and send him to the Senate for trial.

The House was to elect the President if no candidate received a majority of votes in the Electoral College.[36] The Framers thought this was a significant privilege, since they predicted that the Electoral College would be hopelessly fractured in most elections.[37]

Perhaps the most important of the House's prerogatives was set forth in the Origination Clause.[38] This provision mandated that revenue

---

[32] When Gunning Bedford, Sr., the muster-master general of the continental army, challenged congressional delegate John Dickinson Sergeant to a duel because of Sergeant's remarks in the House, several members of Congress wanted Bedford severely punished. However, Congress was satisfied with an apology. 8 J. Cont. Cong. 458–61 & 466–67 (Jun. 12–14, 1777). A speech and debate clause was added to the existing draft of the Articles of Confederation a few months after this incident. 9 *id.* 885, 887 & 893–94 (Nov. 10 & 12, 1777).

Bedford should not be confused with his cousin, Gunning Bedford, Jr., who served as a federal convention delegate and likewise offended the House with intemperate expression. 1 Farrand, p. 492.

[33] Section 1.4.

[34] Article I, Section 5, Clause 4.

[35] Article I, Section 2, Clause 5.

[36] Article II, Section 1, Clause 3.

[37] See Section 7.3 for the presidential election procedure.

[38] Article I, Section 7, Clause 1. This discussion is based on Robert G. Natelson, *The Founders' Origination Clause*, 38 Harvard J.L. & Pub. Policy 629 (2015).

The rule requiring money bills to originate in the lower house also appeared in drafts of the Confederation Congress' Northwest Ordinance, governing federal territories. 30 J. Cont. Cong. 405 (Jul. 13, 1786); 31 *id.* 672 (Sep. 19, 1786), but

bills originate in the House of Representatives. In other words, each revenue bill had to be introduced in the House and clear that chamber before the Senate could act on it.

The Constitutional Convention almost didn't insert the Origination Clause into the Constitution. Its final inclusion was due to the persuasive powers of Edmund Randolph and John Dickinson, both of whom who argued that the Origination Clause would fortify the Constitution against charges that it would create an aristocracy. In Dickinson's most memorable convention speech, he explained that, however logical or illogical House origination might be, its practical value had been proven in Britain. "Experience must be our only guide," he admonished. "Reason may mislead us."

However, the Constitution's origination rule was narrower than the British version. The Constitution's Origination Clause applied only to "Bills for raising Revenue." This meant specifically tax bills—bills justified by no enumerated power other than Article I, Section 8, Clause 1.[39] The Clause did not, as in Britain, apply to appropriations or to levies for regulatory purposes. Moreover, in Britain the upper house was forbidden, at least in theory, to amend such bills; it could vote only aye or nay. By contrast, the Constitution's Origination Clause granted the Senate authority to amend revenue bills. The extent of this authority is treated below.[40]

Most of the powers granted the House were legislative, as the Founders understood that term. There were some exceptions. For example, impeachment could be seen as a judicial function. In addition, the House shared with the Senate certain prerogatives that, in Britain, had been within the executive authority of the king, including the power to issue letters of marque and reprisal, strike and regulate coinage,[41] and fix weights and measures. In the executive category also was the power to

---

was removed for the draft presented on May 10, 1787, 32 *id.* 281, and from all later versions. The removal was not surprising, since Congress itself was to have a leading role in appointing the upper house. The final version of the Ordinance is found in *id.* 334–43 (Jul. 13, 1787).

[39] A "Bill for raising Revenue" included any change in the tax code, whether it increased or reduced revenue.

[40] Section 4.7.

[41] As a practical matter, Parliament assisted in the striking and regulation of coinage.

declare war. Because of the grave nature of any decision to go to war, the Framers decided that it should be approved by the people's House. However, that body did not have a comparable role in making peace.[42]

4.7 The Senate—In General

Although serving with the House of Representatives as part of Congress, the Senate was different in conception, composition, and authority.

One forerunner of the Senate was the *Senatus*, or council of elders of the Roman Republic. The Roman Senate injected wisdom and caution into government process, tried impeachments, vetted proposed laws, exercised a major foreign policy role, and eventually became a legislative body.

Two other forerunners of the American Senate were the Confederation Congress and the British House of Lords. At the federal convention, John Dickinson argued for state legislatures choosing Senators, just as most of them had chosen members of the Confederation Congress. This, he contended, would give the Senate some of the force of the House of Lords.

Yet another model for the federal Senate was the state senate in Maryland. Its members were indirectly elected and served for five-year terms, then the longest legislative terms in the country. Some Framers gave the Maryland Senate credit for restraining excessive popular passions.

As finally crafted, the U.S. Senate was a smaller, more deliberative body than the House, and expected to sit more continually. The six-year term was a compromise between the extremes of one year (prevailing in

---

[42] Peace was to be made by the President and Senate, exercising the Treaty Power. Rufus King and Nathaniel Gorham stated that this was because,

> . . . war is not to be desired and always [is] a great calamity, [so] by increasing the Checks the measure will be difficult— but as peace is forever to be desired, and can be alone obtained by Treaty it seemed preferable to trust it with the President & Senate.

Farrand-Supp., p. 284.

most states), and life appointment (prevailing in Britain and favored by Framers such as Alexander Hamilton and Gouverneur Morris). The personal qualifications for the Senate were residence in the state represented, a minimum age of 30, and U.S. citizenship for nine years.[43] Senators were elected by the state legislatures. When a vacancy occurred during the recess of the state's legislature, the state's governor filled it until the legislature elected a replacement[44]—perhaps a relic of the Crown's power to create new members of the House of Lords and some colonial governors' power to designate upper house members.

Like Representatives, Senators were banned from other federal employment.[45]

Although each state enjoyed equal representation in the Senate,[46] its members cast votes individually rather than as members of state delegations. In the absence of a constitutional provision or Senate rule to the contrary, the "rule of decision" was a majority of those voting.[47]

In its capacity as the upper chamber of Congress, the Senate exercised legislative authority in conjunction with the House. However, its power over "Bills for raising Revenue" (taxes)[48] was limited:[49] It could not originate bills that raised or lowered taxes or otherwise changed the tax code; such bills had to come from the House. Moreover, once the House sent the Senate a tax bill, the Senate was limited to proposing "Amendments."

An "amendment" might largely rewrite or change the political thrust of an underlying bill, but it had to address the same subject(s) as the underlying bill. Taxes, of whatever kind, were considered the same general subject. Thus, the Senate could amend a tax bill by making any tax-related changes it wished. In American legislative usage, appropri-

---

[43] Article I, Section 3, Clause 3.

[44] Article I, Section 3, Clause 2.

[45] Article I, Section 6, Clause 2.

[46] Article I, Section 3, Clause 1.

[47] Section 1.4.

[48] "Bills for raising Revenue" meant taxes under Article I, Section 8, Clause 1. See Section 6.1.

[49] This discussion is based on Robert G. Natelson, *The Founders' Origination Clause*, 38 Harvard J.L. & Pub. Policy 629 (2015).

ations comprised another subject, and regulations spanned many other subjects.[50] If the House had inserted appropriations or regulations in an underlying tax bill, the Senate could alter or remove them. On the other hand, the Senate could not add regulations unrelated those in the original. Nor could it add regulations or appropriations to a tax bill that had none.[51]

4.8 Special Prerogatives of the Senate

Just as the Constitution granted the House certain prerogatives as a separate chamber, it granted similar prerogatives to the Senate. One was a veto over a House effort to adjourn for more than three days.[52] Another was the right to choose its own officers—other than its president, who was always the Vice President of the United States.[53] The Senate received power to judge the elections, returns, and qualifications of its own members and compel the attendance of absent members;[54] to establish its own rules;[55] to punish and expel members;[56] and to deny publication of those parts of its journal that it believed, in its unfettered discretion, should remain secret.[57] As the House was to select the President if the Electoral College had not, the Senate was to select the Vice President if two or more people were tied for second place in the Electoral College.[58]

---

[50] Several sections of the Constitution manifest the common understanding that revenue and appropriations were single (large) subjects distinct from other legislation. Article I, Section 7, Clause 1 (revenue); Article I, Section 9, Clause 6 ("Regulation of Commerce or Revenue"); Article I, Section 9, Clause 12 (appropriations); Article I, Section 9, Clause 7 (appropriations).

[51] Thus, the Senate might be prevented from adding by amendment proposals it had power to originate. For example, the Senate could originate a measure providing for a post office in Pittsburgh, but it could not add such a provision to an unrelated tax bill.

[52] Article I, Section 5, Clause 4.

[53] Article I, Section 3, Clause 5.

[54] Article I, Section 5, Clause 1.

[55] Article I, Section 5, Clause 2.

[56] Article I, Section 5, Clause 2.

[57] Article I, Section 5, Clause 3.

[58] Article II, Section 1, Clause 3.

As the House was to impeach, the Senate was to judge.[59] Senators received the same immunity from arrest and protection for speech as House members.[60]

4.9 The Senate's Executive Powers

Balancing the authority of the House over money bills was the Senate's right to "Advise and Consent" to certain executive decisions. Article II, Section 2, Clause 2 read as follows:

> [The President] shall have Power, by and with the Advice and Consent of the Senate, to make Treaties, provided two thirds of the Senators present concur; and he shall nominate, and by and with the Advice and Consent of the Senate, shall appoint Ambassadors, other public Ministers and Consuls, Judges of the Supreme Court, and all other Officers of the United States, whose Appointments are not herein otherwise provided for, and which shall be established by Law: but the Congress may by Law vest the Appointment of such inferior Officers, as they think proper, in the President alone, in the Courts of Law, or in the Heads of Departments.

Three phrases in this passage require definitions: "public Ministers", Consuls", and "Advice and Consent".[61] For the first two, we turn to the Founders' favorite authority on international law, the Swiss scholar, Emer de Vattel. He wrote of the phrase "public ministers:"

> This term, in its more extensive and general sense, denotes any person entrusted with the management of public affairs, but is more particularly understood to designate one who acts in such capacity at a foreign court.[62]

According to Vattel, there were several kinds of foreign-service

---

[59] Article I, Section 3, Clause 6.

[60] Article I, Section 6, Clause 1.

[61] On the meaning of "Heads of Departments," see Section 7.7.1.

[62] Vattel, p. 682.

public ministers. Ambassadors were those of the greatest dignity. Below them were envoys and residents. There also were diplomatic representatives who did not fit into any of those categories, and were called merely public ministers. This explains why the Constitution refers to "Ambassadors" and "other public Ministers," both here and in Article III.[63]

"Consuls" were not public ministers and generally enjoyed fewer diplomatic privileges.[64] Vattel explained that consuls were,

> persons residing in the large trading cities, and especially the seaports, of foreign countries, with a commission to watch over the rights and privileges of their nation and to decide disputes between her merchants there.[65]

The fact that consuls were not public ministers explains why they were mentioned separately, both here and in Article III.[66]

The other phrase in Article II, Section 2, Clause 2 requiring explanation is "Advice and Consent". This did not mean the President should visit the Senate and engage its members in a roundtable discussion. Rather, in this context, the meaning of "to advise" was "to deliberate"—to take under advisement. The Senate's constitutional power to "Advise and Consent" was to take legislative-style action: Once the President submitted a decision to the Senate, that chamber would deliberate over it and then either approve or disapprove. It might be politically prudent for a President to consult leading Senators in advance, but the Constitution

---

[63] Article III, Section 2, Clauses 1 & 2. Similarly, a report presented to the Continental Congress in 1778 by Gouverneur Morris loosely stated that the three levels of public ministers were 1. ambassadors, 2. ministers plenipotentiary and envoys, and 3. residents. 11 J. Cont. Cong. 698 (Jul. 17, 1778).

[64] 33 J. Cont. Cong. 551–52 698 (Sep. 29, 1787) (report of Foreign Secretary John Jay).

[65] Vattel, p. 279. See also 26 J. Cont. Cong. 77 (Feb. 11, 1784); 29 *id.* 860 (Oct. 31, 1785) (report by Foreign Affairs Secretary John Jay); *id.* 886–87 (Nov. 25, 1785) (report by Jay).

[66] Article III, Section 2, Clause 2. In the federal convention's Committee of Detail, John Rutledge, the chairman, added "& Consuls" to the jurisdiction of the Supreme Court. 2 Farrand, p. 172. See also *id.* 424. The language was inserted into the Appointments Clause later. *Id.* 539.

did not require it.⁶⁷

The Senate's power to approve key executive decisions rendered it an executive, as well as a legislative, body. During the constitutional debates, Anti-Federalists cited this blending of powers as a reason for rejecting the Constitution. Many feared that the Senate could use its blended powers to give the new government an aristocratic cast. Federalists conceded that the Senate's powers were mixed. But they argued that granting the Senate such authority was necessary to balance the President (representing the monarchical principle) and the House (representing democracy). This is another illustration of how the Founders often abandoned separation of powers to accomplish more important goals.⁶⁸

Unlike the House of Representatives, the Senate could not elect its own speaker. The Constitution prescribed that the Vice President was to be President of the Senate.⁶⁹ A precedent was the English Lord Chancellor, who was ex officio speaker of the House of Lords.

Under the original (pre-Twelfth Amendment) constitutional plan, the Vice President usually would be the runner-up in the presidential election.⁷⁰ Thus, he probably would be a gifted politician, the President's rival,⁷¹ and, in those days of shorter life expectancies, a likely successor. Some of the Framers may thought that positioning the Vice President as leader of the Senate would strengthen the Senate's position as a check on the President and on the House of Representatives.

4.10 The Vice President

The qualifications for the office of Vice President (the original Constitution placed no hyphen in the title)⁷² apparently were the same as

---

[67] See Bibliography for sources.

[68] See also Section 1.3.5.

[69] Article I, Section 3, Clause 4.

[70] Article II, Section 1, Clause 3.

[71] Of their potential rivalry, Gouverneur Morris quipped at the federal convention that, if the Vice President turned out to be intimate with the President, "[t]he vice-president then will be the first heir-apparent that ever loved his father."

[72] The Twelfth and Fourteenth Amendments inserted a hyphen, but subsequent amendments have not.

those of the President.[73] His principal function was to serve as speaker ("president") of the Senate.[74] As noted in the previous section, one reason for making the Vice President the leader of the Senate may have been to increase the power of that body.

The Vice President voted as a Senator when the chamber was tied.[75] He also presided over the joint session of Congress that counted the votes of presidential electors.[76]

Thus, as originally conceived, vice presidency was more of a legislative than an executive officer.

If the President were to die, resign, or become disabled, the Vice President succeeded him.[77] Even aside from the possibility of succession, the position was a potentially powerful one: As leader of the Senate, he might enjoy great influence over affairs, and unlike the Speaker of the House, he could not—absent impeachment and conviction—be dislodged from this post. Indeed, some Founders may have expected the Vice President to serve as a counterweight to the President, and perhaps even lead a loyal opposition. However, any such expectations were overturned by the Twelfth Amendment,[78] which induced candidates for

---

[73] This was implicit in the election procedure and made explicit by the Twelfth Amendment.

[74] Article I, Section 3, Clause 4.

[75] Article I, Section 3, Clause 4.

[76] Article II, Section 1, Clause 3 ("The President of the Senate shall, in the presence of the Senate and the House of Representatives, open all the [sealed] Certificates, and the Votes shall then be counted.") This sentence was reproduced verbatim in the Twelfth Amendment.

In the aftermath of the 2020 presidential elections, some constitutional scholars contended that the Vice President could resolve disputes among rival slates of electors or postpone proceedings pending resolution of disputes. However, it is unlikely that the Constitution-makers would have given that much power to one person, especially one who might himself be a candidate The more likely interpretation is that the Vice President is merely the presiding officer of the joint session and that his rulings can be appealed from the floor and reversed by a simple majority.

[77] Article II, Section 1, Clause 6. Whether the Vice President would succeed to the office of President or merely exercise its powers was left uncertain.

[78] The Twelfth Amendment separated the election of the President and Vice President, so they were no longer direct electoral rivals:

President and Vice President to run as a ticket. This rendered the second office in the land largely dependent on the first.

The Electors ... shall name in their ballots the person voted for as President, and in distinct ballots the person voted for as Vice-President, and they shall make distinct lists of all persons voted for as President, and of all persons voted for as Vice-President. ...

CHAPTER FIVE

About the Grants of Powers to Congress

5.1 The Enumerated Powers

This chapter describes the Constitution's general scheme for granting authority to Congress. It also provides some guidelines for interpreting congressional powers. The next chapter examines individual grants in more detail.

Eighteen of the powers granted to Congress—about half of the total sum—were listed in Article I, Section 8. The rest, listed below,[1] were

---

[1] Located outside Article I, Section 8 were the congressional powers to:

• Manage federal property;

• Dispose of federal property;

• Govern the federal territories;

• Authorize the President to fill designated inferior offices without senatorial consent;

• Provide for the decennial census;

• Fix the pay of members of Congress and of federal officers;

• Override state laws regulating the times, places, and manner of congressional elections, other than the place of senatorial elections;

scattered throughout the Constitution. These powers were in addition to the prerogatives granted to the House or Senate as single chambers, discussed in Chapter Four. The lengthy nature of these lists would suggest that congressional powers were limited to those enumerated—even if we didn't know this from other sources.

5.2 Limitations on Powers

In addition to granting powers to Congress, the Constitution imposed restrictions on those powers. Each restriction was structured in one of three ways: (1) interwoven into the words of the grant, (2) added to the grant as a subordinate clause, or (3) located elsewhere in the document because it was intended to limit more than one grant.

Restrictions interwoven into a grant sometimes are called *internal limitations*. One internal limitation was the power to "establish an uniform Rule of Naturalization." The addition of the word "uniform" shows that the clause did not grant authority to establish non-uniform rules of naturalization. In like manner, the power to "establish . . . post Roads" did not grant authority to establish non-post roads.[2]

• Set the time for choosing electors and a uniform day for the electors to vote;

• Establish who succeeds to the presidency after the Vice President;

• Create exceptions to the Supreme Court's appellate jurisdiction;

• Fix the jurisdiction of federal courts inferior to the Supreme Court;

• Declare the punishment for treason;

• Consent to admission of new states or the combination of existing states;

• Defend states from invasion, insurrection, and non-republican forms of government;

• Propose constitutional amendments;

• Prescribe the oath for federal officers;

• Authorize a federal officer to receive benefits from a foreign nation; and

• Establish the rules by which the records and judgments of states were to be proved in other states.

[2] There are many other examples of this form within the Constitution. See, *e.g.*, Article IV, Section 3, Clause 2 (limiting regulations of federal property to "needful" ones).

The second kind of restriction appeared in subordinate clauses immediately after words containing one or more grants. For example, the phrase containing the grant (or, arguably, the two grants) of power to "raise and support Armies" was followed by the restriction, "but no Appropriation of Money to that Use shall be for a longer Term than two Years."[3] This book calls such restrictions *quasi-external limitations*.

Quasi-external limitations were, in turn, of two kinds—the special limitation and the proviso. A *special limitation* is a restriction that, whatever its actual wording, can be expressed by the phrase "so long as." For example, Congress could "promote the Progress of Science and useful Arts"—by [so long as it was done by] "securing for limited Times to Authors and Inventors the exclusive Right to their respective Writings and Discoveries."[4] Similarly, Congress could call forth the militia, but only so long as it did so to "execute the Laws of the Union, suppress Insurrections [or] repel Invasions."

A *proviso* is a clause imposing a condition that can terminate or reduce the scope of a previously listed power or right.[5] Provisos generally are introduced by words such as "but," "reserving," or "provided that." The Constitution qualified the grant of power "[t]o provide for organizing, arming, and disciplining, the Militia" with the proviso, "reserving to the States respectively, the Appointment of the Officers, and the Authority of training the Militia."[6]

The differences between a special limitation and a proviso are subtle, but in close questions of interpretation, a special limitation might be read more broadly than a proviso. To illustrate, consider the Taxation Clause, which includes both a special limitation and a proviso:

---

[3] Also in this category is Article III, Section 3, Clause 3 (granting Congress the power to "declare the Punishment of Treason, but no Attainder of Treason shall work Corruption of Blood. . . .") and Article I, Section 8, Clause 17, where the proviso is placed in parentheses ("not exceeding ten Miles square").

[4] Article I, Section 8, Clause 8. James Madison confirmed that the later phase was drafted deliberately as a limitation (Letter to Tench Coxe, Mar. 28, 1790, in Farrand-Supp. 298).

[5] A proviso also is called a condition subsequent—that is, a condition placed subsequent to the right or power.

[6] Article I, Section 8, Clause 16.

The Congress shall have Power To lay and collect Taxes, Duties, Imposts and Excises, *to pay the Debts and provide for the Common Defence and general Welfare of the United States*; <u>but all Duties, Imposts and Excises shall be uniform throughout the United States</u> . . .[7]

The special limitation is italicized. It meant that a tax was valid only so long as it was imposed to raise revenue for the general welfare. A levy imposed to raise revenue purely to benefit local or special interests was not permitted. The proviso is underlined. It meant that if Congress imposed a duty, impost, or excise, it could not enact one rate in Connecticut and another in New York.[8]

Suppose a taxpayer challenged an impost on the grounds that (1) it was not levied for the "general Welfare," but merely to raise revenue for a special interest and (2) it was not uniform. Suppose further than the government denied both charges. If the case was a close one, a traditional judge might give the benefit of the doubt on the special limitation to the taxpayer, and the benefit of the doubt on the proviso to the government. As skilled attorneys, the majority of the Framers and leading Ratifiers would have been familiar with this practice.

The third kind of restriction was placed entirely outside any one grant, because it applied to two or more grants. Such restrictions sometimes are called *external limitations*. The Bill of Rights was composed mostly of external limitations. So also was Article I, Section 9, which listed prohibitions applicable to Congress. Another external limitation was the clause requiring apportionment both for representation and direct taxes.[9]

5.3 Construing Congressional Powers

During the Founding era, statutes and documents typically were interpreted either strictly or liberally. *Strict construction* meant that if wording could be interpreted reasonably in more than one way, one adopted

---

[7] Article I, Section 8, Clause 1. Italics and underlining added.

[8] Notice this this proviso applies only "Duties, Imposts and Excises," not to direct taxes. For the difference, see Section 6.1.

[9] Article I, Section 2, Clause 3.

the narrower reading. Statutes defining and punishing crimes typically were strictly construed—as they still are today.

Liberal construction did not necessarily mean to interpret broadly. Rather, it meant to interpret according to the intent of the makers. The reader resolved doubts by consulting that intent, irrespective of whether this resulted in a broader or narrower interpretation.[10] The framers wrote the Constitution to be interpreted liberally.

For example, the Coinage Clause[11] granted Congress power "to coin Money." You could read this as meaning "to make money in the form of metallic coins." Alternatively, you could read "to coin" in the broader sense of "to fabricate" (as in "to coin a phrase"). An interpreter following the rule of strict construction would resolve the ambiguity with the narrower reading, thereby denying Congress the power to issue paper (or electronic) money. However, Founding-era jurists would have applied liberal construction—that is, they would have sought the understanding of the Ratifiers ("intent of the makers") and applied that. As it happens, the Ratifiers' understanding was that "to coin Money" meant to strike money in any medium.[12] According to the founding generation's interpretive methods, therefore, the Coinage Clause does confer power to issue non-metallic money.

5.4 The Fiduciary Nature of Congressional Powers

As discussed earlier,[13] the Founders tried to create a fiduciary-style government in which public officials would be the agents or trustees of the people. They often compared the Constitution to instruments creating private fiduciary relationships. Indeed, as observed in Chapter Four, the structure of Article I follows a common form then used for fiduciary documents conferring authority. According to reigning Whig political theory, a government action violating fiduciary duties was void.

---

[10] Intent-based construction was mandated by the doctrine of incidental powers. See Section 5.5. A Founding-era case applying intent-based construction to a state constitution is *Commonwealth v. Caton*, 8 Va. (4 Call) 5 (1782).

[11] Article I, Section 8, Clause 5.

[12] Section 6.3.2.

[13] Section 1.3.5.

5.5 The Necessary and Proper Clause(s) and Congressional Discretion

The Necessary and Proper Clause provided that Congress could "make all Laws which shall be necessary and proper for carrying into Execution" its other powers.[14] This language was adapted from similar wording used in 18th-century documents whereby one person granted enumerated powers to another.[15]

The fundamental purpose of the Necessary and Proper Clause was to communicate to the reader that the powers of Congress were to be read as the Ratifiers intended them rather than under the rules of strict construction.[16] A key legal tool used to promote this intent-based reading was the *doctrine of incidental powers*. The Necessary and Proper Clause was composed of language commonly used to embody the doctrine of incidental powers.

The best way to grasp this is through a simple example. Suppose the owner of a small grocery store signs a contact entrusting management of the store to an agent. Assume the contract says that the agent may "manage the store, hire and fire employees, and purchase and sell products." Managing, hiring and firing, and purchasing and selling are explicitly enumerated. They are called *principal powers* or *express powers*. Most people would understand, however, that the contract probably includes some authority not mentioned explicitly, such as employing a janitorial company or advertising products in newspapers or on the Internet. Just to be sure, though, a careful drafter might add a phrase such as "and to do all other things necessary and proper for managing the store." This additional phrase tells us that the store manager also has implied or incidental powers.

Now, imagine you are the manager and the owner is unavailable for an extended time. You want to know whether the contract permits you to pay property taxes on the land occupied by the store. Paying property taxes is not mentioned explicitly in the enumeration of powers. How do you know whether it is included? Put another way: If this scenario had

---

[14] Article I, Section 8, Clause 18.

[15] Common words used besides "necessary" and "proper" were "needful," "fit," "expedient," "convenient," and "meet" (in the sense of "appropriate").

[16] On strict construction, see Section 5.3.

been presented to the parties at the time they entered the contract, how would they have responded?

That might depend on local custom: Is it customary for store managers in the locality or in the business to pay property taxes? Or it might depend on whether there is an emergency: Can payment be delayed till the owner comes back? Thus, custom and degree of necessity can suggest whether an unstated power is, or is not, incidental.

During the Founding era (as today), the doctrine of incidental powers was subject to some common-sense limits.

The first limit was that an agent could act only for the purpose of carrying out his principal responsibilities. A store manager might pay taxes to save the store, but could not invade the till to pay for his social life. The courts did not tolerate any pretexts: A manager could not invade the till to pay for his social life on the pretext that management required that the manager stay happy.[17]

The second limit on incidental powers was that the agent's actions had to be either reasonably necessary to the enumerated powers or a customary way of carrying them out. A grocery store manager probably could not diversify into a sideline of selling carriages, since selling carriages was neither reasonably necessary for, nor customarily associated with, management of a grocery store.

The third limit (and this is crucial) was that incidental powers never included authority as important as the listed powers.[18] A store manager might have incidental authority to pay taxes to save the business from a tax sale, but he probably would not have power to sell the entire enterprise.

Although the law recognized incidental powers even without "necessary and proper" language, drafters routinely inserted such language as

---

[17] Lord Coke's expression was apt here: *Praetextu liciti non debet admitti illicitum* ("An illegal thing should not be admitted on a legal pretext").

[18] This was in accordance with the maxims *Accessorius sequitur naturam sui principalis* ("The accessory follows the nature of its principal") and *Derivativa potestas non potest esse major primitiva* ("The derivative power cannot be greater than its source"). It was sometimes said that the principal had to be "more worthy" than its incident.

In *Nat'l Fed. of Independent Business v. Sebelius*, 567 U.S. 519 (2012) (the "Obamacare" case), the Supreme Court explicitly recognized this crucial rule for the first time in nearly two centuries.

recitals—that is, as material for information purposes only. Its purpose was to alert readers that they should construe the enumerated powers as intended rather than strictly. The Framers thought the Necessary and Proper Clause particularly advisable because the Articles of Confederation had specifically barred Congress from exercising any incidental powers, and the Framers wanted to communicate that the Constitution was different.

The Necessary and Proper Clause has been widely misunderstood. Some have called it "the elastic clause," and suggested that it granted Congress vast authority that Congress otherwise would not have. Leading Federalists, including Madison and Hamilton, explicitly denied this. Even John Marshall, the Ratifier who as Chief Justice was accused of taking an overly broad view of the Clause, affirmed that it was a mere recital.[19]

Eighteenth-century law tells us that the word "necessary" would have been sufficient to reference the doctrine of implied, incidental powers. Why, then, did the Framers add the further requirement that a law be "proper"? The probable reason was to limit incidental laws to those that complied with the rules of public trust. The Founders would have considered any laws violating Congress's fiduciary duties to be *improper*.

According to prevailing political theory, moreover, laws violating Congress's fiduciary duties would have been outside its rightful authority even without a Necessary and Proper Clause. So the word "proper" did not change the Clause's role as a recital. To the extent that the word "proper" embodied the fiduciary duty of impartiality, it also recognized an equal protection rule for federal legislation similar to the one imposed on the states by the Fourteenth Amendment (1868).

In addition to referring to "the foregoing Powers," the Clause also refers to "all other Powers vested by this Constitution in the Government of the United States." Some commentators argue that (1) the Constitution did not grant explicitly any powers to the U.S. Government as such, but only to officers and departments, so therefore (2) this phase must refer to unenumerated authority derived from sources outside the document.

---

[19] John Marshall's Defense of *McCulloch v. Maryland* (Gerald Gunther, ed. 1969) contains Marshall's writings on this point. He was effectively applying the legal maxim *Expressio eorum quae tacite insunt nihil operatur* ("The expression of those things that already are inherent has no effect").

Of course, one problem with this hypothesis is that the Clause was limited explicitly to powers vested *"by this Constitution."* They could not come from elsewhere. Another problem is that several of the Constitution's provisions did, in fact, grant enumerated powers to the U.S. Government as such[20]—thereby rendering it unnecessary to speculate about unenumerated ones.

The Necessary and Proper Clause was not the Constitution's only reference to incidental powers. The Enclave Clause granted Congress—in addition to the express power to build "Forts, Magazines, Arsenals, [and] dock-Yards"—authority to construct "other needful Buildings."[21] In 18th-century drafting practice, the word "needful" also communicated a grant of incidental authority, thereby allowing Congress to construct buildings other than forts, magazines, arsenals, and dock yards. But incidental authority had to be "needful" for carrying out enumerated powers. An office building for revenue officers would be "needful" for executing the taxing power.[22] A museum or zoo would not.

The Constitution used three kinds of clauses to define how much discretion officials enjoyed. To avoid the requirement that a state impost receive congressional consent, the revenue from the impost had to be "absolutely necessary" to fund a state's inspection laws.[23] That clause permitted only minimal discretion.

On the other hand, Congress could propose constitutional

---

[20] The Guarantee Clause of Article IV imposed several obligations on the U.S. Government, and therefore necessarily granted power to fulfill them. Section 1.3.5. Also, Article VI imposed on the government the duty—and therefore, necessarily the power—to honor the Confederation's "Debts" and other "Engagements." Article I, Section 8, Clause 2 also granted power to pay debts, but only the obligatory language of Article V granted authority to fulfill pre-constitutional "Engagements."

The untenable claim that the Necessary and Proper Clause recognizes a reservoir of unenumerated congressional powers resembles the similarly-untenable doctrine of "inherent sovereign authority." See Section 3.2.

[21] Article I, Section 8, Clause 17 (emphasis added).

[22] The Property Clause, Article IV, Section 3, Clause 2, also uses the word "needful," but this is not an expression of incidental powers because it is not an addition to a previous express list, as are the Necessary and Proper and the Enclave Clauses.

[23] Article I, Section 10, Clause 2.

amendments, "whenever two-thirds of both Houses shall deem it necessary." Similarly, the President could "recommend to [Congress's] Consideration such Measures as he shall judge necessary and expedient."[24] Those clauses granted unlimited discretion. The courts could not second-guess congressional decisions to propose amendments or presidential recommendations to Congress.

The Necessary and Proper and Enclave Clauses lay between the two extremes of "minimal discretion" and "unlimited discretion." By encapsulating the doctrine of incidental powers, they required that laws and buildings be subordinate means—and customary or reasonably necessary means—for exercising enumerated powers.

---

[24] Article II, Section 3.

CHAPTER SIX

The Authority of Congress

This chapter addresses the Constitution's specific grants of powers to Congress. To save space and promote better overall perspective, I have combined the grants into seven broad categories:

- Revenue-raising
- Spending and borrowing
- Powers over the economy
- Judicial and criminal powers
- Federal land
- Promoting concord among the states
- Congressional administrative powers

6.1 Revenue-Raising

Several federal powers enabled Congress to raise revenue. Like the Confederation Congress, the new Federal Congress could market federal lands,[1] sell stamps at post offices,[2] and set a legal-tender value for its

---

[1] Article IV, Section 3, Clause 2 (granting power to dispose of federal lands).

money in excess of the cost.³ However, the most important provision for revenue-raising, at least over the long term, was the Taxation Clause.

The Taxation Clause replaced the ineffective requisitions device of the Articles, which had contemplated Congress receiving most of its funds from grants by the state legislatures. The Taxation Clause authorized Congress "[t]o lay and collect Taxes, Duties, Imposts and Excises" directly from the people. The money was to be used "to pay the Debts and provide for the common Defence and general Welfare of the United States."⁴ Some background is needed to fully understand the Taxation Clause.⁵

Government may impose financial exactions on people to raise money, influence behavior, or for both purposes. In Founding-era discourse, a *tax* was an exaction imposed predominantly to raise revenue.⁶ The Taxation Clause authorized taxes, but not financial impositions designed primarily to influence behavior.

To illustrate: Suppose that Congress levied a tariff on imported diamond jewelry. If the tariff generated significant revenue, then the Taxation Clause authorized it, even if it had the incidental effect of discouraging the importation of diamond jewelry.⁷ But if the tariff was so high it closed off practically all importation of diamond jewelry—and

---

² Article I, Section 8, Clause 7.

³ Article I, Section 8, Clause 5. The profit made when a government imposes a legal tender value for more than the cost is called *seigniorage*. During the Founding era, seigniorage was a recognized prerogative incident to the power to issue money. See Robert G. Natelson, *Paper Money and the Original Understanding of the Coinage Clause*, 31 Harvard J.L. & Pub. Policy 1017 (2008).

The Confederation Congress had issued bills of credit, and was well on the way toward establishing a metallic coinage, *e.g.*, 30 J. Cont. Cong. 162–82 (Apr. 12, 1786); 31 *id.* 503–04 (Aug. 8, 1786) & 876–78 (Oct. 16, 1786); 32 *id.* 160–64 (Apr. 9, 1787) & 223–25 (Apr. 21, 1787).

⁴ Article I, Section 8, Clause 1.

⁵ See Robert G. Natelson, *What the Constitution Means by "Duties, Imposts, and Excises"—and Taxes (Direct or Otherwise)*, 66 Case Western Res. L. Rev. 297 (2015).

⁶ These were the measures subject to the Origination Clause. See Section 4.6.

⁷ At the federal convention Oliver Ellsworth observed that taxes could be imposed to discourage excessive eating and drinking, but only insofar as "the regulation of eating & drinking can be reasonable." 2 Farrand, p. 344.

thereby generated no revenue—it was a regulation of foreign commerce, not a tax.[8] It probably was authorized by the Commerce Clause,[9] but not the Taxation Clause. If the tariff raised some revenue, but the proceeds were not used for the general support of government but instead funded an inspection program for imported diamond jewelry, it was not a tax but a regulation of foreign commerce.

Suppose, on the other hand, that Congress levied a charge on the *domestic* ownership of diamond jewelry so steep that it effectively prohibited the ownership of diamond jewelry—and thus raised no money. This levy would not be valid outside federal territories and enclaves. The Constitution did not authorize it as a tax, for it raised no revenue. The Constitution did not authorize it as a regulation of interstate commerce, because it was not imposed on trade. Instead, it was a rule of property ownership, and therefore within the sphere of exclusive state power.[10]

Founding-era discourse classified taxes as either *direct* or *indirect*. Great Britain and the American colonies and states typically imposed direct taxes through general statutes often called "land tax laws." These were omnibus revenue statutes that usually assessed and taxed far more than land. Their tax base included individuals ("heads"), property and wealth, businesses and trades, and income and profit of all kinds. Direct taxes were levies on status, living, livelihood, and production.[11]

Indirect taxes were levied on consumption of goods and services and

---

[8] Reports in the Confederation Congress discussed the use of duties and imposts to restrict trade. 26 J. Cont. Cong. 269–71 (Apr. 22, 1784); 31 *id.* 495 (Aug. 7, 1786). At the federal convention, George Clymer of Pennsylvania made a motion based on the revenue-commerce distinction. 2 Farrand, p. 363. James Madison once questioned the viability of the distinction, but he seems to have been alone in doing so.

[9] Article I, Section 8, Clause 3.

[10] At the Constitutional Convention, George Mason of Virginia—recognizing that the Taxing Power and Interstate Commerce Power would not accomplish his goal of limiting consumption—argued that the convention should add a federal power to limit consumption directly. Of course, the convention did not do so.

[11] British and American direct tax statutes are collected at Robert G. Natelson, *More Evidence That Direct Taxes Include Levies on Wealth and Income*, https://reason.com/volokh/2024/07/19/more-evidence-that-direct-taxes-include-levies-on-wealth-and-income/.

on certain specific transactions, such as importing and exporting and creating legal documents. Britain's notorious Stamp Tax, which imposed a fee on each newspaper sale and official document, was a kind of indirect tax.

In American (although not British) practice, the term *duties* encompassed all indirect taxes—although that word also could refer to impositions to regulate commerce rather than produce revenue.

The Constitution mentioned several specific kinds of duties: excises (levies on consumption of domestic goods), duties on exports, import duties or imposts, and a specialized impost called *tonnage*. This was a tax on the cargo of ships.

The Founders believed that, except in time of war, the federal government would limit itself to indirect taxes, which would generate sufficient revenue. Most educated men had read Thucydides' history of the Peloponnesian War and would have remembered an experiment by the Athenian empire during that war. In 413 B.C., Athens abolished direct taxes on her own citizens (the eisphorá) and on her allies (the hated phóros, or tribute). Instead, she imposed a five percent ad valorem levy on imports and exports. In the wake of the change, public resistance dropped and revenue increased.

The Framers inserted two quasi-external restrictions[12] on the revenue-raising power. The first was in the form of a special limitation and the second in the form of a proviso. The special limitation provided that tax money not used "to pay the Debts" of the government had to be employed to "provide for the common Defence and general Welfare" rather than for local or special interest purposes. Supreme Court Justice Joseph Story later observed that the General Welfare Clause prevented taxes from being imposed for local or special interest purposes or

> for ... objects wholly extraneous as, for instance, for propaganding [sic] Mahometanism among the Turks, or giving aids

---

[12] For quasi-external restrictions, special limitations, and provisos, see Section 5.2.

and subsidies to a foreign nation, to build palaces for its kings, or erect monuments to its heroes.[13]

The terms "common Defence" and "general Welfare" encapsulated the fiduciary requirements that government spend for the benefit of the people as a whole, and not play favorites.

The proviso in the Taxation Clause required that "all Duties, Imposts and Excises shall be uniform throughout the United States." This meant that in levying indirect taxes Congress could not impose different rates on different sections of the United States. Congress could not levy a ten-percent tariff on imports at Charleston and a twenty-percent tariff at New York, while leaving imports into Boston tax-free. The proviso was supplemented by additional rules requiring uniformity in indirect taxes and apportionment of direct taxes, all in pursuit of the ideal of impartiality.[14]

6.2 Borrowing and Spending

The Constitution endowed Congress with power to "borrow Money on the credit of the United States."[15] It further imposed a mandate on the U.S. government requiring and empowering it to pay existing Confederation debt:

> All Debts contracted and Engagements entered into, before the Adoption of this Constitution, shall be as valid against the United States under this Constitution, as under the Confederation.[16]

No borrowing limits were imposed.

Spending was to be undertaken only through congressional appropriations: "No Money shall be drawn from the Treasury, but in Conse-

---

[13] 1 Joseph Story, Commentaries on the Constitution of the United States 673 (1833).

[14] Section 1.3.5.

[15] Article I, Section 8, Clause 2.

[16] Article VI, Clause 1.

quence of Appropriations made by Law."[17] The common understanding was that appropriating money was within the legislative sphere.

Some enumerated powers included spending authority within their core language. For example, the powers to "support Armies,"[18] "maintain a Navy,"[19] and "establish Post Offices and post Roads"[20] all contemplated spending money. Monetary expenditures were customary or reasonably necessary for the exercise of most other powers, and thus authorized by the Necessary and Proper Clause.[21]

The Constitution did not authorize spending for unenumerated purposes. How is it, then, that the federal government spends trillions of dollars for unenumerated purposes? The answer begins with Alexander Hamilton.

Hamilton's "high Federalist" views were the most extreme of any leading Founder. At the 1787 convention, he urged his fellow delegates to propose a national government empowered to "pass all laws whatsoever." He further suggested that the chief executive and the senate be elected for life.[22] When his colleagues disregarded his proposals, he went home. Later in the convention, he returned, but confessed on the floor his "dislike of the [Constitution's] Scheme of Govt in General."[23] He admitted that "No man's ideas were more remote from the plan than his own were known to be."[24]

Despite his distaste for the Constitution, Hamilton decided to support its ratification. His personal notes show that he hoped to be part of a new federal administration that would "triumph altogether over the state governments and reduce them into an entire subordination, dividing

---

[17] Article I, Section 9, Clause 7.

[18] Article I, Section 8, Clause 12.

[19] Article I, Section 8, Clause 13.

[20] Article I, Section 8, Clause 7. See Section 6.3.5 for a discussion of the post-road power.

[21] Article I, Section 8, Clause 18.

[22] 1 Farrand, p. 291.

[23] 2 *Id.*, p. 524.

[24] 2 *Id.*, pp. 645–46.

the large states into smaller districts."[25]

Hamilton fought hard for the Constitution. He authored most of *The Federalist*. He also led the pro-Constitution forces during the first part of the New York ratifying convention.[26] When explaining the Constitution to the public, he emphasized that the federal government would enjoy only limited powers.

But once the battle was won, Hamilton changed his message. While serving as Secretary of the Treasury in December, 1791, he issued his *Report on Manufactures,* in which he argued that the "general Welfare" language of the Taxation Clause empowered Congress to spend money on almost anything:

> [T]he power to raise money is plenary and indefinite and the objects to which it may be appropriated are no less comprehensive than the payment of the public debts, and the providing for the common defence and general welfare.

Of course, this clashed with many Federalist representations made during the ratification debates, including his own.[27]

It also clashed with the Constitution's text. In 18th-century English, the phrase "to provide . . . for the general Welfare" did not mean "to spend for the general welfare." It meant "to store up provisions for [in other words, tax for] the general welfare."[28] Moreover, Hamilton's interpretation made no sense in light of the Constitution's listing of such additional powers as to "support Armies," "maintain a Navy," and "establish Post Offices and post Roads." Hamilton's interpretation of the Taxation Clause also would have rendered nugatory the two-year limit on

---

[25] 13 Documentary History, p. 278.

[26] Hamilton was forced to step back when John Lansing, Jr. and Robert Yates, who had been his New York colleagues in Philadelphia, informed the ratifying convention delegates what Hamilton had proposed there.

[27] Section 1.2.

[28] See Robert G. Natelson, *The General Welfare Clause and the Public Trust: An Essay in Original Understanding*, 52 U. Kan. L. Rev. 1 (2003). Compare the Navy Clause, Article I, Section 8, Clause 13: "to provide and maintain a Navy." To "provide" a navy means to pass laws authorizing it; to "maintain" it means to spend what is necessary to carry out the plan.

miliary appropriations in the Armies Clause.[29]

Although Hamilton's new hypothesis won almost no support among his contemporaries, it did pick up some during the 19th century. Then in 1936, the Supreme Court issued dicta (side comments) adopting it,[30] and the next year, the court declared those dicta to be authoritative.[31] It thereby licensed Congress to spend money on almost anything it chose.[32]

Some commentators who admit Hamilton's interpretation is wrong nevertheless try to rescue the cause of unlimited domestic spending by arguing that it is authorized by the Constitution's Article IV Property Clause.[33] Their argument runs like this:

- The Property Clause granted Congress power to "dispose of . . . other Property belonging to the United States;"
- the Founders believed money was property;
- the Property Clause imposed no limits on the disposal power; so
- Congress may spend any of its money for any purpose.

But this line of reasoning suffers from some of the same problems that afflict Hamilton's interpretation: It would render several other congressional powers useless. It would allow Congress to evade the two-year appropriation limit in the Armies Clause. And it contradicts how the Constitution was represented to the Ratifiers.[34] Furthermore, there is almost no Founding-era evidence that the Ratifiers thought the Property Clause had anything to do with spending.

Actually, the phrase "other Property" in Article IV seems to have

---

[29] Article I, Section 8, Clause 12.

[30] *United States v. Butler*, 297 U.S. 1 (1936).

[31] *Helvering v. Davis*, 301 U.S. 619 (1937).

[32] "Almost anything" because in theory an expenditure must be for the common defense or general welfare. The Supreme Court has never enforced this limitation, but some federal spending programs are so frivolous or special-interest oriented they arguably violate it. Robert G. Natelson, *A Constitutional Rule on Federal Spending*, https://lawliberty.org/a-constitutional-rule-on-federal-spending/ (2025).

[33] Article IV, Section 3, Clause 2.

[34] Chapter Three.

been limited to real estate. It was part of the larger phrase "Territory and other Property," and at least two Founding-era rules of construction direct us to interpret "Property" as being in the same general class as "Territory."[35]

This reading is supported by major reasons behind Article IV: to enable the federal government to take possession of, manage, and sell state land claims west of the Appalachians and convert them into new states. In pursuit of such ends, Article IV addressed the disposition and regulation of federal territories outside the states, the admission of new states, the division of states into smaller states, and the possible consolidation of states. Article IV added that the Constitution would not "be so construed as to Prejudice any Claims of the United States, or of any particular State." All of those issues involved real estate rather than spending.

In sum: The original Constitution granted Congress authority to spend money when executing its enumerated powers. But it granted no authority to spend on unenumerated subjects.

6.3 Congressional Economic Powers: Commerce across Political Lines, Bankruptcy, the Postal Clause, Patents, Copyrights, and Money and Other Weights and Measures

6.3.1 Preliminary Note

The original Constitution divided economic responsibilities between the federal government and the states. The economic subjects conceded to Congress were money and other weights and measures, bankruptcy, patents and copyrights, the mails, intercity highways, and much of the area of law known as the *law merchant*.

---

[35] *Noscitur ex socio qui non cognoscitur ex se* ("What is not known by itself alone is known by its associate"); *Copulatio verborum indicat acceptionem in eodem sensu* ("A connection of words implies taking them with the same meaning.") (Sir Francis Bacon).

6.3.2 Money and Other Weights and Measures

In 18th-century law, "regulating commerce" included overseeing weights and measures and issuing and governing money. As explained below, however, the Constitution granted Congress power to "regulate Commerce" only across political boundaries. By inserting a separate clause on money and measures, the Framers enabled Congress to govern those subjects unimpeded by state lines. The clause provided, "The Congress shall have Power . . . To coin Money, regulate the Value thereof, and of foreign Coin, and fix the Standard of Weights and Measures."[36]

The power to "coin Money" and to "regulate . . . foreign Coin" included money forged in any medium, not merely metallic coin—a point repeatedly affirmed during the ratification debates. While many of the Founders did not much care for paper money, they denied only the states, not the federal government, the prerogative of issuing it.

Regulating the value of money meant principally setting legal tender values. Legal tender values were the prices at which creditors had to accept the money. They usually they were more than the money's intrinsic values: A coin with an intrinsic worth of a penny might have a legal tender value of 25¢. The authority of governments to create such differences and profit from them was called *seigniorage*. The Constitution also granted the closely related power to define and punish counterfeiting.[37]

---

[36] Article I, Section 8, Clause 5. It has been suggested facetiously that Congress could prolong its two-year term by using its weights and measures power to increase the length of the year. To some in the founding generation, the possibility was not altogether facetious: An Anti-Federalist delegate to the Massachusetts ratifying convention suggested the federal government might meddle with the Constitution's terms of office. 6 Documentary History, p. 1195. There were precedents, including the Roman government's manipulation of the official calendar and Oliver Cromwell's edict altering the word "month" for some purposes to mean the 28-day military month. DeLolme, pp. 281–82,

For further discussion, see Robert G. Natelson, *Does the Constitution Have a Hidden Flaw That Could Create Tyranny? About "Gödel's Loophole"*, https://i2i.org/does-the-constitution-have-a-hidden-flaw-that-could-create-tyranny-about-godels-loophole/.

[37] Article I, Section 8, Clause 6.

6.3.3 Bankruptcy

Congress received authority to "establish ... uniform Laws on the subject of Bankruptcies throughout the United States.[38] Like the governance of weights and measures and the issuance of money, bankruptcy law was part of "regulating commerce," but the separate grant enabled Congress to exercise this authority within state boundaries.

The Bankruptcy Clause did not require Congress to adopt a law on the subject—and, indeed, Congress intervened only gradually throughout the 19th century. The adjective "uniform" is an internal limitation:[39] Congress may not adopt different bankruptcy standards for different parts of the country.

6.3.4 Patents and Copyrights

The provision we now call the Intellectual Property Clause enabled Congress to "promote the Progress of Science and useful Arts"—but only by granting patents and copyrights.[40] This was the sole area of property law not left primarily to state supervision.

6.3.5 The Postal Clause

The Postal Clause granted Congress power to "establish Post Offices and post Roads."[41] A post road was an inter-city thoroughfare with stations called "posts" or "stages," each supervised by a post office. The posts or stages contained facilities for hiring and changing horses and vehicles—hence the expressions "stage wagon" and "stage coach." Many posts also featured inns and taverns, offices for handling the mail, and newspaper offices—hence the still-common appearance of "post" in newspaper names.

---

[38] Article I, Section 8, Clause 4.

[39] See Section 5.2 (defining "internal limitation").

[40] James Madison confirmed that this as an internal limitation on Congress. Farrand-Supp., p. 298 (Letter to Tench Coxe, Mar. 28, 1790). Although this clause denominated patents and copyrights as "rights," in fact, they were privileges. In the language of the time, as today, the term "right" without the adjective "natural," could refer to a privilege.

[41] Article I, Section 8, Clause 7. See Robert G. Natelson, *Founding-era Socialism: The Original Meaning of the Constitution's Postal Clause*, 7 Brit. J. Am. Legal Studies 1 (2018).

City streets, cross-roads, and lesser highways were not post roads even if a courier might carry mail over them. Ratification-era debate confirms that they were to remain solely the responsibility of state and local governments.[42]

The phrase "establish Post Offices and post Roads" was borrowed from British practice. In this context, the word "establish" included building and maintaining post offices and post roads, operating them, and fixing penalties for such offenses as violating the postal monopoly or interfering with the mail.

6.3.6 The Commerce Clause—in General

In 18th-century law, to "regulate commerce" was to supervise trade and certain closely associated activities. The body of jurisprudence applied to commercial regulation was called the *law merchant*.[43] The chief subjects addressed by the law merchant were

- weights and measures;
- money;
- bankruptcy
- buying and selling goods, particularly by professional traders (merchants);
- prices, markets, quality of goods, and terms of sale;
- navigation and, to a lesser extent, other forms of transportation;
- trading ethics, mercantile insurance, and commercial paper;[44] and

---

[42] Modern interstate highways have no posts or stages for the rental of horses, so by the rules of strict construction (see Section 5.3) they are not "post roads." But they do provide speedy travel between distinct localities with discrete "stages" for refueling and refreshment, and they help assure speedy delivery of the mail. Accordingly, interstate highways qualify as post-roads by the rules of intent-based construction, the method of constitutional interpretation favored by the Founders. *Id.*

[43] The phrase "law merchant" is of French origin, and, as in other phrases of French origin such as "attorney general" and "court martial," the adjective comes after the noun. The law merchant was mercantile law.

[44] Commercial paper consists of instruments by which money is promised or ordered. Examples are promissory notes and checks.

- tariffs and other restrictions to promote or discourage particular economic activities.[45]

Notice that the Constitution granted Congress general power over the first three items on the list—weights and measures, money, and bankruptcy—irrespective of political boundaries. But it granted power over the other items only insofar as they crossed political boundaries: "with foreign Nations, among the several States, and with the Indian Tribes."[46] In thus splitting commercial jurisdiction between the federal government and the states, the Framers essentially adopted the central/local division advocated by the colonists when Americans were still part of the British Empire.

6.3.7 More Information about the Commerce Clause

This section examines some specific aspects of commercial regulation, and explains the extent to which the original Constitution entrusted them to Congress.

Transportation. The law merchant's (and therefore Congress's) power over navigation was sweeping:[47] It extended to construction, ownership, and maintenance of harbors, lighthouses, and piers. Authority over land transportation was less extensive. It included regulation of land transport, but not the creation or ownership of the modes of transportation. Most road creation remained exclusively within the authority of the states, which is why the Framers enumerated a separate power to establish "post Roads." Some Framers wanted the federal government to cut canals, but their proposal to add an enumerated power for that purpose was unsuccessful.

---

[45] On the content of the law merchant, see Robert G. Natelson, *The Original Understanding of the Indian Commerce Clause: An Update*, 23 Federalist Soc'y Rev. 209 (2022) and Robert G. Natelson, *The Meaning of "Regulate Commerce" to the Constitution's Ratifiers*, 23 Federalist Soc'y Rev. 307 (2022).

[46] Article I, Section 8, Clause 3.

[47] Some writers have assumed that Chief Justice Marshall was being inventive—perhaps employing an expansive version of the Necessary and Proper Clause—when holding that regulating commerce included regulating navigation. But as Marshall pointed out, this had always been true. *Gibbons v. Ogden*, 22 U.S. 1, 190 (1824).

Incorporation. The Founding-era record suggests that the law merchant included power to issue charters of incorporation for regulatory purposes.[48] However, the Framers rejected a proposed power to authorize incorporation of canal companies.

The Indian Commerce Clause. The portion of the Commerce Clause commonly called the Indian Commerce Clause, granted Congress power to "regulate Commerce . . . with the Indian Tribes." It enabled Congress to supervise the same activities it supervised under the remainder of the Commerce Clause. In the case of the Native Americans, these activities included the behavior of merchants in the Indian trade, commercial finance, price-setting, commercial travel across political lines, and related activities.

Modern writers often claim that the Indian Commerce Clause granted Congress plenary power over all (not merely commercial) Indian affairs and that this power was exclusive—that is, the states retained none. These claims are inaccurate. Under the Constitution, the states retained concurrent, although subordinate, power over commerce with the Indian tribes, and exclusive authority over other Indian affairs, except where preempted by the federal government pursuant to other constitutional provisions, such as the Territories and Treaty Clauses.[49]

Tariffs and Other Trade Restrictions. Congress's power to administer the law merchant included imposing tariffs for regulating trade. Tariffs authorized by the Commerce Clause might be restrictive in nature—that is, adopted to limit or stop the import of certain goods. Alternatively, tariffs might raise revenue for narrowly defined regulatory activities, such as the inspection of goods and the maintenance of harbors.

Tariffs for regulating trade usually were called "duties" or "imposts," but they should not be confused with duties or imposts levied to raise general revenue. Revenue-raising duties and imposts were authorized by the Taxation Clause rather than by the Commerce Clause. Because the uniformity rule in the Taxation Clause did not apply to tariffs for regulat-

---

[48] Or so Elbridge Gerry claimed at the federal convention, without contradiction (2 Farrand, pp. 633 & 635–36).

[49] See Section 7.9.2 (treaty power) and Section 3.4 (concurrent jurisdiction). See also Robert G. Natelson, *The Original Meaning of the Indian Commerce Clause*, 85 Denver U. L. Rev. 201 (2007) and *The Original Understanding of the Indian Commerce Clause: An Update*, 23 Federalist Soc'y Rev. 209 (2022).

ing trade, the Constitution added another rule of uniformity, the Port Preference Clause. It read as follows:

> No Preference shall be given by any Regulation of Commerce or Revenue to the Ports of one State over those of another: nor shall Vessels bound to, or from, one State, be obliged to enter, clear, or pay Duties in another.[50]

Today, economists are skeptical of restrictive tariffs, but during the Founding era, most people thought they helped a nation compete economically with other nations. Through restrictive tariffs, many believed, Congress could stimulate American agriculture and manufacturing. Congress also could use commercial regulations as diplomatic leverage to induce other nations to open their markets to our products. Thus, Congress could employ the Commerce Power to impact economic activities, such as agriculture and manufacturing, outside the scope of the word "commerce." Further, Congress could use the Commerce Power to achieve non-economic goals, including goals that were moral or cultural. For example, the power to regulate "Commerce with foreign Nations" enabled Congress to restrict the importation of slaves. (Article I, Section 9, Clause 1 imposed a twenty-year ban on full use of this power.)

When pursuing non-commercial goals under the Commerce Power, however, Congress had to do so through the regulation of commerce, not by laws directly governing non-commercial activities such as manufacturing or agriculture.

The Necessary and Proper Clause. There was one exception to the last statement. There were some cases in which Congress could regulate activities not specifically enumerated. These cases were covered by the Necessary and Proper Clause.

The Necessary and Proper Clause is discussed in Section 5.5. Suffice to say here that Congress could enact laws regulating some non-commercial activities if doing so was incidental to exercising enumerated powers. Laws passed under Congress's incidental powers, unlike regulations of enumerated subjects, could be adopted only to achieve enumerated purposes. Congress could not pass a law regulating some aspect of agri-

---

[50] Article I, Section 9, Clause 6 (italics added).

culture as incidental to commerce if Congress's real purpose was to regulate agriculture and not commerce.[51]

6.3.8 More on the Limits of Congress's Economic Powers

Modern Supreme Court doctrine purports to grant Congress virtually unlimited authority over economic activity and some writers would extend this to all interrelationships among people.

These notions are profoundly ahistorical. As we have seen, the Anglo-American concept of regulating commerce across political boundaries had well-defined limits. Several exhaustive studies have confirmed that these limits were understood during the ratification-era.[52]

Buttressing those studies are three other factors.

- A very broad meaning of "Commerce" is not a permissible reading of the Constitution because it would render many, or most, of the other congressional powers irrelevant.
- During the ratification debates, the Commerce Power was relatively uncontroversial. If the Commerce Power were as broad as modern commentators say it is, the Constitution never would have been ratified.
- During the ratification debates, the Constitution's advocates publicly listed examples of activities over which the federal government would have no authority. Among these were marriage, divorce, domestic life, manufacturing, agriculture, land use, land titles, land conveyancing, commerce wholly within state lines, state and local government, regulation of most crimes and civil suits, social services, training the militia and appointing militia officers, religion, and education.[53] Obviously, these represen-

---

[51] Since 1941, when the Supreme Court stopped enforcing limits on the Commerce Power, Congress frequently has violated this rule. For example, Congress adopts laws regulating the environment on the grounds that the environment "substantially affects" commerce, but actually with the goal of regulating the environment, not regulating commerce. See, *e.g.*, *Hodel v. Indiana*, 452 U.S. 314 (1981).

[52] See the bibliography for this chapter.

[53] See the bibliography for this chapter.

tations are inconsistent with extravagant modern claims for the Commerce Power.

On the other hand, those who claim the Commerce Power was limited to "making commerce regular"—that is, creating an unfettered open national market—interpret it too narrowly. As explained above, the Constitution granted Congress authority to adopt all sorts of restrictions and prohibitions on trade, including those intended to influence non-commercial activities indirectly.

6.4 Congressional Military Powers

History taught the Founders that nations were tempted to launch wars for aggressive purposes. The Revolution taught them that Congress needed power to tax for the common defense. Classical Greco-Roman history informed them that federations combining monarchical with republican states were inherently unstable, because the monarchical states sought to dominate their neighbors. Both Greco-Roman and British history informed them of the danger from military strongmen, so the legislature should retain power over military finance and serve as a check on the executive's war-waging authority. All these lessons appear in the Constitution's handling of military matters.

In general, the Constitution's warfare protocol was that Congress would "provide for" (in the future-looking 18th-century sense) military operations, and the President would carry them out.

Defensive war. During the Founding era, wars were classified as defensive or offensive. The Constitution's fundamental authorization for the federal government to engage in defensive war was the Guarantee Clause of Article IV:

> The United States shall guarantee to every State in this Union a Republican Form of Government, and shall protect each of them against Invasion; and on Application of the Legislature, or of the Executive (when the Legislature cannot be convened) against domestic Violence.[54]

---

[54] Article IV, Section 4.

The Guarantee Clause enabled and obliged the government to use military force (1) against a non-republican state government, (2) against invaders into state territory, and (3) upon state request, against domestic violence. Additionally, the Territories and Property Clause of Article IV implicitly authorized defensive war to protect federal property and territory outside state boundaries.[55]

Complementing the Guarantee Clause was a congressional power to utilize state militias for defensive war purposes: "To provide for calling forth the Militia" for "execut[ing] the Laws of the Union, suppress[ing] Insurrections and repel[ling] Invasions."[56] To ensure against state neglect of the militia, the Constitution authorized Congress to "provide for organizing, arming, and disciplining, the Militia, and for governing such Part of them as may be employed in the Service of the United States," while prescribing the rules by which the militia was to be trained.[57]

Another branch of Congress's defensive war power was its ability to suspend the writ of habeas corpus "when in cases of rebellion or invasion the public safety may require it."[58] Legislative suspension of the privilege of habeas corpus was a recognized incident of the power to conduct war: In times of military emergency, the British Parliament had sometimes suspended citizens' ability to obtain the writ,[59] and during the Revolutionary War, the Continental Congress did the same. Suspension authorized military detention and punishment for citizens who otherwise could have

---

[55] Article IV, Section 3, Clause 2. ("The Congress shall have Power to dispose of and make all needful Rules and Regulations respecting the Territory or other Property belonging to the United States.")

[56] Article I, Section 8, Clause 15.

[57] Article I, Section 8, Clause 16. Despite the Supreme Court's claim to the contrary in *Perpich v. Dep't of Defense*, 496 U.S. 334 (1990), the text does not authorize the federal government to "nationalize" the militia for training purposes. The states, not the federal government, are to train the militia: "reserving to the States respectively ... the Authority of training the Militia according to the discipline prescribed by Congress." *Id.* Also, there does not seem to be any constitutional sanction for employing the militia in offensive war.

[58] Article I, Section 9, Clause 2.

[59] DeLolme, p. 277.

demanded a hearing in a civilian court.[60]

Because the power to suspend habeas corpus was an incident to the federal government's war power, there was no need for the Framers to add it to the list of express congressional powers: It was encompassed by the Necessary and Proper Clause.[61] Limits on suspending the writ of habeas corpus are discussed in Section 9.10.2 .

Offensive war. During the Founding era, a nation entering into an offensive war was expected to "declare war."[62] Doing so signaled that the offensive conflict was a just war rather than merely an effort to conquer or loot other countries. As Charles Pinckney said at the federal convention: "Conquest or superiority among other powers is not or ought not ever be the object of a republican system."[63] This did not prevent the federal government from taking foreign territory as a customary incident of a just war and of the Treaty Power.

The Constitution granted Congress the following powers primarily relevant to offensive war, but employable in defensive conflicts as well:

- "declare War,"[64]
- "grant Letters of Marque and Reprisal,"[65] which authorized private entities to wage naval war,
- "make Rules concerning Captures on Land and Water,"[66]

---

[60] *E.g.*, 9 J. Cont. Cong. 784 (Oct. 8, 1777) (citing fact of invasion and temporarily authorizing the commander-in-chief to court-martial civilians for dealing with the enemy within geographic limits); *id.* 1068 (Dec. 30, 1777) (extending that power); 10 *id.* 204–05 (Feb. 27, 1778) (authorizing the death sentence via court martial for U.S. "subjects" who assisted the enemy in certain ways within seventy miles of U.S. armed forces).

[61] Article I, Section 8, Clause 18.

[62] Vattel, pp. 501–503.

[63] Farrand-Supp., p. 113.

[64] Article I, Section 8, Clause 11.

[65] Article I, Section 8, Clause 11. Letters of Marque and Reprisal were abolished by international convention during the nineteenth century. Thus, this power is now unexercised.

[66] Article I, Section 8, Clause 11.

- "raise and support Armies,"[67] although military appropriations had to be renewed at least every two years,[68]
- "provide and maintain a Navy,"[69]
- enlist and conscript soldiers and sailors—powers that, while unmentioned, were recognized incidents of raising armies and navies,[70] and therefore within the Necessary and Proper Clause; and
- "make Rules for the Government and Regulation of the land and naval Forces."[71]

In the British Empire, making "Rules for the Government and Regulation of the land and naval Forces" was a prerogative of Parliament. That body established permanent rules of conduct for the Royal Navy, and it annually passed a "Mutiny Act," which prescribed rules for the army. Traditionally, the English courts recognized martial law only in time of war, but these parliamentary acts imposed martial law on servicemen even in time of peace. During the pre-constitutional era, the Continental Congress exercised precisely the same power, adopting military regulations entitled "Articles of War" in 1776 and amending them the following year.[72]

There has been controversy over the extent to which Congress could, in its "Rules for the Government and Regulation of the land and naval Forces," deny servicemen the protections of the Bill of Rights. That subject is discussed in Section 9.12.1.

---

[67] Article I, Section 8, Clause 12.

[68] Article I, Section 8, Clause 12.

[69] Article I, Section 8, Clause 13.

[70] Vattel, p. 473.

[71] Article I, Section 8, Clause 14.

[72] The Continental Congress' principal Articles of War are in 5 J. Cont. Cong. 788–807 (Sep. 20, 1776), amended at 7 *id.* 264–66 (Apr. 14, 1777) and 9 *id.* 476–77 (Jun. 18, 1777).

6.5 Congressional Judicial, Criminal, and Immigration Powers

The common law divided crimes into *mala in se* and *mala prohibita*. A crime *malum*[73] *in se* was one that was "evil in itself," for it violated natural law. Examples were murder, theft, and treason. A *malum prohibitum*—"a prevented (or prohibited) evil"—was a crime only because it violated some scheme of legislative regulation. An example was violation of a commercial restriction.

As the Federalists explained during the debate over the Constitution, congressional authority over crimes *mala in se* would be very limited. Congress could "define and punish Piracies . . . committed on the High Seas, and Offenses against the Law of Nations"—the latter encompassing control over the emigration and immigration of free persons.[74] It could "make Rules for the Government and Regulation of the land and naval Forces."[75] The Constitution further authorized Congress to define and state the punishment for felonies on the high seas,[76] to specify (within limits) the punishment for treason,[77] and to legislate within federal territories and within the District of Columbia and other federal enclaves.[78] In addition, the Constitution granted Congress authority to "provide for the Punishment of counterfeiting the Securities and current Coin of the United States"[79]—arguably a *malum in se* crime, because counterfeiting is a

---

[73] *Malum* in this context is a noun meaning "evil." *Mala* is the plural form.

[74] Article I, Section 8, Clause 10. On governance of emigration and immigration as part of the law of nations, see Robert G. Natelson, *The Constitution's Define and Punish Clause: The Source of the Power to Regulate Immigration*, 11 Brit. J. Am. Leg. Studies 209 (2022). Congress's power over immigration was limited until 1808. Article I, Section 9, Clause 1.

[75] Article I, Section 8, Clause 14.

[76] The Articles of Confederation authorized Congress to appoint courts to try piracy, but not to define or punish piracy. Confederation Foreign Secretary John Jay concluded that authority to define and punish piracy was implied, but authority over felony in general was not. 29 J. Cont. Cong. 797–805. A congressional committee later proposed an amendment to the Articles clarifying the issue. 31 *id.* 497 (Aug. 7, 1786).

[77] Article III, Section 3, Clause 2.

[78] Article I, Section 8, Clause 17.

[79] Article I, Section 8, Clause 6. The Confederation period witnessed notorious cases of forgery of congressional securities. *E.g.*, 28 J. Cont. Cong. 61 (Feb. 11, 1785).

form of theft. In a few cases, congressional authority over *mala in se* crimes, such as mail theft, was inherent in expressly granted powers.[80] Otherwise, only the states could legislate on *mala in se* crimes within their borders.

Congress received considerable authority to create *mala prohibita*. For example, Congress could legislate criminal penalties for violating its rules pertaining to taxation, appropriation, commerce, intellectual property, and other subjects within the federal sphere.[81] Presumably, Congress could declare it a crime to violate its regulations governing federal property within state boundaries[82] or to disregard its full faith and credit rules.[83]

Congressional creation of crimes could not exceed the scope of the enumerated powers. Regulation of manufacturing and agriculture, for example, generally was not within the scope of the Commerce Power, so Congress could not render it a crime to violate federal manufacturing or agricultural standards.

6.6 Congressional Powers over Federal Land—the Enclave Clause and the Territories and Property Clause

The Enclave Clause authorized Congress:

> To exercise exclusive Legislation in all Cases whatsoever, over such District (not exceeding ten Miles square) as may, by Cession of particular States, and the Acceptance of Congress, become the Seat of the Government of the United States, and to exercise like Authority over all Places purchased by the Consent of the Legislature of the State in which the Same shall be, for the

---

[80] For example, dealing with mail theft was a recognized part of "establishing" post offices. Section 6.3.2. When regulating the post office, the Confederation Congress provided for punishment of mail theft, 32 J. Cont. Cong. 48 (Feb. 14, 1787), and for infringing the postal monopoly. *Id.* 50.

[81] Article III, Section 3, Clause 2.

[82] Article IV, Section 3, Clause 2.

[83] Article IV, Section 1.

Erection of Forts, Magazines, Arsenals, dock-Yards, and other needful Buildings.[84]

The Framers inserted this provision to allow the federal government to maintain installations free of state control. In June, 1783, when the Confederation Congress was meeting in the State House (now Independence Hall) in Philadelphia, Continental soldiers surrounded the building, peacefully but firmly demanding back pay. When Pennsylvania authorities refused to disperse the troops, Congress was sufficiently disquieted to leave Philadelphia for Princeton, New Jersey. Congress soon began to consider the desirability of a national capital over which it would have sole control, so it would not need to rely on state authorities.[85]

The Enclave Clause authorized acquisition of ten miles square (one hundred square miles) for a national capital. This, like all enclaves, was to be located within state boundaries and acquired with the consent of the state.

The Enclave Clause also authorized acquisitions to carry out enumerated powers: It empowered Congress to acquire land for "needful" buildings. The word "needful" in enumerations of powers generally referred to items incidental to express grants. That fact, together with the structure of the Constitution, suggested that enclaves could be held only for enumerated purposes. In case there was any doubt on the point, the Constitution listed four specific examples of "needful Buildings"— "Forts, Magazines, Arsenals, [and] dock-Yards"—all incidental to powers expressly enumerated. Under the rule of construction known as *ejusdem generis* ("of the same kind"),[86] the phrase "other needful Buildings" denoted structures of like character.

---

[84] Article I, Section 8, Clause 17.

[85] 24 J. Cont. Cong. 410–14, 418 (Jun. 21-Jul. 1, 1783). The first mention in the Journal of a capital district was on July 8, 1783. *Id.* 428. At one point, Congress voted for an impractical plan for two capital districts. 25 *id.* 712–14 (Oct. 21, 1783).

[86] The rule of *ejusdem generis* is that the content of a general phrase is defined by the nature of specific items listed. For example, if you were given a choice of "animal, vegetable, or mineral," you might classify a tree as "vegetable." But given a list of "cabbage, lettuce, radishes, cucumbers, and other vegetables," *ejusdem generis* suggests that on this list, the phrase "other vegetables" does not include trees.

"Buildings" did not include undeveloped land. Contemporaneous dictionaries defined the word much as we would—as edifices or fabricated enclosures for purposes of shelter and security.

How large could the "Places" be that Congress acquired "for the Erection of . . . needful Buildings"? That would depend on the circumstances. Land supporting an office building might be limited to the land on which the building was located and a surrounding yard. But other enclaves could be a good deal more extensive. Some Founding-era treaties with Indian tribes provided for large enclaves around forts and trading posts in potentially hostile Indian country: The most common size was six miles square, although some enclaves were five or two miles square. Presumably, the courts could invalidate an effort to create an enclave of excessive size.[87]

The ratification-era record suggests that a state negotiating the cession of an enclave could negotiate terms of governance that would bind Congress. For example, a state could insist that citizens of the prospective enclave be guaranteed certain rights. One reason the Bill of Rights was adopted was to assure that the liberties of citizens in the capital district were protected.[88]

The other constitutional provision directly relevant to federal land was the Territories and Property Clause.[89] During the federal convention, the delegates struggled with several issues pertaining to the Western Territories. One of these was how to enforce congressional claims over those territories. Another was the extent to which the Constitution would recognize state claims. A third was whether new states carved out of these lands would have to be admitted on an equal footing with the original states (as promised in the Northwest Ordinance), or whether

---

[87] Modern courts have not done so, even when the Enclave Clause is used to justify massive federal holdings of raw land for unenumerated purposes. See, *e.g.*, *Collins v. Yosemite Park*, 304 U.S. 518 (1938). The popularity of national parks may be one cause of this reluctance, although government ownership of those parks is not necessary to preserve them, since they could be held by perpetual charitable trusts, as in some other countries.

[88] During the ratification battle, there were complaints that without a bill of rights, the federal government might deprive residents of the capital district of basic rights, such as trial by jury and freedom of religion.

[89] Article IV, Section 3, Clause 2.

Congress could impose conditions on the admission of those states. On August 29, at the request of Gouverneur Morris, the convention voted to drop the equal-footing requirement. The following day, the convention adopted language proposed by Morris that preserved both congressional and state claims in the West. With some minor changes, Morris' proposal eventually became the Territories and Property Clause—often called merely the "Property Clause":

> The Congress shall have Power to dispose of and make all needful Rules and Regulations respecting the Territory or other Property belonging to the United States; and nothing in this Constitution shall be so construed as to Prejudice any Claims of the United States, or of any particular State.

The "Territory . . . of the United States" originally comprised land ceded by Great Britain to the states in the Treaty of 1783. It was land located outside of core state boundaries; most state claims to that land were ceded to Congress. Land within a "Territory of the United States" might be titled to the federal government, to states, or to private parties. But however titled, all of it was subject to federal governmental authority. The Constitution impliedly authorized the federal government to acquire additional "Territory" from foreign nations, because land acquisition was a customary incident of the Treaty Power.[90]

"[O]ther Property" referred only to real estate, not to other kinds of property.[91] Specifically, it was land within state boundaries titled to the federal government, but not qualifying as an enclave. Congress had power to "make all needful Rules and Regulations respecting . . . other Property." Because "other Property" was land within state boundaries over which the states had not yielded jurisdiction, it is unlikely the Constitution granted Congress the unconditional authority it enjoyed over enclaves and territories. The Founding-era records do not say what the line was to be between state and federal jurisdiction over "other Property." But the Founders surely would not have approved of the modern Supreme Court's doctrine granting Congress such broad power to

---

[90] Section 7.9.2.

[91] Section 6.2.

manage "other Property" that it becomes a virtual enclave.[92]

The Property Clause granted Congress unconditional power to dispose of federal property. Under the "proper" requirement of the Necessary and Proper Clause and prevailing political theory, rules of public trust applied to disposition. This meant that, although Congress enjoyed wide discretion as to the terms of disposition, it could not convey federal land to states or other parties without obtaining some sort of fair value (which need not be money). The terms of the disposal had to serve the interest of the entire country.

Although the Property Clause granted power to dispose and manage, it granted no power to acquire or retain. The Founding-era records disclose a universal belief that most federal lands would be sold promptly. The federal government could acquire and retain land only as an incident to other powers. In other words, every tract of federal land had to serve some enumerated power, and presumably Congress's "needful" rules and regulations also had to be directed toward serving enumerated powers.

Once an enclave or other land no longer served an enumerated power, disposition was mandatory.

Most of the Founders would have seen permanent federal land ownership for unenumerated purposes as subversive of the constitutional scheme. This was partly because the government was to enjoy only enumerated powers and partly because extensive federal land ownership would render many people dependent on the government. It also was because the Founders constructed the Constitution for a country in which land was owned by the common people rather than by the nobility or the government. If much of the land was to be government-owned, the document would have been drafted differently.[93]

To summarize: The original Constitution contemplated three kinds of federal control over land:

---

[92] *E.g., Kleppe v. New Mexico*, 426 U.S. 529 (1976).

[93] For example, during the ratification controversy, Federalist Noah Webster wrote that the reason the Constitution did not guarantee a specific right to hunt and fish was because land would be individually owned and owners had the right to hunt and fish on their own land. Noah Webster, A Collection of Essays and Fugitiv [sic] Writings 149 (1790).

- General governmental jurisdiction over the capital district and other enclaves, irrespective of whether or not particular land within those enclaves was titled to the federal government, to a state, or to private parties;
- general governmental jurisdiction over federal territories, irrespective of whether or not particular land within those territories was titled to the federal government, to a state, or to private parties; and
- rule-making authority over "other Property" situated within states, but titled to the federal government.

Enclaves and "other Property" were to be held only for enumerated purposes.

6.7 Congressional Powers to Promote Concord among the States

Several federal powers were designed to promote good relations among the states. Some of these appeared in the enumeration of congressional powers in Article I, Section 8. The Commerce Clause, for example, would enable Congress to end the interstate trade wars that had marred the Confederation. The Coinage Clause would reduce interstate conflicts over paper money. The Enclave Clause would prevent any state from exercising undue influence over federal operations. Congressional authority to enact uniform naturalization and bankruptcy laws was directed at other potential sources of interstate conflict.

In addition, Article I, Section 10 granted Congress authority to block some state actions that might endanger relations with other states. Congress could veto or revise state taxes on imports and exports, veto state efforts to build peacetime military forces other than the militia, and veto compacts between states and between states and foreign powers.

Although the states had initial power to set the times, places, and manner of elections for Senators and Representatives, Congress could revise those laws or make its own, except that it could not change the place of choosing Senators.[94]

Article IV was devoted to rules mitigating interstate conflict. Section 1, the Full Faith and Credit Clause, enabled Congress to prescribe

---

[94] See Section 6.8.1.

uniform rules for authenticating out-of-state legal documents. Section 2 contained the Privileges and Immunities and Fugitive Slave Clauses, which are discussed elsewhere.[95] Section 3 granted Congress power to admit new states, to veto the combination and division of states, and to manage and sell federal land both inside and outside state boundaries. Finally, Section 4, the Guarantee Clause, authorized Congress, in conjunction with other branches, to ensure that some states did not become monarchies and thereby threaten the republican members of the union.

6.8 Congressional Administrative Powers

Scattered throughout the Constitution were congressional powers related to the administration of the federal government itself. We already have discussed the grants to Congress of power to manage federal enclaves[96] and "other Property."[97] This section summarizes the remainder.

6.8.1 A Limited Power over Elections

The Constitution granted Congress some authority over federal elections. Congress could determine the time for selecting presidential electors and the day on which they were to vote.[98] With regard to congressional elections, regulation in the first instance was reposed in the state legislatures. But under the Times, Places and Manner Clause Congress could alter the "Times, Places and Manner" of electing Representatives and the times and manner of electing Senators.[99] This provi-

---

[95] See Section 3.10.2 on the Privileges and Immunities Clause and Sections 4.4 and 9.4 on the Fugitive Slave Clause.

[96] Article I, Section 8, Clause 17.

[97] Article IV, Section 3, Clause 2.

[98] Article II, Section 1, Clause 4.

[99] Article I, Section 4, Clause 1. This provision has received various names. I have chosen "Times, Places, and Manner Clause" as the most descriptive. Recent Supreme Court decisions have referred to it as the Elections Clause. However, that term is insufficiently specific, because the Constitution contains several other clauses regulating elections. They are Article I, Section 3, Clause 1 (for Senators, superseded by the Seventeenth Amendment); Article II, Section 1,

sion was designed to protect the integrity of those elections by erecting mutual checks between the states and the federal government. Under its terms, states enjoyed the initial regulatory power, but Congress could override it. Congress consisted of a Senate beholden to state legislatures and a House beholden directly to the people, and the approval of both would be necessary before a state decision could be superseded.

To understand the scope of the congressional power over elections, one must know something of 18th-century election law and practice. English and American election laws, American state constitutions, and other documents frequently referred to regulating the *manner of election*. The manner of election was understood to encompass:

- Setting the qualifications of electors and of candidates;
- regulating the times of election—that is, the date for voting and the terms of office;
- establishing the places of election—the voting location and legislative districts; and
- determining the election procedures—that is, whether the election was direct or indirect, whether a plurality or majority was necessary for victory, whether voting was viva voce or by secret ballot, how voting lists were kept and how elections were publicized, which officers oversaw elections, the ballot's design and how votes were counted, and what punishments applied for election-day misconduct.

The Constitution did not use the broad phrase "the manner of election" to cover all four of these categories. Instead, it provided separately for each category. It specified the qualifications and terms of office. It addressed "Times" and "Places" individually. And it covered other election procedures with the new phrase, the *Manner of holding Elections*.

The primary reason for granting Congress power to fix the *time* of election was to enable Congress to set a single nationwide day for popular, legislative, and electoral college balloting. Different polling days in different states and lengthy polling times in any one state would invite political manipulation, disparate treatment of ballots, and other miscon-

---

Clauses 2 & 3 (for the President and Vice President); and the Twelfth Amendment (also for the President and Vice President).

duct.¹⁰⁰ During the ratification struggle, there was little, if any, opposition to the congressional power to fix uniform days.

Congressional authority to alter the *places* at which Representatives were elected included two components: (1) drawing boundaries for congressional districts and (2) identifying voting locations. This power was a check on state legislative gerrymandering and on state efforts to manipulate elections through strategic location of voting places. Congress received no authority to alter the places at which Senators would be elected, because Senators would be elected by their respective state legislatures.

During the ratification debates, Anti-Federalists attacked the congressional power to alter the place of elections for the House of Representatives. They argued that Congress might gerrymander legislative districts or choose polling places to favor the urban vote. In response, Federalists pointed to the mutual checks afforded by the different composition of House and Senate.

Anti-Federalists also expressed concern that a congressional majority might manipulate the times, places, and manner of holding elections to entrench itself in power. For example, some argued that Congress could alter qualifications or terms of office—a contention clearly wrong, because the Constitution addressed those directly. Other Anti-Federalists raised the more reasonable concern that Congress might rig the dates, places, and procedures to favor incumbents.¹⁰¹

The Constitution's advocates explained that the principal purpose of congressional power under the Times, Places and Manner Clause was to enable the central government to preserve itself in the event one or more states refused to hold federal elections or—perhaps as a result of foreign invasion—were unable to do so. Hamilton wrote in Federalist No. 59 that the "propriety [of the Clause] rests upon the evidence of this plain

---

¹⁰⁰ During the 2020 presidential election, many states dispensed with the congressionally mandated Election Day and permitted mail-in voting over an extended period. The ensuing disputes vindicated the Founders' caution.

¹⁰¹ One might argue that this fear has been vindicated, because Congress has adopted incumbent-favoring campaign finance laws under its "Manner of holding Elections" power. As the foregoing explanation of the constitutional text makes clear, however, that power is not broad enough to authorize regulation of congressional campaigns; and the Constitution contains no language at all supporting congressional regulation of *presidential* campaigns.

proposition, that every government ought to contain in itself the means of its own preservation." Thus, Federalists predicted that the power would be exercised rarely, and only to correct serious state abuses.

The Federalists also discussed the limited scope of the regulations Congress could issue under this Clause. Their illustrations matched standard contemporaneous manner of election rules: whether the ballot would be open or secret, what officer would oversee the election, and whether election would be by a plurality or majority. William Davie, a former Philadelphia convention delegate serving as a Federalist spokesman at the North Carolina ratifying convention, parsed the Clause grammatically to demonstrate to his fellow delegates its narrow scope.[102] His ally, John Steele, added, "The power over the manner only enables [Congress] to determine how these electors shall elect—whether by ballot, or by vote, or by any other way."[103]

This narrow construction was relied on by several of the state ratifying conventions and formally adopted by New York, North Carolina, and Rhode Island. Narrow construction would help guard against abuse by a self-interested congressional majority. It was clearly part of the ratification bargain.

6.8.2 Other Administrative Powers

Congress enjoyed seven other administrative powers. They were:

- To set rules for the decennial census—necessary to determine how Representatives and direct taxes would be allocated among the states.[104]

---

[102] 30 Documentary History, p. 282–83:

> I am willing to appeal to grammatical construction and punctuation. Let me read this, as it stands on paper, [Here he read the clause different ways, expressing the same sense.] Here, in the first part of the clause, this power over elections is given to the states, and in the latter part the same power is given to Congress, and extending only to the time of holding, the place of holding, and the manner of holding, the elections. Is this not the plain, literal, and grammatical construction of the clause?

[103] 30 Documentary History, p. 290.

[104] Article I, Section 2, Clause 3.

- To decide when a federal official could accept an emolument, office, or title from a foreign government.[105]
- To set the order of presidential succession following the Vice President.[106]
- To dispense with senatorial approval of lesser executive officers.[107]
- To fix the pay of all federal officers, provided that the President's salary not be altered during his term[108] nor a judge's salary lowered.[109]
- To erect and govern the federal court system, including power to limit the appellate jurisdiction of the Supreme Court and to determine where trials were to be held for crimes allegedly committed outside state boundaries.[110]
- By a two-thirds vote of each house, to propose constitutional amendments to the states and, by a majority of each house, choose among two different modes of ratification.[111]

---

[105] Article I, Section 9, Clause 8.

[106] Article II, Section 1, Clause 7.

[107] Article II, Section 2, Clause 2.

[108] The power to compensate is inherent in the various enumerated powers. For the rule pertaining to the President, see Article II, Section 1, Clause 8.

[109] Article III, Section 1.

[110] Chapter Eight.

[111] See Chapter Twelve.

CHAPTER SEVEN

The Executive

7.1 Introduction

Article II of the Constitution outlined the nature, selection, powers, and duties of the executive branch. In drafting Article II, the Framers were influenced by the executive provisions in existing state constitutions. They also were influenced by the documents—commissions and instructions—by which the Crown had granted executive power to governors of the American colonies.[1]

The drafting of Article II was the least satisfactory of any in the Constitution. After only four presidential elections, the procedure for choosing the President had to be substantially rewritten. This was done through the Twelfth Amendment, adopted in 1804. Article II was patched up further by the Twentieth and Twenty-Fifth Amendments.

Two other difficulties emerged in the first session of the First Congress, held in 1789. Article II provided for the appointment of subordinate executive officers, but did not specify how they were to be removed in cases other than impeachment. Chapter Eleven explains how

---

[1] Writers on the Constitution generally have overlooked the connection between Article II and the royal commissions. The bibliography for this chapter explains how to obtain sample commissions.

that issue was resolved. The other difficulty was that the first sentence in the first section was ambiguous. We now turn to that issue.

7.2 Executive Designation Clause or Executive Vesting Clause?

The first sentence of Article II reads as follows: "The executive Power shall be vested in a President of the United States of America."[2] This sentence communicated that there would be only one executive and stated his title. The Framers had rejected proposals for an executive council of the kind existing in most states. The Framers believed a council would impair the secrecy, efficiency, and dispatch required of a national executive. Responsibilities for executive actions would be diffused among its members, and it would be more difficult to constrain than a sole executive.[3]

The question arising in the First Congress was whether that sentence, in addition to designating a unified executive, also acted as a grant. Did it confer "the executive Power"? Disagreement over that issue continues even today.

Those who contend that the first sentence of Article II granted to the President "the executive Power" argue that the language conveyed broad authority of the sort traditionally enjoyed by Anglo-American chief executives, and particularly by the King of England. They have named that sentence the "Executive Vesting Clause." We shall call their position the "vesting-clause theory." Their opponents contend that the first sentence of Article II did no more than identify and name the executive, and that the President received his authority from enumerations in other parts of Article II.

The answer to this question controls how we read the remainder of Article II. If the first sentence was merely a designation clause and did not grant authority, then the structure of the Article was as follows:

- Designation of the President as chief executive (first sentence in Section 1).
- Organizational details (remainder of Section 1).

---

[2] Article II, Section 1, Clause 1.

[3] *Cf.* DeLolme, pp. 150–52.

- Enumerated powers of the President (Sections 2 and 3).
- Removal from office (Section 4).

Under this interpretation of Article II, the President enjoyed only the powers specified in Sections 2 and 3 and a few others located elsewhere in the Constitution, such as the veto.

On the other hand, if the vesting-clause theory is correct, the structure of the Article was as follows:

- Designation and a wide grant of power (first sentence in Section 1).
- Organizational details (remainder of Section 1).
- Restrictions, explanations, and qualifications of the power granted earlier (Sections 2 and 3).
- Removal from office (Section 4).

If this is the proper reading, then the first sentence of Article II granted the President an undefined, but presumably regal, pool of executive authority, which Sections 2 and 3 then cut down to republican proportions. Unsurprisingly, most presidents and their supporters have favored the vesting-clause theory.

The arguments for both sides are too intricate to discuss at length, but here is a sample:

Vesting-clause advocates point out that the first sentence of Article II, unlike its counterpart in Article I (which identified Congress as the legislative branch), did not refer merely to powers "herein granted." This difference suggests that the first sentence of Article II conferred broad, unspecified powers. Opponents respond that under the Constitution's governmental scheme, the scope of the executive power was defined by the scope of the legislative. Because the legislative powers were limited to those "herein granted," there was no need to add similar words to the executive power.

Advocates of the vesting-clause theory further argue that treating the first sentence as merely a designation results in that sentence being worthless surplus, thereby violating the rule that the reader should favor an interpretation that does not result in surplus.[4] The opposition

---

[4] Section 2.6.

responds that a designation is not surplus. They add that treating the sentence as a grant of king-like executive authority would turn the power-grants of Section 2 and 3 into surplus. Vesting-clause advocates rejoin that Sections 2 and 3 were not surplus, because they were limitations and explanations of the vesting clause. They prevented the President from having all the authority of a king. They add that the "executive Power" encompassed not merely execution of legislative acts, but general supervision of foreign affairs—and because Sections 2 and 3 did not provide adequately for foreign affairs, the first sentence of Section 1 must have granted power.

Much more has been said on this subject. Both sides, however, have overlooked a very strong piece of evidence. That evidence is how 18th-century lawyers (such as most of the Framers) actually wrote legal documents bestowing power.

Instruments by which one person or entity conveyed enumerated powers to another were very common during the Founding era. They included powers of attorney, trusts, wills, charters, statutes, royal commissions, state constitutions, and, of course, the Articles of Confederation. As one might expect, those instruments tended to be organized in set ways. There were two dominant patterns. One of the two patterns is not relevant here,[5] but the other was (1) designation, followed by (2) organizational details, followed by (3) enumerated powers. Drafters employed the same pattern in most of the colonial charters, in the king's commissions granting powers to colonial governors, in the Articles of Confederation, and in several of the pre-1787 state constitutions. The Framers followed it for the first eight sections of Article I as well. As explained in Chapter Eight, the Framers also followed it in Article III, the judiciary Article.

If, however, the first sentence of Article II was a vesting clause, then it did not follow either of the two common drafting patterns. While such a departure was not impossible, the conservatism of legal drafters renders it unlikely.

There are several other reasons for believing that the first sentence of

---

[5] This pattern was used mostly for simple documents. It combined in one section the designation of the recipient of authority and the enumeration of powers without intervening material—i.e., "I hereby grant John Doe the power to sell, lease, manage, etc."

Article II conveyed no power. Here are a few:

First: A clause simply conveying the "executive Power" would have been unclear to the Founders because there was no uniform understanding as to the exact scope of the executive power. The British Crown, the British colonial royal governors, and the thirteen state executives all enjoyed somewhat different spheres of authority.[6]

Second: The provisions of Sections 2 and 3 were worded as grants, not as mere explanations and qualifications. They included phrases such as "He shall have Power . . ."

Finally: At least one item in Article II's enumeration could not be a qualification of royal-style authority, because it granted a prerogative the British king did not have. This was the President's power to recommend specific measures to the legislature.[7] The British king could, in his speech from the throne, draw Parliament's attention to general subject areas, but had no authority to make specific recommendations.[8] So the Constitution's power to recommend must have been a grant of new authority—which suggests that the enumerated items paralleling it were grants as well.[9]

Although some have argued that the President's list of enumerated powers was too skimpy to have been agreeable to the founding generation, that is a misunderstanding; in fact, the enumeration was not skimpy at all.[10] Anti-Federalists fiercely attacked the office as too powerful.

During the ratification debates, no one suggested that the first sentence of Article II would bestow any authority. Alexander Hamilton, writing in The Federalist, assumed the contrary.[11] The vesting-clause

---

[6] For example, colonial governors could remove members of the legislature's upper house. Had the first sentence of Article II granted the "executive Power" as (presumably) then understood, the President might have been able to remove Senators, for nothing in the Constitution expressly limited that power.

[7] Article II, Section 3.

[8] *DeLolme*, pp. 164–65, 184 & 283.

[9] *Noscitur ex socio qui non cognoscitur ex se* ("What is not known by itself alone is known by its associate").

[10] Sections 7.5 through 7.9.2.

[11] *The Federalist* No. 77 (Hamilton) (presenting an analysis of some enumerated presidential powers, and then introducing a brief discussion of the rest by stating, "The only remaining powers of the Executive are . . .").

theory was not mentioned until after the Constitution had been ratified.[12]

On balance, therefore, the evidence suggests that the impartial reader would have interpreted Article II as having the following structure:

- Designation of the President as chief executive (first sentence in Section 1).
- Organizational details (remainder of Section 1).
- Enumerated powers of the President (Sections 2 and 3).
- Removal from office (Section 4).

7.3 The Term of the President and Vice President and the Presidential Election Procedure

The President and Vice President were to be elected for concurrent four-year terms. Initially, there was no limit on the number of times they could run for re-election.[13]

The election procedure consisted of four distinct stages:

- Presidential electors were chosen in each state in the manner prescribed by that state's legislature;
- the electors by ballot voted for the President and Vice President and certified their ballots to the President of the Senate (the sitting Vice President);
- Congress met in joint session under the chairmanship of the President of the Senate, counted the vote, and declared the result; and
- if no presidential candidate received sufficient votes, there was a run-off in the House of Representatives; if no vice-presidential candidate received sufficient votes, there was a run-off in the Senate.

---

[12] Thornton Anderson, *Creating the Constitution: The Convention of 1787 and the First Congress* 186–87 (1993). The first mention (in *Annals of Congress*, Volume 1 at p. 388) was by John Vining of Delaware, who had been neither a Framer nor a ratifier. However, members of Congress who had been Framers or ratifiers later adopted it, including Hamilton in his first "Pacificus" essay. Hamilton thereby contradicted his position in *The Federalist*.

[13] They were limited to two terms by the Twenty-Second Amendment.

Constructing the presidential election system was probably the Framers' most difficult task. They had to accomplish goals that often competed against each other. Among those goals were: (1) preserving the independence of the President from Congress and the states, (2) ensuring state and congressional acceptance by giving the states and Congress some power in the process, but not enough to compromise the President, (3) ensuring that the winner enjoyed wide national, rather than merely regional, support, (4) ensuring that the system should not be too cumbersome, (5) ensuring that electors were knowledgeable about the candidates, (6) guarding against foreign and undue special interest influence, (7) avoiding "stampeding" and other mob-like behavior, and (8) producing Presidents capable of doing the job.

Although it is frequently charged that the presidential election system was the product of slavery, during the Framers' deliberations on presidential elections, slavery was almost never mentioned. Convention voting patterns on the presidential election system were unrelated to slavery. The two states most committed to slavery—South Carolina and Georgia—split on the vote to adopt the Electoral College.

Proposals early in the federal convention envisioned the President being elected on a joint ballot by both houses. The delegates ultimately rejected this approach for fear that it might render the President too dependent on Congress—especially if he was permitted to seek re-election. (Most of the Framers favored giving the President an opportunity to seek re-election as an incentive to good performance.) A trace of congressional selection did remain in the final version, however: Each state could appoint as many electors as it had both Senators and Representatives. The number of electors was thus the same as the number in Congress.

The Constitution granted Congress power to regulate "the Manner of holding Elections" for Congress,[14] but each state legislature determined how its electors were to be chosen.[15] This exclusive state governance was a survival from an earlier proposal at the Constitutional Convention that the states nominate candidates for President.

The whole body of electors has come to be called the Electoral

---

[14] Article I, Section 4, Clause 1.

[15] Article II, Section 1, Clause 2.

College, although the Constitution does not use that term. "College" in this context derives from the Latin word *collegium*, meaning an association or guild. The specific phrase "electoral college" had been applied to groups of electors in the Holy Roman Empire and the Roman Catholic Church.

Presidential electors were to use their own judgment in voting for President and Vice President. Although appointed by the states, the states could not control them any more than the President who appoints judges can dictate their future judgments. And while some have contended that elector discretion was caged by the Twelfth Amendment (1804), nothing in the amendment's language suggests this. On the contrary, the congressional debate over the Twelfth Amendment discloses a general understanding that elector deliberation would be unfettered.[16]

The Founders were determined to preserve the quality of electoral deliberation. To preserve electors' independence from outside undue influence, no Congressman or federal employee was to serve as an elector.[17] To prevent mob behavior, the electors were not to convene in any one place: Each state delegation was to meet in its own state.[18] To prevent bandwagon voting, all electors were to vote on the day, if any, specified by federal law.[19] To prevent them from voting merely for candidates from their own states, each was to vote for two persons, at least one of whom had to be from another state.[20] The hope was that while each state might have a favorite son, a majority would fix upon a candidate who was everyone's second choice. Finally, the electors were to vote

---

[16] Robert G. Natelson, *Why the Constitution mandates that presidential electors exercise best judgment*, SCOTUS Blog, https://www.scotusblog.com/2020/04/symposium-why-the-constitution-mandates-that-presidential-electors-exercise-best-judgment. However, the Supreme Court ruled in *Chiafolo v. Washington*, 140 S.Ct. 1269 (2019) that states could dictate electors' votes. In doing so, the court disregarded most of the Founding-era evidence and all of the Twelfth Amendment evidence. Perhaps the court reached its decision to protect the Electoral College from further political attack.

[17] Article II, Section 1, Clause 2.

[18] Article II, Section 1, Clause 3.

[19] Article II, Section 1, Clause 4.

[20] Article II, Section 1, Clause 3.

"by Ballot"—which during the Founding era invariably meant secret ballot.

After tabulating, certifying, and sealing the vote, each state's delegation was to transmit its results to the President of the Senate—that is, to the Vice President of the United States—at the national capital.[21] Of course, the Vice President might well be a candidate for President himself, so he was not permitted to open the ballots until the entire Congress was assembled in one chamber, thereby forming a joint session of both houses. The Constitution granted this joint session, chaired by the Vice President, power to oversee the count.[22]

If every elector voted properly, there would be twice as many votes as members of Congress—two for each elector. The person with the most votes won if he had a majority of the electors and if he had more votes (rather than was tied with) any other candidate.[23]

The thirteen original states were entitled to send 65 Representatives and 26 Senators to the first Congress, for a total of 91 members. Since the number of electors was the same as the number of Congressmen and each elector cast two votes, there were 182 votes in all. For purposes of illustration, assume an election with the following results:

Candidate A	50 votes
Candidate B	44 votes
Candidate C	42 votes
Candidate D	28 votes
Candidate E	18 votes

In this case, Candidate A would be the winner, since his votes, while not a majority of all votes cast, did represent a majority of all electors (50 of 91) and more than any other candidate. As runner-up, Candidate B

---

[21] Article II, Section 1, Clause 3.

[22] Founding-era state constitutions frequently directed joint legislative sessions to perform election duties. The U.S. Constitution did not grant this function to Congress as a legislative body, but as a special joint assembly. That joint assembly probably was not bound by standing congressional laws purporting to prescribe rules for future counts.

[23] Article II, Section 1, Clause 3.

would become Vice President even if in a run-off election one of the other candidates would have been chosen for Vice President.

If Candidate A had a majority of electors but (because each elector had two votes, not one) Candidate B was tied with him, then there was a run-off election between the two of them in the House of Representatives. This would occur in the following election:

Candidate A	49 votes
Candidate B	49 votes
Candidate C	38 votes
Candidate D	28 votes
Candidate E	18 votes

In this case, the person with the most electoral votes, other than the person chosen as President, would become Vice President. Thus, if the House selected Candidate A, then Candidate B would become Vice President.

If no candidate for President had a majority, then there was a run-off in the House. This time, however, the House selected from all the top five vote-getters.[24] Consider the following results:

Candidate A	45 votes
Candidate B	44 votes
Candidate C	44 votes
Candidate D	31 votes
Candidate E	18 votes

Here, the House would choose among the top five—in this case, all the candidates with votes. Conceivably, the House could choose E as President, even though he had obtained only eighteen electoral votes. The remaining candidate with the most votes would become Vice President. If the House chose Candidate E as President, then Candidate A would become Vice President. If the House chose Candidate A as President, however, the two remaining candidates with the most votes were B and C, who were tied at 44 each. In that case, the Senate selected between

---

[24] Article II, Section 1, Clause 3.

them—the only time the Senate could choose its own presiding officer.[25]

The federal convention considered designating the Senate rather than the House as the back-up forum for electing the President, but ultimately decided that this would leave the Senate with too much power and encourage collusion between the Senate and an incumbent President seeking re-election. So the convention opted for the House, but preserved the principle of equal representation among states. For this purpose only, the House would vote by state, with each state entitled to one vote, irrespective of how many members of Congress or electors it had. Two-thirds of state delegations had to be present to elect the President.

The electoral scheme blended what James Madison and others called the federal and national aspects of America's new government.

As soon as President Washington left the political scene, Article's II electoral system began to crack. Presidential/vice-presidential rivalry proved unacceptable in practice. In the election of 1796, John Adams became President and Thomas Jefferson Vice President. But they headed rival political parties, and they soon were at each other's throats. In the following election, two candidates running for President and Vice President on the same ticket (Jefferson and Aaron Burr) each received the same number of electoral votes. Because the Constitution provided for no designation of which votes were cast for which man for which office, a lengthy deadlock ensued in the House of Representatives—broken only when the good sense of Alexander Hamilton's High Federalists overcame their disgust, and they broke the deadlock by voting for Jefferson.[26] Two electoral crises in two consecutive elections produced the Twelfth Amendment.

7.4 The President's Qualifications, Compensation, and Oath

The Constitution imposed certain qualifications on the President. The Constitution implied, although it did not state explicitly until adoption of the Twelfth Amendment, that the same qualifications applied to the Vice President. Both had to be at least 35 years old, which was a significant requirement in an age in which people often did not live

---

[25] Article II, Section 1, Clause 3.

[26] Burr later repaid Hamilton by killing him in a duel.

beyond their 50s. The idea was to better assure a certain amount of maturity and wisdom. Also, both had to have resided within the country for the previous fourteen years.

Most importantly, the President and Vice President had to be natural-born citizens or citizens at the time of ratification. The Founders adopted the phrase "natural-born citizen" from the English legal term, "natural born subject," which defined who could serve in Parliament or the Privy Council. Essentially, a natural-born citizen was one who met either one of two requirements. First, a person usually qualified (there were narrow exceptions)[27] if born within the United States or within American territory, even if the person's parents were aliens. Alternatively, an individual qualified even if born outside the country if the individual's father was an American citizen not then engaged in traitorous or felonious activities.[28]

These birth and residence requirements were designed better to assure that the President and Vice President were truly sympathetic to those they were to govern, and to guard against the risk that they might be sympathetic to a foreign power.[29]

There was no constitutional requirement that a President or Vice President be male. The pronoun "he" used throughout the Constitution was generic.[30]

The primary reason for paying the President a salary was to assure that people of modest means could serve. Congress was to set the salary.

---

[27] The exceptions applied to the children of foreigners within the territorial limits of the United States whom the law did not deem to be in "allegiance" to the United States. Foreigners within the country but not in allegiance included (1) foreign diplomats, (2) Indians whose primary loyalty was to their tribes, (3) invaders, and (4) persons within the country illegally. For a discussion of these categories, see Robert G. Natelson & Andrew T. Hyman, *The Constitution, Invasion, Immigration, and the War Powers of States*, 13 Brit. J. Am. L. Stud. 1 (2024).

[28] Since the publication of the first edition, several readers have contacted me to argue that "natural born" should be defined as Vattel defined it. Invariably they are driven by hope that using Vattel's definition would disqualify from the presidency a politician they dislike. However, the Constitution's meaning does not depend on one's political hopes. The document generally employed legal terms according to English usage— and as Vattel acknowledged, the English standard for "natural born" varied from that used in other nations.

[29] On the principle of *sympathy*, see Section 1.3.5.

[30] On the gender-neutral aspect of the Constitution, see Section 4.4.

However, Congress could not increase or diminish the compensation of a sitting President during his term. This was to encourage independence from Congress and free exercise of executive judgment. For a similar reason, the Presidential Emolument Clause barred the President from receiving any other emolument from either the nation or any state.[31] Section 4.5 discusses the meaning of "emolument."

The nondenominational oath[32] required of the President was designed to solemnize the occasion of his taking office and to impress upon him the gravity of the position and that malfeasance in office had potential consequences in the next world. Because an oath was seen as a call to God to witness the truth of what one said, an atheist was legally disqualified from taking a lawful oath. The effect was to limit the presidency to people who believed in God.[33]

7.5 The Enumerated Powers of the President—In General

7.5.1 The Scheme of Enumeration

The presidency was not modeled on any one office. It bore some similarity to the British Crown, but it was a republican magistracy distinctly less powerful than the Crown. The British king or queen (at least in theory) enjoyed an absolute veto over legislation, could declare war, make treaties, appoint Lords, and, to a certain extent, employ members of the House of Commons. The President enjoyed only a qualified veto, had no power to declare war, shared the treaty-making power with the Senate, appointed no Senators, and could not employ members of Congress in his service. On the other hand, the President enjoyed the opportunity of making specific recommendations to the legislature, in a manner the king could not.

Although not as potent as the British monarch, the President was more powerful than the governor of any American state. At the time, few

---

[31] Article II, Section 1, Clause 7.

[32] Article II, Section 1, Clause 8.

[33] On this controversial point, see my article, *The Original Meaning of the Establishment Clause*, 14 Wm. & Mary Bill Rights J. 73 (2005). A legal maxim stated, *Jurare est Deus in testem vocare, et est actus Divini cultus* ("To swear is to call God as a witness and is an act of divine reverence").

state governors could veto laws, and their discretion was commonly limited by an executive council. Moreover, most were dependent on the state legislature, because the lawmakers selected them—usually annually. The governorships defined by the 1777 New York constitution and the 1780 Massachusetts constitution were somewhat stronger than most, and they served as partial models for the President.

The Constitution granted the President sixteen express enumerated powers.[34] Most were located in Sections 2 and 3 of Article II. Some of these were, strictly speaking, not executive, but legislative—particularly the right to veto bills and resolutions[35] and to recommend measures to Congress.[36]

---

[34] Here is the list:

- the qualified veto (I-7-2 & I-7-3);
- serving as Commander-in-Chief of armed forces (II-2-1);
- requiring the written opinions of executive officers (II-2-1);
- granting reprieves and pardons (II-2-1);
- making vacancy appointments (II-2-3);
- receiving representatives of foreign powers (II-3);
- executing the laws (II-3);
- commissioning U.S. officers (II-3);
- making treaties (II-2-2), subject to the advice and consent of the Senate;
- appointing foreign affairs officers (II-2-2), subject to the advice and consent of the Senate;
- appointing domestic affairs officers (II-2-2), subject either to the advice and consent of the Senate or pursuant to law;
- appointing judges (II-2-2), subject to advice and consent of the Senate;
- giving Congress information (II-3);
- making recommendations to Congress (II-3);
- convening Congress on extraordinary occasions (II-3); and
- adjourning Congress if it could not agree on a time (II-3).

[35] Article I, Section 7, Clauses 2 & 3.

[36] Article II, Section 3, Clause 1.

7.5.2 The President's Incidental Powers

In addition to granting the President express (stated) powers, the Constitution granted incidental, implied powers. Chapter Five explained the Founding-era doctrine of incidental/implied authority and the role of the Necessary and Proper Clause as a useful but legally unnecessary acknowledgement that Congress had such authority.[37] The Constitution contained no explicit Necessary and Proper Clause applicable to the President, but legally that made no difference. Unless incidental authority was explicitly withheld (as in the Articles of Confederation), the effect was the same as if the Constitution stated that "The President may issue all orders which shall be necessary and proper for carrying into Execution his enumerated powers."

The following discussion of presidential powers rests both on express and on implied authority.

7.6 Presidential Powers—Arguably Legislative or Judicial

7.6.1 The Veto

Like the British king, the colonial governors, and the governor of Massachusetts, the President could veto measures adopted by the legislature.[38] The Founders sometimes called this the "revisionary power," but this did not mean the President could re-write bills. In the 18th century, "to revise" meant only to review or re-examine.

Vetoes by the king and colonial governors had been absolute. The President's veto was qualified: A two-thirds majority of each house of Congress usually could override it.

When a President received a measure passed by Congress, he had four options:

- He could sign the measure and make it law.
- He could exercise a qualified veto by returning the measure to the chamber of its origin with his reasons for disapproval, in

---

[37] Article I, Section 8, Clause 18.

[38] Article I, Section 7, Clauses 2 & 3.

which case only affirmative votes of two-thirds of each chamber could make it law.

- If 10 or more days (Sundays excepted) elapsed between the time he received the measure and the time Congress adjourned, he could (as an alternative to signing or vetoing it) let it become law without his signature.
- If fewer than 10 days (Sundays excepted) elapsed between receipt and congressional adjournment, he could (as an alternative to signing or vetoing it) exercise an absolute veto by not signing it.

The Constitution granted the President a veto for three principal reasons. First, the Founders hoped that the President—as the representative of the entire American people—would block legislation designed to serve only special interest purposes. Second, the veto power reduced the chances of unconstitutional legislation being enacted. Third, the President could use the veto to defend the independence of the executive branch: A President without a veto might be at the mercy of a hostile Congress.

The veto is an example of how the Founders disregarded the principle of separation of powers when that principle did not serve the more basic value of inter-branch independence.[39]

7.6.2 Other Quasi-Legislative and Quasi-Judicial Authority

The President enjoyed quasi-legislative and quasi-judicial powers that, like the veto, were suggested by British and American precedents. The king, the royal governors, and some state governors could call their legislatures into session. The President also could convene either or both chambers of Congress—but only "on extraordinary Occasions."[40] Similarly, the king and colonial governors could dissolve their legislatures at any time (although they did not receive the financial appropriations they wanted if they acted too quickly). The President could adjourn Congress only if the two chambers could not agree between themselves on an adjournment time.[41]

---

[39] On the principle of independence, see Section 1.3.5

[40] Article II, Section 3.

[41] Article II, Section 3.

The President was to deliver to Congress from time to time a message on the state of the union. He could recommend "such Measures as he shall judge necessary and expedient."[42] The language in this Necessary and Expedient Clause looked somewhat like the Necessary and Proper Clause of Article I; both phrases were variations on common language in 18th-century agency agreements. However, the Necessary and Expedient Clause gave more discretion to the President than the Necessary and Proper Clause gave to Congress. The latter authorized only laws "which shall be necessary and proper." The former authorized the President to make any recommendations that he personally "judge[d] necessary and expedient." A court might review whether Congress had acted in a necessary and proper way, but it never could question the President's personal judgment as to what measures to recommend to Congress.

The British sovereign, colonial governors, and some state governors could pardon or reprieve those guilty of crime, with varying exceptions. The President also could pardon, subject to another set of exceptions.[43] His pardon power extended only to federal, not state, crimes, and could have no effect on impeachment proceedings. A pardon extended only to crimes already committed, not those that might be committed in the future.

The President, like the king, could appoint judges for life (or, technically, during "good behavior").[44] However, no permanent appointment would be valid unless either (1) approved by the Senate or (2) the judgeship was one for which Congress had dispensed with the need for senatorial consent.[45]

---

[42] Article II, Section 3.

[43] Article II, Section 2, Clause 1.

[44] Article II, Section 2, Clause 2; Article III, Section 1. Good behavior meant until committing an offense meriting impeachment and removal from office.

[45] Article II, Section 2, Clause 2. The President also could make temporary judicial appointments pursuant to the Recess Appointments Clause. Article II, Section 2, Clause 3. See Section 7.7.2.

7.7 Domestic Executive Powers

7.7.1 Executing the Laws

The phrase directing the President to "take Care that the Laws be faithfully executed" was based on language by which the Crown had instructed colonial governors. The Continental Congress often had adopted such language when instructing its own agents. "Faithfully" meant "in good faith"—that is, honestly.

To aid the President's execution of his responsibilities, the Constitution granted him authority to demand written reports from heads of departments.[46] The term "departments" referred to major offices, such as the treasury, the war department, the navy department, and the Attorney-General's office.[47]

7.7.2 Appointing Subordinate Executive Officers

To execute the laws, the President had to operate through subordinate officials. Because the Founders' experience with the British monarchies had made them wary of potent executives, most early state constitutions vested appointments in the legislature or required that state presidents and governors make appointments in conjunction with an executive council. The U.S. Constitution vested the President with appointment power, but still provided checks.

Executive branch positions below the President (other than the Vice President, who was mostly a legislative officer) were created and paid for by Congress. In the absence of congressional legislation to the contrary, the President's appointment of an individual for any permanent job was subject to the "Advice and Consent" (deliberation and approval)[48] of the Senate. However, Congress could authorize the President (or the courts or heads of departments) to dispense with senatorial approval when filling positions below the rank of ambassador, judge, or department head.[49]

---

[46] Article II, Section 2, Clause 1.

[47] *E.g.*, 19 J. Cont. Cong. 126–28 (Feb. 7, 1781).

[48] The President rather than President-and-Senate technically made the appointment. Section 11.2. For the meaning of "advice and consent," see Section 4.8.

[49] Article II, Section 2, Clause 2.

The Constitution further authorized the President unilaterally to appoint temporary officers to fill "Vacancies that may happen during the Recess of the Senate.⁵⁰ This provision is called the Recess Appointments Clause. In Founding-era legislative practice, a "recess" could refer to any legislative break, but the specific phrase "the Recess" referred only to formal breaks between scheduled legislative sessions. In other words, "the Recess" was the regularly scheduled period, usually extending for months at a time, during which lawmakers went home to their districts. The phrase did not apply to shorter breaks during which lawmakers generally remained at the capital and could be summoned to act on appointments.

For a vacancy to happen during the recess, the vacancy must have been created during the recess. If someone resigned, was removed, or died when the Senate was in session, the Recess Appointments Clause did not apply, even if the vacancy carried over into the recess.

Thus, for the President to use his authority under the Recess Appointments Clause, he had to fill a position that became vacant when the Senate was on its regularly scheduled inter-session break. Any recess appointment expired at the end of the next session of the Senate unless the Senate, after taking advice (deliberating), approved the appointment.[51]

Finally, the Constitution granted the President the power and duty of commissioning officers of the United States.[52] In other words, the President signed the document empowering them. As to executive officers, the power to commission carried with it the incidental power to instruct. This power was incidental because it was customary for commissioning

---

[50] Article II, Section 2, Clause 3. The language in this Clause is explained in Robert G. Natelson, *The Origins and Meaning of "Vacancies that May Happen During the Recess" in the Constitution's Recess Appointments Clause*, 37 Harvard J. of L. & Pub. Pol'y 199 (2014).

[51] In *National Labor Relations Board v. Noel Canning*, 573 U.S. 513 (2014), a 5-4 majority of the Supreme Court held that the recess could be an intra-session break and that a vacancy need not be created during the recess if the vacancy continued into it. These conclusions conflict with the Founding-era meanings of the terms "the Recess" and "happen." The majority paid little heed to Founding-era evidence, however, and relied instead on purported subsequent practice. The other four justices contested the majority's version of subsequent practice, and cited the article referenced in the previous footnote.

[52] Article II, Section 3.

executives to instruct. It was incidental also because it was necessary: If the President could not instruct the executive officers he commissioned, there would be no way for him to "take Care that the Laws be faithfully executed."[53]

7.7.3. Removal of Executive Officers

Executive officers below the President could be removed from office in one of two ways. One was by impeachment by the House of Representatives, followed by trial and conviction by the Senate. The other was by presidential dismissal. Chapter Eleven examines both impeachment and presidential dismissal.

7.8 Military Powers

The first specifically executive presidential power on the Constitution's list was to serve as "Commander in Chief of the Army and Navy of the United States, and of the Militia of the several States, when called into the actual Service of the United States."[54] This power was constrained by the rules that only Congress could declare war, establish regulations for the governance of the armed forces, set the terms for calling forth the militia, and "provide for organizing, arming, and disciplining, the Militia, and for governing such Part of them as may be employed in the Service of the United States."[55] Similarly, Congress established the rules governing federal military installations.

The President's power to "take Care that the Laws be faithfully executed"[56] gave him more discretion in deploying military force against disturbances at home (insurrection, invasion, widespread disregard for the law) than in deploying force abroad.

In the actual theater of battle, the customs of war granted the commander-in-chief broad incidental powers. These included authority to impose harsh military discipline on soldiers, martial law upon civilians, and detention and summary trial and punishment—including capital

---

[53] Article II, Section 3.

[54] Article II, Section 2, Clause 1.

[55] Article I, Section 8, Clause 15. See also Section 6.4.

[56] Article II, Section 3.

punishment—by military tribunal.[57] The President could suspend the writ of habeas corpus within the battle theater as part of martial law. This authority was different from the separate congressional power to suspend the writ over a broader territory, an incident of the war power limited by the Suspension Clause (Article I, Section 9).

More information about habeas corpus is provided in Section 9.10.2.

7.9 Foreign Affairs and Treaties

7.9.1 Powers of the President Over Foreign Affairs

The Constitution divided federal foreign affairs powers between Congress, the Senate, and the President. Congress was to declare and finance war. The Senate was to approve treaties and the appointment of diplomats. But most foreign policy authority was in the President.[58]

The Constitution empowered the President, "by and with the Advice and Consent of the Senate, to make Treaties, provided two thirds of the Senators present concur."[59] It further stated that he could

> nominate, and by and with the Advice and Consent of the Senate ... appoint Ambassadors, other public Ministers and Consuls ... and all other Officers of the United States, whose Appointments are not herein otherwise provided for, and which shall be established by Law.[60]

In this context, to "advise" the President meant to deliberate on or

---

[57] The Continental Congress' Articles of War, for example, authorized such actions. 5 J. Cont. Cong. 788–807 (Sep. 20, 1776), amended in 7 *id.* 264–66 (Apr. 14, 1777) and again in 9 *id.* 476–77 (Jun. 18, 1777).

[58] A leading commentator once argued that the Framers intended the Senate to direct foreign policy because they referred to the President as an "agent." Leonard W. Levy, Original Intent and the Framers' Constitution 38 (1988). But during the founding era, "agent" often had the Latinate meaning of "one who acts" rather than a representative or subordinate. *Cf.* 2 Farrand, p. 539 (referring to the Senate's own "agency" in the treaty-making process).

[59] Article II, Section 2, Clause 2.

[60] Article II, Section 2, Clause 2.

consider his proposals, not to offer recommendations.[61]

The Constitution further provided that the President, "shall receive Ambassadors and other public Ministers" and "shall take Care that the Laws be faithfully executed, and shall Commission all the Officers of the United States."[62] Thus, the President was to appoint, subject to senatorial approval, all senior federal employees with foreign affairs responsibilities. Those employees included front-line diplomats ("Ambassadors, other public Ministers and Consuls") and those among the "other Officers of the United States" who worked in the foreign policy arena. Front-line diplomats had to be approved by the Senate. Of the lesser officers, Congress could "vest the Appointment" in the President alone or in the Secretary of State.[63] The President was to commission all of them.[64] The power to commission included the power to instruct.[65]

The records of the Continental Congress show that the duties of foreign affairs employees were defined by law to include international negotiation, research, record-keeping, communication, and departmental administration.[66] As the one with responsibility to "take Care that the Laws be faithfully executed," the President would determine how foreign affairs officials executed their legal duties.

The Constitution further specified that the President was "to receive Ambassadors and other public Ministers."[67] The power to "receive" foreign diplomats included the power, for good cause, to place conditions upon their reception or to refuse recognition.[68] So although the Constitution did not state explicitly that the President would have general control over foreign policy, his enumerated powers and their incidents clearly gave him such control—subject to some checks from the Senate.

---

[61] Section 4.8.

[62] Article II, Section 3.

[63] Article II, Section 2, Clause 2.

[64] Article II, Section 3.

[65] See Section 7.7.2.

[66] 19 J. Cont. Cong. 43–44 (Jan. 10, 1781) (outlining the duties of employees in the Department of Foreign Affairs).

[67] Article II, Section 3.

[68] Vattel, p. 686 (discussing when a sovereign can or should refuse to receive).

7.9.2 Power of the President Over International Compacts and Treaties

Founding era international law distinguished between a "compact," which was any agreement between governments, and a "treaty," which was a compact among sovereigns to be executed over an extended period of time.[69] The Constitution authorized the President to enter into short-term executive agreements for exchanges of prisoners or ambassadors,[70] so long as such exchanges were not encumbered by long-term obligations.[71] The President's responsibility to enforce the laws (including treaties) also gave him some power to enter into short-term agreements with other nations.

But treaties had long-term consequences and were the "supreme Law of the Land." So the President's power to "make Treaties" was checked by the requirement that they be approved by two-thirds of the Senate.[72]

The check was necessary. During the Confederation era, James Madison noted that Congress's treaty power could be used to grant Congress authority to regulate commerce, even though the Articles of Confederation did not otherwise bestow that power on Congress. Madison recognized that treaty-making authority carried with it incidental power over a range of subjects that might not otherwise be enumerated.

Of course, the Constitution, unlike the Articles, did grant Congress power to regulate foreign commerce. However, the Constitution's grant of treaty-making authority carried with it other powers the Constitution did not otherwise enumerate.[73] For example, although the Constitution expressly enumerated the government's power to declare war,[74] it did not

---

[69] Section 3.7.

[70] Article II, Section 2, Clause 1 (commander-in-chief power); Article II, Section 3 (power to "receive Ambassadors and other public Ministers").

[71] Not comporting with original understanding are *United States v. Belmont*, 301 U.S. 324 (1937) and *United States v. Pink*, 315 U.S. 203 (1942), which held that an executive agreement for exchange of ambassadors can include long-term obligations without Senate approval.

[72] Article II, Section 2, Clause 2.

[73] This is the source of the common, but erroneous, belief that the federal government can employ treaties to override the Constitution.

[74] Article I, Section 8, Clause 11.

mention authority to make peace. This is because making peace was incidental to the treaty power. The Framers' decision to apply different procedures for initiating war and peace was a carefully considered one.

The power to acquire and cede territory also was incidental to treaty making. One of many precedents was the pact between Charles II of England and Louis XIV of France, whereby Charles had sold Dunkirk to France for five million livres. Another—mentioned by George Mason at the federal convention—was British cession of holdings in the West Indies. Still another was the 1783 treaty with Great Britain, which ceded British territory south of Canada and east of the Mississippi River to the United States.[75]

The possibility of land cessions by treaty became an issue at the Virginia ratifying convention, because the delegates from Kentucky (then part of Virginia) feared for their access to the Mississippi. To quiet those fears, Governor Edmund Randolph argued that any land transfer uniquely disadvantageous to a major group of citizens would violate the public trust duty of impartiality and—according to Whig political theory—would be void. Still, everyone acknowledged that the Treaty Power could be used to alienate or acquire territory. If Thomas Jefferson been in the country for the constitutional debates, he might not have agonized over whether the federal government had authority to acquire the Louisiana Territory.

In addition to transferring real estate, treaties could provide for payments from one nation to another. In the secret Treaty of Dover, signed in 1670 but not made public until shortly before the American Revolution, Louis XIV granted Charles II a revenue stream designed to free Charles from dependence on parliamentary appropriations. This was the event, perhaps, that moved James Wilson to admonish to the federal convention that, "The power of making Treaties involves the case of subsidies."[76]

Another common subject of treaties was religion. In exchange for the payments granted in the Treaty of Dover, Charles II promised Louis XIV

---

[75] G. Rous, in the pamphlet entitled Omega, Observations on the Opinion of Mr. G. Rous, p. 8 (1780) ("to arrange the limits of territory between the respective states, is the ordinary subject of every treaty of peace"). See also the response from "Omega," *id.* 30 (not disputing the point).

[76] 2 Farrand, p. 523.

to restore Roman Catholicism as the official religion of England. During the confederation era Congress adopted a treaty with the Netherlands that, a congressional committee admitted, contained some restrictions on freedom of religion.[77] Anti-Federalists opposing the Constitution argued that the federal government might employ its treaty power to erect a national church.

Some Founders held a narrower view of the treaty power: During the federal convention, George Mason and John Francis Mercer both contended that treaties would not contradict prior statutes. But the prevalent assumption was that the power to make treaties carried with it a great deal of unmentioned, incidental authority. The Ninth and Tenth Amendments did not restrict use of this incidental authority because that authority inhered in the Treaty Clause, itself an enumerated power.

Treaties were either "self-executing" or not. A self-executing treaty required no legislation to carry it out. A non-self-executing treaty required legislation. This brings us to the still-controversial question of whether a treaty could empower Congress to legislate on a subject the Constitution does not list among its powers.

The leading Supreme Court case on the matter is *Missouri v. Holland*.[78] The United States and Great Britain (then acting for Canada) had adopted a treaty regulating human behavior toward North American migratory birds. Congress executed the treaty by passing a statute—even though the Constitution did not list the regulation of wildlife on non-federal land as a congressional power.

---

[77] 24 J. Cont. Cong. 69 (Jan. 14, 1783). A committee of Congress reviewing the proposed treaty noted that "it imposes some degree of restraint on religious worship," but nonetheless recommended ratification (*id.* 65). Religious freedom also was addressed in Congress's 1786 treaty with Prussia. 30 *Id.* 275 (May 17, 1786). At the North Carolina ratifying convention, Federalist James Iredell argued that the Treaty Power could *not* be used to "establish a foreign religion among ourselves." 30 Documentary History, p. 405, but cited no reason for this conclusion.

[78] 252 U.S. 416 (1920). For a more recent example of the continuing controversy, see *Bond v. United States*, 572 U.S. 844 (2014), in which four justices argued that Congress's power to implement treaties was limited and five justices interpreted the statute to avoid the issue.

The Supreme Court held the statute valid because the Necessary and Proper Clause granted Congress authority to pass laws "necessary and proper for carrying into execution" the Treaty Clause.

Some scholars argue that the court was wrong. They point out that the Necessary and Proper Clause can be used only to assist officers and departments in carrying out their constitutional duties. The Treaty Clause, they say, refers only to the President's power to *make* treaties not to any power to *execute* treaties. So Congress may not legislate to help the President execute a treaty unless Congress can point to some other enumerated power to support the measure.

Unfortunately,[79] there at least two weaknesses in that argument. One is that, as we have seen, it conflicts with the Founding-era understanding of the Treaty Power. The other is that it conflicts with the Constitution's text. The Constitution does, in fact, grant the President power to execute treaties: Under Article VI, treaties are part of the "supreme Law of the Land," and under Article II, the President must "take Care that the Laws be faithfully executed." Congress may use the Necessary and Proper Clause to assist him in that responsibility.

Readers discomforted by the idea that the federal government can use treaties to expand its reach beyond its other enumerated powers may seek solace in three constitutional safeguards. First, the Constitution rendered it fairly difficult to make a treaty. It required both the President and two-thirds of all Senators present—not just two-thirds of those voting. The President protected the national interest, while the Senate (then selected by the state legislatures) could protect state interests.

Second, the Necessary and Proper Clause encompassed only incidental powers,[80] so it did not authorize Congress to adopt legislation significantly altering the constitutional design. Congress could not, for example, "execute" a treaty with Spain by assuming complete command over all the real estate in America, even if the treaty called for it. Moreover, the doctrine of incidental powers generally restricted laws executing treaties to matters ordinarily subject to international agreement.

---

[79] My own sympathies are with those who wish to restrict Congress's implementation to powers otherwise enumerated. However, the legal and historical evidence is to the contrary.

[80] Section 5.5.

Third, other parts of the Constitution limited how the treaty power could be exercised. Because the power was restricted by the Second through Eighth Amendments, no treaty could abolish the right to jury trial, authorize unreasonable searches and seizures, infringe the right to keep and bear arms, or compromise other protected rights. Other constitutional provisions blocked Congress from passing ex post facto laws, suppressing free speech, or funding a national church—no matter what a treaty might say on the matter.

7.10 Limitations on the President

The Constitution constricted the President's powers with internal limitations, quasi-external limitations, and external limitations.[81] An example of an internal limitation was that his power to appoint executive branch officials suggested that he could not appoint Senators. In this respect, the President was weaker than the British king, who selected members of the British House of Lords and the members of most colonial upper houses.[82]

Among the quasi-external limitations were the following: He was commander-in-chief of the militia—but only when it was "called into the actual Service of the United States."[83] He could pardon or reprieve prisoners, but not in cases of impeachment.[84] He could "make Treaties," but they were effective only if approved by a two-thirds vote of Senators present.[85] He could appoint officers, but his appointments were effective only if (1) approved by a majority vote of the Senate, (2) the office was one for which Congress had dispensed with that requirement, or (3) the vacancy had been created when the Senate was in "the Recess," in which

---

[81] See Section 5.2 for definitions of internal, quasi-external, and external limitations.

[82] But the king could not remove members of the upper house, as colonial governors could—further evidence that the first sentence of Article II did not grant the "executive Power," since that phrase was of variable scope. Section 7.2.

[83] Article II, Section 2, Clause 1.

[84] Article II, Section 2, Clause 1.

[85] Article II, Section 2, Clause 2.

case the appointment expired at the end of the next senatorial session.[86] His power to convene Congress was limited to extraordinary occasions, and his power to adjourn Congress was limited to cases in which the two chambers could not agree among themselves on a proper time.[87]

External limitations on federal powers also applied to the President. Thus, the Second Amendment prevented him from disarming the people or state militias. The Third Amendment, protecting against the quartering of troops, was directed principally at the President and his functionaries.

Finally, as discussed Chapter Eleven, the President was constrained by possible impeachment and removal from office.

7.11 The Meaning of "Officers"

The Constitution seems to place offices and officers into several different categories. These include offices and officers "of the United States," "under the United States," "under the Authority of the United States," and "of Profit or Trust under the United States." The Framers' level of professional draftsmanship was such to render it unlikely that these differences were meaningless or random.

Professor Seth Barrett Tillman was the first modern scholar to notice patterns in this usage.[88] For example, the Constitution's listing of impeachable officers ("The President, Vice President and all civil Officers of the United States") implies that the President is not an "Officer of the United States"—but presumably a branch of the government instead. The Constitution's Commissioning Clause suggests the same conclusion.[89]

But if the President is not an "Officer of the United States," is he an "Officer *under* the United States"? If not, then he is not subject to the

---

[86] Article II, Section 2, Clauses 2 & 3. For the Recess Appointments Clause, see Section 7.7.2.

[87] Article II, Section 3.

[88] More recently, he has teamed up with Professor Josh Blackman. See Seth Barrett Tillman & Josh Blackman, *Offices and Officers of the Constitution: Part I: An Introduction*, 61 So. Tex. L. Rev. 309 (2021), and its sequels.

[89] Article, II, Section 3, Clause 4 ("he shall . . . Commission all the Officers of the United States").

Foreign Emoluments Clause,[90] and Professor Tillman has produced Founding-era evidence that he is not. Whether the President is or is not an "Officer of" or "Officer under" also has Fourteenth-Amendment implications.[91]

---

[90] Section 4.5.

[91] The amendment disqualifies from offices *under* the United States insurrectionaries who previous took oaths as officers *of* the United States. U.S. Const., amend. XIV, § 3. This amendment is outside the scope of this book.

CHAPTER EIGHT

The Judicial Branch

8.1 Judicial Powers

Article III was devoted primarily to identifying and defining the responsibilities of the courts. It expanded the rudimentary court system existing under the Articles of Confederation.[1]

Except for skipping the method of selection of judges (which the Constitution prescribed in Article II)[2], Article III followed the same general plan of organization followed in Articles I and II. It began with a designation clause, itemized the terms and conditions under which judges would hold office, enumerated their powers, and restricted their authority.

Article III's first sentence stated that the "judicial Power ... shall be vested in one supreme Court, and in such inferior Courts as the Congress may ... ordain and establish." Some claim this was a vesting clause that granted power as well as identified the courts. However, this is unlikely for several reasons. First, as noted when we addressed Article II, that

---

[1] See 19 J. Cont. Cong. 354–56 (Apr. 5, 1781) (ordinance establishing courts for the trial of piracies and felonies committed on the high seas).

[2] Article II, Section 2, Clause 2.

would have been inconsistent with the drafting customs of the time.³ Additionally, interpreting this sentence to convey power to "such inferior Courts as the Congress may . . . ordain and establish" would violate a fundamental legal rule then applying to grants.⁴

The next sentence of Section 1 provided that judges were to hold their offices during "good Behaviour." This phrase, copied from English practice (and often rendered by the Latin, *quam diu se bene gesserit*),⁵ meant that judges were to hold office until they either died or were convicted of an impeachable offense. The same sentence further provided that each judge was to receive a salary and be immune from pay cuts while in office. The purpose was better to assure judicial independence from political pressures.

Section 2 contained three clauses. The first clause described the judiciary's enumerated powers, although the actual grants came later. This clause listed nine kinds of "Cases" or "Controversies" subject to federal jurisdiction. A "Case" was a lawsuit. Eighteenth-century dictionaries reveal that "Controversy" sometimes was a synonym for "Case," and that the two terms could be employed interchangeably. This is confirmed by how the Constitution employed the words: Several items labeled in the first clause of Section 2 as "controversies" were labeled "cases" in the very next clause.⁶

The constitutional text and the ratification debates indicate that the term "case" (or "controversy") was limited to its 18th-century sense. If a matter wasn't properly a judicial case then, the federal courts would not have jurisdiction over it. For example, the federal courts had no power to give advisory opinions: The federal convention had rejected a proposal by Charles Pinckney to require the Supreme Court to give advisory opinions

---

³ Section 7.2.

⁴ This was the rule against grants *in futuro*, which barred grants to persons or entities that, like the lower courts, might never come into existence

⁵ "So long has he shall have behaved himself well."

⁶ Thus, Article III, Section 2, clause 2 referred to "Cases . . . in which a State shall be a Party," a category that the previous clause called "Controversies." Some writers have hypothesized possible differences between the meaning of "cases" and "controversies." *E.g.*, John Harrison, *The Power of Congress to Limit the Jurisdiction of the Federal Courts and the Text of Article III*, 64 U. Chi. L. Rev. 203 (1997).

in response to inquiries posed by the President or by either house of Congress.

Here were the nine classes of cases within the judicial power:[7]

Cases "in Law and Equity" arising under federal law—that is, cases involving application of the Constitution, congressional statutes, or treaties made either before and after the Constitution become effective. The words "Law and Equity" referred to the two most important branches of Anglo-American jurisprudence. "Law" or "common law" consisted of the principal rules governing such areas as contracts, personal injuries, criminal law, and property. "Equity" consisted of the rules governing corporations, trusts, and fiduciary relationships. Equity also provided some special remedies in areas normally covered by "Law."

Cases involving foreign diplomats. Because of diplomatic immunity, generally only disputes in which foreign diplomats were plaintiffs or had consented to jurisdiction qualified as cases.

"[A]dmiralty and maritime" cases. Admiralty was the branch of Anglo-American jurisprudence dealing with ships and navigation. It was distinct from law and from equity.

Cases in which the U.S. government was a party. Because the United States would be a sovereign entity, it would have to grant permission (most likely by statute) for a private party to sue it. As was true of a claim against a foreign diplomat, a suit by a private party against a sovereign without the sovereign's consent was not a "case" in Anglo-American law. So if the United States did consent, federal courts could hear matters in which the federal government was either the plaintiff or the defendant. If the United States did not consent, then federal courts could hear only matters in which the federal government (or perhaps a state or foreign government) was the plaintiff. An example of a case in which the federal government was a plaintiff would be a prosecution by the government against a person accused of violating federal law.

Cases between two or more states. As sovereigns, states generally could not be sued without their consent. By the Articles of Confederation, the states had agreed to allow Congress to empanel commissioners to judge disputes among them. When the states ratified the Constitution, they

---

[7] Article III, Section 2, Clause 1. Plaintiffs with a case described in Article III did not have to sue in federal court. In almost all instances, they could proceed in state courts instead.

continued this conferral of jurisdiction, but the Constitution transferred such cases from temporary commissioners to permanent federal courts.

Cases between a state and citizens of another state. A valid "case" was one in which the state was the plaintiff or had consented to being sued. Leading Federalists affirmed this during the ratification debates, and a few years later, Congress and the states adopted the Eleventh Amendment to cement this understanding. [8]

Cases between citizens of different states. The reason federal courts received jurisdiction over such matters was to give the plaintiff an alternative to proceeding in the courts of the defendant's state, where he might encounter local hostility. Jurisdiction based on difference in state citizenship is called *diversity jurisdiction.*

Cases between citizens of the same state claiming lands under grants of different states. The reasons for this can be illustrated by an example: At one time, Massachusetts claimed a portion of western New York. Two residents of Connecticut might each assert title to land in the part of New York claimed by Massachusetts. One party might trace his claim to a purported grant from Massachusetts, while the other traced his to a purported grant from New York. A federal tribunal would more likely be impartial in such a case than a state court of Massachusetts or New York, and more likely to be able to enforce its judgment than a state court of Connecticut or Massachusetts.

Cases in which one party was a U.S. state or a U.S. citizen and the other party was a foreign nation or a foreign citizen—assuming that any sovereign state or nation in the case was a plaintiff or otherwise consented to jurisdiction.

After the list of cases and controversies came the formal grant of power to the Supreme Court. Section 2, Clause 2 bestowed on the court two different kinds of jurisdiction—original and appellate. Original jurisdiction is the power to act as a trial court. Appellate jurisdiction is the power to hear appeals from a trial court. The Clause provided:

> In all Cases affecting Ambassadors, other public Ministers and Consuls, and those in which a State shall be Party, the supreme Court shall have original Jurisdiction. In all the other Cases before mentioned, the supreme Court shall have appellate Juris-

---

[8] Section 3.5.

diction, both as to Law and Fact, with such Exceptions, and under such Regulations as the Congress shall make.[9]

Thus, Section 2, Clause 1 enumerated the nine kinds of cases within federal jurisdiction, and Clause 2 referred back to that enumeration to grant the Supreme Court original jurisdiction over some items (diplomatic cases and those in which a state was a party) and appellate jurisdiction over the rest. This pattern was much like a will in which the testator lists items of property first, then bestows gifts to each family member by referring to the preceding list.

The Constitution granted the Supreme Court appellate jurisdiction "both as to Law and Fact." This provision became controversial during the ratification battle. Anti-Federalists argued that the inclusion of "Fact" would empower the Supreme Court to overturn jury verdicts more readily than Anglo-American courts traditionally had been permitted to.[10] To quiet this objection, Congress proposed, and the states ratified, the Seventh Amendment. The Seventh Amendment provided that the Supreme Court could reverse verdicts only to the same extent that courts previously had done.

The Constitution by itself did not create any lower federal courts. Instead, it authorized Congress to "constitute Tribunals inferior to the Supreme Court."[11] This power to constitute gave Congress the flexibility to (1) grant additional jurisdiction to pre-existing tribunals, particularly the state courts, and (2) create and empower new federal tribunals.[12]

Because federal tribunals might not be created for some time, the Constitution did not grant them any powers. Indeed, it was contrary to

---

[9] Article III, Section 2, Clause 2.

[10] In this respect, the Anti-Federalists were on solid ground. This ill-advised language seems to have arisen out of proposals in the Continental Congress for a court of appeals to hear admiralty (maritime) cases, with the goal of allowing that court to overrule juries. 13 J. Cont. Cong. 137.

[11] Article I, Section 8, Clause 9. In the language of traditional conveyancing, this was a "power of appointment."

[12] This was confirmed a few years after the ratification, in an opinion written by Justice William Paterson, one of the Framers. *Stuart v. Laird*, 5 U.S. 299 (1803). Paterson pointed out that the same interpretation had prevailed in 1789, a fact conceded by the attorney for the losing party, former Attorney General Charles Lee.

prevailing legal doctrine to make a grant to take effect only in the future.[13] Instead, the Constitution provided that in six of the nine types of federal cases, the Supreme Court was to hear appeals "under such Regulations as the Congress shall make."[14] In constituting lower courts and in regulating appeals, Congress would grant them their authority.

8.2 Judicial Review

In the course of his judicial duties, a federal judge might encounter a state or federal enactment inconsistent with the Constitution. In that event, the judge would be required to apply the Constitution and disregard the enactment. This could have the effect of voiding the enactment—at least for that case. Today, the practice of voiding unconstitutional state and federal actions is called *judicial review*.

Judicial review has proven controversial. One reason is that it can cause popular legislation to become void. Another is because judges exercising judicial review sometimes make mistakes. Text writers on constitutional law have contributed to the controversy by claiming or implying that judicial review was unknown until Chief Justice Marshall allegedly seized the power for the Supreme Court in the 1803 decision of *Marbury v. Madison*.[15]

Actually, the Founders who expressed pre-ratification opinions on the subject considered judicial review part of proper judging. They did not want a statute that clashed with the Constitution to survive, and they expected judges to grant priority over such statutes to the Constitution. At the Virginia ratifying convention, for example, Anti-Federalists worried about whether the courts would be aggressive enough to strike down unconstitutional laws, while Federalists thought they would.

Americans had a centuries-old acquaintance with the idea that lower-

---

[13] 2 William Blackstone, Commentaries, *441; see also *165. The Founders often thought of government in terms of the law of private legal relationships, such as agency and conveyancing. *E.g.*, Edmund Pendleton to Richard Henry Lee, June 14, 1788, in 10 Documentary History, pp. 1625–26 (comparing the people's grant of power to various real estate conveyances and to agency). See also Section 1.3.5 (analogy between the Constitution and a power of attorney).

[14] Article III, Section 2, Clause 2.

[15] 5 U.S. (1 Cranch.) 137 (1803).

level laws were invalid if they clashed with higher-level laws. As British subjects, they had understood that laws passed by a colonial assembly were void if inconsistent with the colonial charter or with Magna Carta. In the Continental Congress, a congressional committee concluded that some state laws violated the rules under which the United States had been created, and that such laws therefore "ought to be deemed void."[16] By the time *Marbury v. Madison* was decided, there had been about three dozen American court cases—including some high-profile cases before the Constitution's ratification—in which judicial review was applied or assumed.[17]

8.3 Limitations on the Judicial Power

The remainder of Article III was devoted to limitations on the judicial power. One was that Congress could make "Exceptions" to the Constitution's grant to the Supreme Court of "appellate Jurisdiction, both as to Law and Fact."[18] This authority to reduce the Supreme Court's authority sometimes is called the *jurisdiction stripping* power.

Some commentators have argued that the Constitution should be interpreted to limit Congress's ability to engage in jurisdiction stripping. Their assumption is that the Founders could not have intended Congress to have power to hobble the Supreme Court by taking away all or most of its appellate jurisdiction. However, Founding-era practice was to grant legislatures broad authority to define, expand, and narrow the jurisdiction of judicial tribunals. In England, a legal maxim held that, "The designation of the justices is by the King, but ordinary jurisdiction [is defined] by law."[19] In America, state constitutions usually recognized, either implicitly, or explicitly, the power of the legislature broadly to define courts' jurisdiction however the legislature pleased.[20]

---

[16] 13 J. Cont. Cong. 136 (Feb. 2, 1779).

[17] See Bibliography.

[18] Article III, Section 2, Clause 2. In traditional conveyancing terms, this may be thought of as a power of divestment.

[19] *Designatio Justiciariorum est a Rege, Jurisdictio vero ordinaria a Lege.*

[20] For example, the New York and New Jersey constitutions contained almost no restrictions on the legislature's authority to create courts or define their jurisdiction. The Massachusetts, Pennsylvania, and South Carolina Constitutions

On this point, moreover, we have testimony from several leading Founders. During the ratification battle, Rufus King and Nathaniel Gorham, both of whom had represented Massachusetts in the federal convention, wrote that,

> [I]n a few enumerating instances the supreme Court have original & final Jurisdiction—in all other cases which fall within the federal Judicial, the supreme court may or may not have appellate Jurisdiction as congress may direct.[21]

Around the same time, Roger Sherman, who had represented Connecticut at the convention, observed that the judicial powers "cannot be extended beyond the enumerated cases, but may be limited by Congress."[22] During the Virginia ratifying convention, John Marshall (later Chief Justice) stated in the course of defending the Constitution:

> What is the meaning of the term exception? Does it not mean an alteration and diminution? Congress is empowered to make exceptions to the appellate jurisdiction, as to law and fact, of the Supreme Court. These exceptions certainly go as far as the legislature may think proper for the interest and liberty of the people.[23]

So both contemporaneous practice and the Founders' own testimony make it clear that Congress enjoyed discretion to limit the appellate jurisdiction of the Supreme Court.

The Constitution contained four other limitations on the judicial power:

- The requirement of trial by jury, set forth in Article III[24] and

---

explicitly gave the legislature power to erect certain courts and define their jurisdiction.

[21] Farrand-Supp., p. 283. See also 2 Farrand, p. 431 (showing that "Exceptions" modifies "appellate," with "Law and Fact" inserted for other purposes).

[22] Farrand-Supp., p. 288.

[23] 10 Documentary History, p. 1437.

[24] Article III, Section 2, Clause 3.

strengthened in the Sixth and Seventh Amendments. This limitation is treated in Chapter Nine.
- The restrictive definition of "treason." This limited the judicial power because it restricted the traditional prerogative of courts to define common law crimes.[25] Treason also is discussed in Chapter Nine.
- Congress's power to declare the punishment for treason.[26] That topic is discussed in Chapter Six.
- The Supremacy Clause of Article VI,[27] which may be considered a limitation on, or at least a regulation of, federal as well as state judicial power. It is treated in Chapter Three.

---

[25] Article III, Section 3, Clause 1.

[26] Article III, Section 3, Clause 2.

[27] Article VI, Clause 2.

CHAPTER NINE

The Bill of Rights and Other External Limitations on Federal Powers

9.1 The Unamended Constitution's Protections for Liberty, and the Adoption of the Bill of Rights

Chapter Five explained the kinds of restrictions the Constitution imposed on powers granted to Congress. They included *internal limitations* (those expressed as part of a grant), *quasi-external limitations* (those immediately following a grant), and *external limitations* (limitations applying to two or more powers). Chapter Five also surveyed the Constitution's internal and quasi-external limitations. This Chapter surveys its external limitations.

Most of the unamended Constitution's external limitations on Congress were in Article I, Section 9. That section itemized laws that Congress could not pass, even though such laws otherwise might be within express or implied congressional authority. In accordance with standard drafting practice, the Framers placed these external limitations immediately after the principal list of congressional powers.[1]

---

[1] That is to say, after Article I, Section 8, in compliance with the maxim, *Exceptio semper ultima ponenda est* ("An exception should always be placed last").

Other external limitations were scattered throughout the Constitution. They included the requirement that direct taxes be apportioned among the states,[2] the rule against imposing punishments for treason on innocent parties,[3] and the guarantee of trial by jury in criminal cases.[4]

During the ratification debates, Anti-Federalists argued that the Constitution's external limitations were insufficient. They proposed that the document be amended to include a bill of rights.[5]

Federalists contended that a bill of rights was unnecessary. In their view, the new government would not have sufficient authority to oppress individual liberties. For example, they maintained that the new government could not restrict freedom of the press or of religion, because it had no enumerated powers over either the press or religion. Anti-Federalists pointed out, however, that the government could use its enumerated powers to infringe liberty. Congress could use its taxing authority to suppress disfavored printers or religious denominations. It could employ its unlimited authority in the capital district and in the western territories to suppress dissent or establish a national religion there.

Federalists also suggested that enumerating natural rights could be dangerous. No bill of rights could include all natural rights, so some necessarily would be omitted. By following the rule of construction whereby items not on a list were excluded,[6] courts might conclude that Congress had power to do everything the bill didn't specifically prevent it from doing.

Anti-Federalists rejoined that the Constitution already contained a mini-bill of rights (Article I, Section 9) that protected a few important liberties, such as the privilege of habeas corpus. So any danger from a partial enumeration of rights was already in the Constitution. The Federalists could have responded that Article I, Section 9 was qualita-

---

[2] Article I, Section 1, Clause 3.

[3] Article III, Section 3, Clause 1.

[4] Article III, Section 2, Clause 3.

[5] For an explanation of rights and privileges, see Section 3.10.2. Amendments would, in the event they contradicted the original text, override it, in accordance with the legal rule, *Leges posteriores priores contrarias abrogant* ("Later laws override prior ones to the contrary").

[6] *Inclusio unius est exclusio alterius.*

tively different from the sort of bill of rights the Anti-Federalists sought, because its focus was more on good government than on natural rights. But instead of making this argument, Federalist leaders wisely realized they had lost the debate, and that, unless they compromised, the Constitution would not be ratified. They accordingly entered into a "gentlemen's agreement" with political moderates: "Vote for the Constitution, and once it is approved, we, the Federalists, will cooperate in adding a bill of rights."

For the Constitution to come into effect, ratification by nine states was necessary.[7] When the First Federal Congress convened in March, 1789, eleven had ratified. Pursuant to the gentlemen's agreement, on June 8, 1789, Representative James Madison rose on the floor of Congress to introduce a bill of rights. After several months of intermittent consideration, Congress transmitted twelve amendments to the states.[8]

The congressional resolution contained a preamble that explained the method and purpose of the Bill:

> The Conventions of a number of the States, having at the time of their adopting the Constitution, expressed a desire, in order to prevent misconstruction or abuse of its powers, that further declaratory and restrictive clauses should be added: And as extending the ground of public confidence in the Government, will best ensure the benificent [sic] ends of its institution, Resolved. . . .

Thus, some of the proposed amendments were "declaratory . . . clauses" (that is, rules of construction) designed to "prevent misconstruction" of the Constitution by explaining how the instrument should be interpreted. The rest were "restrictive clauses" to prevent "abuse" of federal powers by creating external limitations curtailing those powers. The discussion below explains which amendments served which purposes.

The states never ratified the first proposed amendment, and did not

---

[7] Article VII.

[8] Madison tried to induce Congress to adopt an amendment protecting press, religion, and jury trial from *state*, as well as federal, interference, but without success.

ratify the second until 1992, when it became the Twenty-Seventh Amendment. But the requisite number of states duly approved the third through twelfth. On December 15, 1791, they were proclaimed as the First through Tenth Amendments.

Madison's original plan was to insert much of the Bill of Rights into Article I, Section 9. But some members of Congress objected. Most of the Bill consisted of external limitations on all federal authority, not merely on the power of Congress,[9] and legal drafting practice[10] suggested that such amendments should be located after all enumerated powers, not merely after the powers of Congress. Accordingly, Congress proposed appending them to the end of the document. The two amendments that were rules of construction were—also in accordance with drafting practice—placed last of all. They became the Ninth and Tenth Amendments, and are discussed in Chapter Ten.

The Bill of Rights as ratified contained about two dozen external limitations,[11] all designed to supplement the unamended Constitution's protections for liberty. We can divide them into two broad classes: (1) external limitations protecting what the Founders considered natural rights, and (2) external limitations protecting traditionally valued privileges.

The first class created exceptions in federal powers to prevent those powers from being exercised to infringe natural rights. The rights thus guarded were freedom of religion, freedom of speech, peaceable assembly, the right to petition, possession of arms (and therefore self-defense), and the sanctity of the home and other property. Members of the founding generation sometimes classified freedom of the press as a privilege[12] but more often as a natural right, and the Constitution placed it among the rights.

---

[9] These were contained in the Second through Eighth Amendments.

[10] *Exceptio semper ultima ponenda est* ("An exception should always be put last.").

[11] The exact number depends on how you count.

[12] In 1986, a draft bill of rights prepared by a committee in the First Congress was discovered. It is in the handwriting of Roger Sherman. The committee grouped the natural rights, except for self-defense (not mentioned), together in a single paragraph. Privileges were protected in later paragraphs. Liberty of the press effectively appeared both among the natural rights and among the privileges.

The Bill of Rights and Other External Limitations on Federal Powers : 165

The rules protecting natural rights made up the First, Second and Third Amendments, and parts of the Fourth and Fifth. The rules pertaining to privileges addressed trial by jury, due process of law, limitations on search warrants, the viability of state militias, proportionality in bail and fines, and protection against "cruel and unusual punishments." These external limitations took up most of the Fourth and Fifth Amendments, and all of the Sixth, Seventh and Eighth. The Second Amendment protected the militia as well as the natural right of self-defense.

The remainder of this chapter examines each of the Constitution's external limitations on federal authority, whether in the Bill of Rights or elsewhere in the document.

9.2 "Good Government" Restrictions

Some external limitations imposed fiduciary standards—rules of "public trust"—on the new government. The fiduciary standard the founding generation referenced most was the duty of impartiality. The duty of impartiality required (and still requires) that a fiduciary serving several different beneficiaries treat them all dispassionately, rather than show favoritism to some at the expense of others.

The following illustrates when the duty arises: A man dies leaving a will. The will grants the man's property to a trust, to be managed by a trustee. The will directs that the trustee pay income from the estate to the deceased's widow. It further directs that upon the widow's death, the trustee shall pay what is left of the estate to the deceased's adult children.

In absence of circumstances to the contrary, it is in the widow's interest for the trustee to invest in assets yielding high income, even if that puts the capital amount at some risk. It is in the children's interest for the trustee to invest conservatively to preserve the capital, even if the result is little income. Unless the will states otherwise, fiduciary law requires the trustee to balance investments so as to work a rough justice among the parties. That is the trustee's duty of impartiality.

The widow and children in the illustration have only two different interests. The American people have many. Nevertheless, the Founders saw Congress as being in the position of the trustee, with the people in the position of beneficiaries. Congress had an obligation to try to treat all groups as fairly as possible.

Most of the "good government" restrictions in the unamended

Constitution were inserted to encourage and assist Congress in meeting its obligation of impartiality. The rest—which served various policies (including impartiality)—included oath requirements, limits on retroactive laws, rules pertaining to finances and records, and a ban on federal titles of nobility.

9.2.1 Uniformity of Indirect Taxes

The external limitations imposed on the congressional taxing power were designed primarily to assure that taxation bore impartially on different sections of the country. Article I, Section 9 forbade Congress from imposing taxes (exactions to raise revenue) or duties (exactions either to raise revenue or regulate trade) on exports from the states.[13] If Congress could not tax exports, then Congress would face one fewer temptation to discriminate against some sections of the country. Southern states especially sought this protection, for their economies depended largely on the export of home-grown commodities, such as tobacco. The ban on federal exactions on exports was stricter than the comparable one the Constitution imposed on the states, which remained free to levy taxes on exports if Congress consented.[14]

The Constitution granted Congress power to levy duties on imports, which were called *imposts*. However, imposts had to be uniform throughout the United States.[15] This assured that Congress would not play favorites by levying lower tariffs at some American ports than at others. Moreover, Congress was required to treat all U.S. ports equally when regulating revenue and commerce, and could not adopt import or export tariffs that discriminated among states.[16]

---

[13] Article I, Section 9, Clause 5. Possibly, Congress could tax exports from federal territories, although this might conflict with the rule of Article I, Section 8, Clause 1 that duties, imposts and excises "be uniform throughout the United States."

[14] Article I, Section 10, Clause 2.

[15] Article I, Section 8, Clause 1.

[16] Article I, Section 8, Clause 1; see also Article I, Section 9, Clause 6 ("No Preference shall be given by any Regulation of Commerce or Revenue to the Ports of one State over those of another").

9.2.2 Apportionment of Direct Taxes

Another external limitation encouraging impartiality was the Apportionment Rule. The rule was stated twice—first in the affirmative:

> Representatives and direct Taxes shall be apportioned among the several States ... according to their respective Numbers, which shall be determined by adding to the whole Number of free Persons, including those bound to Service for a Term of Years, and excluding Indians not taxed, three-fifths of all other Persons.[17]

And later in the negative:

> No Capitation, or other direct, Tax shall be laid, unless in Proportion to the Census or Enumeration herein before directed to be taken.[18]

These provisions established the same formula for direct taxes among states as for representation in the House of Representatives. (See Chapter Six, Section 6.1 for an extended explanation of "direct" and "indirect" taxes.)

This formula was based on each state's sum of (1) free persons, including indentured servants and (2) three-fifths of all slaves, but (3) excluding "Indians not taxed." The third category consisted of Native Americans still governed exclusively by their tribes and therefore outside any state political system.[19] Indians living outside of tribal jurisdiction and subject to state laws were counted among as "free Persons."

As explained in Section 4.3, the three-fifths formula for slaves did not originate at the federal convention, but in an earlier congressional study concluding that slave labor was only 60 percent as productive as

---

[17] Article I, Section 2, Clause 3.

[18] Article I, Section 9, Clause 4.

[19] The wording in the congressional proposal originally was "except Indians, not paying taxes," and this version (without the comma) was in the federal convention's first draft. 2 Farrand, p. 571.

free labor and produced proportionately less tax revenue.[20] This judgment was economic in nature and had nothing to do with race. The Apportionment Rule counted both non-tribal Indians and America's 60,000 free African-Americans exactly as it counted whites.

9.2.3 The Oath to Support the Constitution

Article VI, Clause 3 provided that all federal and state legislators and officers

> shall be bound by Oath or Affirmation, to support this Constitution; but no religious Test shall ever be required as a Qualification to any Office or public Trust under the United States.

At the time of the Founding, oaths of office routinely were required of officeholders. In all the states, officeholders were expected to swear or affirm that they were Christians, or at least believed in the divine inspiration of the Old and New Testament.

Under Founding-era law, the oath-taker was calling God to witness the truth of what he or she said.[21] Only those who believed in God (or gods) were qualified to take a valid oath. Because an atheist did not believe in God, the oath had diminished or no force in his or her case.[22]

The reason the oath requirement was considered a good government measure is that it was thought to increase the likelihood that officeholders would be virtuous. It suggested to the oath taker the danger of divine retribution if he should conduct himself improperly.

During the ratification debates, the Federalists proponents explained that, despite the Constitution's proclamation against religious tests, the oath requirement would act as a sort of religious test. Office-holding

---

[20] 24 J. Cont. Cong. 259–60 (Apr. 18, 1783); 25 *id.* 949 (Madison's congressional notes). As of March 8, 1786, nine states had approved the formula. 30 *id.* 103 & 107.

[21] Hence the maxim, *Jurare est Deus in testem vocare, et est actus Divini cultus* ("To swear is to call God as a witness and is an act of divine reverence").

[22] The Constitution's provision allowing a prospective officeholder to "affirm" rather than to "swear" did not validate an atheist's oath. The option of affirming was inserted to accommodate certain Christian sects (such as the Quakers) who believed the New Testament forbade them from swearing (see James 5:12).

would be limited to theists. No other religious test was needed, the Federalists said, because there were worthy men of all religions. It was not necessary to limit federal office to Christians.[23]

9.2.4 Other "Good Government" Rules, including the Emoluments Clauses

The Constitution contained several other good government measures. Three provisions pertained to *emoluments*. The meaning of that term is discussed in Section 4.5. The three emoluments clauses were as follows:

- The Congressional Emoluments Clause,[24] which prevented members of Congress from being appointed to offices created or whose "Emoluments" had been increased during the current term of office.
- The Foreign Emoluments Clause, which barred federal officeholders from accepting, without the consent of Congress, any "present, Emolument, Office, or Title, of any kind whatsoever from any King, Prince, or foreign State."[25] This was designed to prevent government officials from being compromised by foreign governments. In practice, it was difficult to apply to American diplomats: during that era, gift-giving was a core part of diplomatic protocols.
- The Presidential Emoluments Clause,[26] which banned the President from receiving emoluments from the United States or any state, other than his formal compensation.

Like the states, the federal government was barred from granting any

---

[23] Robert G. Natelson, *The Original Meaning of the Establishment Clause*, 14 Wm. & Mary Bill Rights J. 73 (2005).

[24] Article I, § 6, cl. 2.

[25] Article I, Section 9, Clause 8.

[26] Article II, Section 1, Clause 1.

title of nobility.[27] As the successor to the Confederation, the federal government would assume full responsibility for the Confederation's debts.[28] Moreover, regular records had to be kept and published of all receipts and expenditures.[29]

In the British Parliament and American colonies, provisions for revenue (taxes) and for appropriations frequently had been lumped together under the generic names of "money bills" or "supply bills." After Independence, state legislatures began to move in the direction of the modern state "single subject rule," by which each bill is limited to one general topic. The first move in this direction seems to have been using different bills for revenues and appropriations. Although the Constitution did not adopt the modern single subject rule, it promoted the trend in that direction by treating taxes, appropriations, and regulations as separate categories.

The Constitution prohibited the federal government from spending money unless pursuant to a valid appropriation.[30] It required revenue (tax) bills to originate in the House of Representatives.[31] It permitted the Senate to amend revenue bills, but prevented the Senate from adding terms unrelated to revenue unless the House had done so first.[32]

9.3 Restrictions on Federal Retroactivity: The Article I, Section 9 Ex Post Facto and Attainder Clauses and the Fifth Amendment Takings and Due Process Clauses

9.3.1 The Problem of Retroactivity

The Founders believed that, to be republican, a government had to honor the rule of law. They saw it as inconsistent with the rule of law for

---

[27] Article I, Section 9, Clause 8. Section 1.3.3 of this book explains that the probable reason this ban was separate from the guarantee of republican government.

[28] Article VI, Clause 1.

[29] Article I, Section 9, Clause 7.

[30] Article I, Section 9, Clause 7.

[31] Article I, Section 7, Clause 1, discussed in Sections 4.6 and 4.7.

[32] See Section 4.6.

the government to convict a person for an act that was not a crime when the act was performed. They further thought it inconsistent with the rule of law to enforce rules that interfered unduly with settled expectations. In non-criminal matters, government could change a rule retroactively only if the rule had not been relied on. An example of a proper retroactive change was a reduction of scheduled payments to holders of public securities who had purchased them at steep discounts because no one expected the securities to be paid in full.

9.3.2 The Reasons for the Fifth Amendment Takings and Due Process Clauses

The Constitution prohibited both Congress and the states from passing ex post facto laws or bills of attainder.[33] The Constitution banned only the states, not the federal government, from "impairing the Obligation of Contracts" or inflating the currency by declaring paper or base metal legal tender. The Constitution applied the Fifth Amendment's Takings and Due Process Clauses only to the federal government.

Those two clauses apparently derived from the ratification process. Initially, some people believed that the Constitution's ban on federal and state ex post facto laws would prevent governments from taking property without compensation or passing retroactive laws of either a civil or criminal nature. During the ratification debates, Anti-Federalists argued that retroactive civil legislation was sometimes desirable, at least if it furthered rather than upset settled expectations.[34] Federalists responded that the Ex Post Facto Clauses applied only to criminal laws.

On the initiative of John Lansing, Jr.,[35] the New York ratification document incorporated that understanding. But Lansing also seems to have recognized that limiting the ex post facto ban to criminal laws created a risk: It freed Congress to adopt unfair as well as fair retroactive

---

[33] Article I, Section 9, Clause 3 (Congress); Article I, Section 10, Clause 1 (states).

[34] Retroactive civil laws that uphold expectations—such as laws validating marriages unintentionally void due to legal technicalities—sometimes are called "curative statutes."

[35] Lansing had been a delegate to the federal convention, but left early because he thought the convention was crafting a constitution that gave the central government too much power. He later served as New York's chief justice and still later as chancellor—the most prestigious judicial officer in the state.

civil laws. So he induced the New York convention to issue in its ratification instrument another declaration:

> That no Person ought to be taken imprisoned or disseised [i.e., lose possession] of his freehold, or be exiled or deprived of his Privileges, Franchises, Life, Liberty or Property but by due process of Law.

Lansing based this declaration on four separate sections of a state "bill of rights" statute adopted the preceding year. That statute protected citizens whom the state sued either criminally or civilly by requiring the state to follow "due process of law" and "due Course of Law."

James Madison was among those who had believed the Constitution's prohibitions on ex post facto laws would guard against retroactive civil and criminal legislation. Perhaps he was disappointed by the agreement to restrict those prohibitions to criminal laws. In any event, when he offered his proposed bill of rights to Congress in June, 1789, he included both a takings clause to prevent the federal government from seizing property without compensation, and a due process clause based on the New York model. The latter would empower courts to void some unfairly retroactive federal measures.[36]

9.3.3 The Takings Clause

The Fifth Amendment Takings Clause reflects the Lockean/public trust view that costs incurred for public benefit ought to be distributed among the general public, not imposed disproportionately on a minority. The Founding-era legal maxim for this proposition was *Qui sentit commodum, sentire debet et onus*—loosely, "Who feels the gain should feel the pain." The Framers did not find it practicable for the Constitution to follow that principle uniformly, but they did insert several other provisions that furthered it, including the Takings Clause.

There is little specific discussion in the Founding-era record about the Takings Clause, so we must deduce its scope and meaning from the Constitution's text and from other circumstances. It is clear that the Clause is a qualification of the federal government's condemnation or

---

[36] Courts sometimes used the doctrine of "equitable construction" (see Section 2.7) to achieve the same goal. *Ham v. McClaws*, 1 Bay 93 (S.C. 1789).

eminent domain power—that is, the sovereign's prerogative of taking private property for public use.[37] Other issues are less clear, and can be stated in the following questions:

- Did the term "property" extend only to real estate, or did it include personal property, such as goods or money?
- Was compensation due if the taking was merely temporary, with possession restored to the owner after a time?
- Did a "taking" include regulation that reduced property values as well as actual seizure?
- Did the term "public use," restrict the government only to takings that resulted in government possession, or did it encompass other public purposes and benefits?

The first question is whether "property" included only real estate or other forms of property as well. The word "property" appeared twice elsewhere in the Constitution—once in the Property Clause, where it probably was limited to real estate,[38] and once in the Fifth Amendment's Due Process Clause, where it encompassed all kinds of property. The rules of construction suggest that when a word is used twice in a single provision—here the Fifth Amendment—the meanings are the same. This implies that the Takings Clause protected all forms of property.

Other circumstances support this reading. Magna Carta, which was revered among the Founders, mandated that when royal officials requisitioned grain or provisions, those officials had to pay for them. During and after the Revolution, the Continental and Confederation Congresses recognized again and again their obligation to compensate for goods seized or requisitioned, even when currency inflation and the exigencies of war made payment difficult.[39] I have found no good evidence that

---

[37] The federal government's enumerated powers over territories and enclaves certainly included eminent domain, and it was incidental to several other enumerated powers as well. One commentator has argued that eminent domain was too important to be incidental to enumerated powers, but Founding-era law books show this was not the case. See the bibliography for this chapter.

[38] Article IV, Section 3, Clause 2, discussed in Section 6.6.

[39] 7 J. Cont. Cong. 145–46 (Feb. 22, 1777) (requisitioning of carriages to be paid for); 8 *id.* 752 (Sep. 17, 1777) ("provisions and other articles" taken to be paid for); 9 *id.* 905 (Nov. 14, 1777) ("even the disaffected will be paid a reasonable

"property" in the Fifth Amendment was limited to land.

The second question is whether compensation was due if the taking was temporary. In other words, if the government eventually restored the item to its owner, did it still owe compensation?

The probable answer is yes. For nearly three hundred years, the Anglo-American legal system had understood property to include leaseholds and other forms of temporary possession. During the Revolution, the Continental Congress made explicit provision for compensation for temporary takings.[40]

The third question is whether the Takings Clause required compensation only when government actually seized possession or whether compensation also was required when government merely regulated in a way that reduced the property's value. The plain meaning of the word "take" suggests only the former, and history supports the plain meaning: Founding-era governments did not customarily compensate for the impact of regulations on market value.

The fourth and final question is whether the term "public use" restricted the federal government to taking property only for public possession (as for a fort, office building, or post road) or whether it could take for any public benefit. This is a difficult issue that has provoked a great deal of modern controversy.[41]

Some commentators argue that the natural meaning of "use" limited takings to seizures for government possession. Others maintain that Founding-era governments could take land from its owner and convey possession or title to others, so long as there was a public benefit and the government paid the owner full compensation.

For better or worse, the latter group has the better of the argument. The claim that the Founding-era meaning of "use" was limited to possession is simply wrong. Samuel Johnson's Dictionary, for example, offered

---

price" for articles taken); 18 *id.* 980 (Oct. 26, 1780) (compensation for taking salt); 27 *id.* 543 (Jun. 3, 1784) (compensation for taking wood, forage, and other property).

[40] 14 J. Cont. Cong. 867–68 (Jul. 23, 1779) (compensation for use of real property during the period of the war only).

[41] In recent years, the controversy has centered on the Supreme Court's decision in *Kelo v. City of New London*, 545 U.S. 649 (2005), which held that "public use" essentially meant public benefit.

several meanings of "use," with the most common being "the act of employing any thing [sic] to any purpose," and another being "Advantage received." On a more specialized level, Giles Jacob's Law Dictionary defined "use" as "the profit or benefit of lands or tenements," and other law dictionaries featured similar wording.

The definition of "use" as benefit or purpose was the product of an extensive history: The English Statute of Uses (1536) governed arrangements in which one person, X, held title to property "for the use of" some other person, Y. This phrase meant that X held title merely for the purpose of benefiting Y. Y might, or might not, be in possession of the land, but its profits went to benefit him.

The Constitution employed the word "use" to mean "benefit" or "purpose" in two other places as well. Article I, Section 8, Clause 12 granted Congress the power to "raise and support Armies, but no Appropriation of Money to that Use shall be for a longer Term than two Years." Article I, Section 10, Clause 2 denied states power to tax imports or exports without congressional consent. But it further provided that even if Congress had consented, "the net Produce" of such taxes "shall be for the Use of the Treasury of the United States." In other words, the money was to be for the benefit of the Treasury of the United States. Clearly the state would not have to give the U.S. Treasury actual possession of the precise dollars received, but it had to ensure the Treasury benefited accordingly.[42]

In summary: The Takings Clause of the Fifth Amendment allowed the federal government to seize real or personal property for any public reason, so long as the government paid "just compensation." Compensation was due even if the taking was temporary. But no compensation was due if the federal government reduced the value of property by enacting a regulation. Of course, a regulation might be invalid for some other reason, such as failure to follow due process of law.

---

[42] The law of uses eventually evolved into the law of trusts. Traditionally, first year law students learn about the special meaning of "use." But for some reason legal commentators and judges seem to have forgotten this information when discussing the Fifth Amendment Taking Clause.

9.3.4 The Due Process Clause

By a provision in Magna Carta (1215), King John promised as follows:

> No free person shall be captured, or imprisoned, or dispossessed, or outlawed or exiled or in any way destroyed; nor shall we [the king] go against him or proceed against him, except by a legal judgment of his peers, or by the law of the land.

In subsequent years, the term "due process of law" became a recognized synonym for "law of the land." Some American documents, such as the Massachusetts Constitution of 1780, used the phrase "law of the land"; others, such as the Northwest Ordinance of 1787, employed "due process of law." In 1776, the Continental Congress protected accused Tories in language reminiscent of Magna Carta, providing that no one,

> [b]e injured in his person, or property, or in any manner whatever disturbed, unless the proceeding against him be founded on an order of this Congress, or the Association, convention, council or committee of safety of the colony. . . .[43]

The Fifth Amendment Due Process Clause stated, "No person shall . . . be deprived of life, liberty, or property, without due process of law."[44] From its history, it is quite clear what it meant: If the government sought to execute, imprison, or fine a person, it could not make up the rules as it went along, but had to proceed in accordance with the pre-established proper procedure or "law of the land." This rule applied whether the government was prosecuting a criminal or civil case.

As noted above, John Lansing, Jr. of New York and James Madison of Virginia share credit for inserting the Due Process Clause into the Constitution. The history and wording demonstrate that the due process guarantee applied to all branches of the federal government, not merely to the executive and judicial branches, as in England.

The due process guarantee enabled the courts to invalidate particu-

---

[43] 5 J. Cont. Cong. 464 (Jun. 18, 1776).

[44] DeLolme, p. 80, listed these as property, personal security, and the "locomotive faculty."

larly harsh retroactive civil legislation, thereby partially restoring a safeguard Lansing and Madison apparently thought had been lost when the Ratifiers construed the Ex Post Facto Clauses to apply only to criminal laws.[45] The Fifth Amendment Due Process Clause effectively banned Congress from punishing citizens for "breach of legislative privilege." The clause also expanded the prohibition on federal bills of attainder to include "bills of pains and penalties," by which legislatures imposed punishments other than attainder on named persons alleged to have committed crimes.[46]

Hence, if federal authorities sought to execute or imprison Mr. Jones for treason, they had to prosecute him in accordance with pre-existing legal procedures. Similarly, if Mrs. Jones duly acquired title to land in the District of Columbia by following the procedures set forth in the District's conveyancing law, Congress could not change those rules retroactively to deprive Mrs. Jones of title. If Congress imposed a tax on transactions already completed, the courts would limit how far into the past Congress could go. Congress could change the law prospectively—to cover future events—but (except in limited cases)[47] not retroactively.

Many commentators, as well as the modern Supreme Court, assert that the constitutional guarantee of due process mandates more than merely following pre-established procedures. That was assuredly not the Founders' understanding. It is true that the celebrated 17th-century legal writer Sir Edward Coke once suggested that due process required that those accused of serious crimes be formally accused by grand jury indictment rather than by a prosecutor's "information," but that was because standing law required grand jury indictment. The Founders did not believe that due process compelled a grand jury, for in the Bill of Rights they listed the grand jury guarantee separately. They also listed separately other procedural guarantees the modern Supreme Court claims are part of due process: the right to fair trial, trial by jury, the right to an attorney,

---

[45] Section 9.3.2.

[46] Section 3.12. Similar state legislation was prohibited by the Fourteenth Amendment Due Process Clause, adopted in 1868.

[47] The Due Process Clause did not prevent passage of curative legislation—measures that protected, or at least did not interfere with, people's expectations. An example might be curing a technical defect in certain marriages contracted within the District of Columbia.

and the right to be free of warrantless searches. The Founders itemized these in the Constitution because they considered them valuable protections that were not encompassed in the phrase "due process."

Since the late 19th century, the Supreme Court has claimed that the due process guarantee also empowers it to strike down state and federal laws that the court believes unreasonably infringe on its view of personal liberty. This doctrine passes by the oxymoronic name of "Substantive Due Process."[48] Although a handful of writers have tried to demonstrate that the Founders believed in Substantive Due Process,[49] their arguments are not very convincing. For example, one of their arguments is that a few Founding-era jurists argued that a statute in violation of "higher law" was void. However, the higher law those jurists cited was not due process.[50]

To recapitulate: The Due Process Clause of the Fifth Amendment was one of a series of procedural guarantees in both the unamended Constitution and the Bill of Rights. It was essentially an anti-retroactivity guarantee, ensuring that, when proceeding against citizens in or out of court, the federal government would follow pre-established law rather than make up the rules as it went along.

---

[48] During the late 19th and early 20th centuries, the Court wielded Substantive Due Process to void laws infringing on "conservative" values, such as economic and parental rights. After (purportedly) abandoning the doctrine in the mid-20th century, the Court returned to it to invalidate laws infringing on "progressive" values. At time of publication, it was unclear whether *Dobbs v. Jackson Women's Health*, 597 U.S. 215 (2022), which reversed the ruling that abortion was protected by Substantive Due Process, signaled a wider retreat from the doctrine.

[49] See the bibliography to this chapter.

[50] *Bowman v. Middleton*, 1 Bay 252 (S.C. Com. Pl. 1792) and *Butler v. Craig*, 2 H. & M.H. 214 (Md. 1787), sometimes cited as forerunners of Substantive Due Process, actually relied on Magna Carta rather than due process. *Ham v. McClaws*, 1 S.C.L. (1 Bay) 93 (S.Ct. Ct. Com. Pl. 1789) relied on equitable construction (see Section 2.7). A few 18th-century judges argued hypothetically that a statute might be invalid if it violated natural law—but not due process. See *Calder v. Bull*, 3 U.S. (3 Dall.) 386 (1798) (dictum by Justice Chase).

Some writers contend the Due Process Clause of the Fourteenth Amendment, ratified in 1868, has a different meaning than that in the Fifth Amendment. That issue is outside the scope of this book, although I have commented on it in the bibliography for this chapter.

9.4 Protecting "Property" in Slaves

Illustrating the fact that the Constitution was principally a document of positive law rather than one of natural law is how the Framers treated the issue of slavery.

When the federal convention met, the English-speaking peoples were already well into their century-long process of becoming the first major ethnic group to abolish slavery. In 1772, a judicial decision prohibited slavery within England.[51] When the federal convention met, all the states except Georgia and the Carolinas had abolished the African slave trade outright, and North Carolina had imposed steep imposts on it. Several northern states were in the process of ending slavery itself. Without foreknowledge of the invention of the cotton gin, many Framers believed that slavery was on the path to extinction.[52] Almost all of them agreed that slavery was contrary to natural law and harmful to both slaves and their masters.

But they also realized that some states were committed to slavery and that two, South Carolina and Georgia, were committed to importing more slaves. Thus, the Framers felt compelled to make unsavory bargains, without which the Union might have fragmented into multiple republics.

The Taxation and Commerce Powers enabled Congress to discourage or ban the slave trade.[53] As part of a compromise with South Carolina and Georgia, the Framers qualified congressional power with a clause prohibiting Congress before 1808 from either banning the trade or imposing a "Tax or Duty" in excess of ten dollars per person imported.[54] This provision was made unamendable.[55]

Also, the Fugitive Slave Clause provided that any slave escaping from

---

[51] Section 9.10.

[52] For example, Roger Sherman of Connecticut stated that "the abolition of slavery seemed to be going on in the U.S. & that the good sense of the several States would probably by degrees compleat [sic] it." 2 Farrand, p. 369. Oliver Ellsworth, also of Connecticut, opined that "Slavery in time will not be a speck in our Country." *Id.* 371.

[53] See Section 6.3.6.

[54] Article I, Section 9, Clause 1.

[55] Article V.

one state to another had to be returned to his master.⁵⁶ The Apportionment Clause reduced both congressional representation and direct taxes for states with slaves.⁵⁷

9.5 The First Amendment: Preliminary Comments

The First Amendment explicitly protects six rights from congressional interference:

- Freedom from patronizing an established religion;
- free exercise of religion;
- freedom of speech;
- freedom of the press;
- peaceful assembly; and
- the right to petition for redress of grievances.

Over the past century, the First Amendment has become one of the most heavily litigated portions of the Constitution. However, much modern First Amendment law is unconnected to its original constitutional meaning.

The text of the First Amendment clearly limits its effect to actions by "Congress." Yet the Supreme Court applies it to all branches of the federal government and to the states. Additionally, most of what the Supreme Court calls First Amendment law is a judge-made scheme of balancing tests and policy preferences. This scheme misdefines some rights and creates distinctions that have no basis in the Constitution's text or its history.

One key to understanding how the Founders conceived the First Amendment is to understand that the listed rights—with the incidental right of free association—often were exercised together. The following scenario depicts events common throughout the Founding era:

In September, 1765 during his regular Sunday church service, a

---

⁵⁶ Article IV, Section 2, Clause 3.

⁵⁷ Article I, Section 2, Clause 3.

dissenting minister[58] gives a sermon criticizing Parliament's Stamp Act. After the service, members of the congregation meet with the minister. All agree to jointly subscribe to a letter of protest to Parliament and to contribute to a fund to print the sermon so it can be sold as a pamphlet.

Consider the scenario again, with the relevant rights flagged:

In September, 1765 during his regular Sunday church service [*free exercise of religion, assembly*] a dissenting minister [*no establishment of religion*] gives a sermon criticizing Parliament's Stamp Act [*free exercise of religion/free speech*]. After the service, members of the congregation meet with the minister [*assembly, free speech*]. All agree to jointly subscribe [*association*] to a letter of protest to Parliament [*petition, press*] and contribute to a fund to print the sermon so it can be sold as a pamphlet [*association, press, perhaps some religious exercise*].

Note how these rights, and the financial contributions necessary to effectuate them, are intertwined. Here is another common scenario:

In 1781, three brothers meet together (*assembly*) and agree (*speech*) to create a partnership (*association*) to acquire a newspaper (*press*). One will provide financing, one will contribute anonymous columns to the newspaper, and the third will edit it and run the print shop (*press*). As was common in the day, the newspaper will include snippets of spiritual guidance (*free exercise of religion*).

The following discussion necessarily divides the First Amendment into its separate clauses. But the reader should remember that in real life, they usually were exercised in combinations of two or more. It follows that the content of each right influenced the content of the others.

9.6 The First Amendment Religion Clauses

The First Amendment Religion Clauses provided that "Congress

---

[58] *I.e.*, a Protestant minister not affiliated with the Church of England.

shall make no law respecting an establishment of religion, or prohibiting the free exercise thereof." The portion of this language before the comma is called the Establishment Clause, and the latter part is called the Free Exercise Clause.

Like the rest of the First Amendment—but unlike the remainder of the Bill of Rights—the Religion Clauses protected only against actions by Congress. They did not apply to the other branches of government. One likely reason was to leave the executive branch free to promote Christianity among the Indians. Another reason may have been to leave the President and Senate free to address religious matters by treaty.[59] Indeed, Anti-Federalists warned that the federal government might enter into a treaty to establish a particular religion.

The Establishment Clause barred Congress from erecting a national church or national religion, establishing a religious creed, or funding or otherwise favoring one faith or set of faiths. It also prevented Congress from interfering with established churches in states where they existed. The Establishment Clause did not erect a "wall of separation" between religion and state, if that phrase means preventing the federal government from aiding religion on a non-preferential basis.

The Free Exercise Clause guarded the freedom of theists to worship God or gods as they wished. It did not protect atheists or other non-believers,[60] although non-believers enjoyed overlapping protection under the First Amendment's Free Speech, Free Press, and Assembly and Petition Clauses.[61]

9.7 The First Amendment Speech and Press Clauses

The First Amendment provided that "Congress shall make no law . . . abridging the freedom of speech, or of the press . . ." The verb "abridge" meant "diminish" or "lessen." A law that reduced freedom of speech or of the press to any degree violated the First Amendment.

This absolute protection extended to "the freedom of speech" and

---

[59] Section 7.9.2. Still another reason for exempting the President may have been the needs of military discipline.

[60] See bibliography.

[61] However, outright denial of God was not protected by the Free Speech or Press Clauses. See Section 9.7.2.

"the freedom ... of the press" as those terms were understood at the time. It did not extend to expression outside the understood scope of "the freedom of speech" and "the freedom of the press."

9.7.1 Freedom of Speech

In this context, "speech" meant direct in person communication, as opposed to communication through a medium. The phrase "freedom of speech" might refer either to debate in the legislature or to the speech rights of ordinary citizens. The Constitution protected lawmakers through the Speech and Debate Clause.[62] The First Amendment was designed primarily for other citizens.

There were few reported freedom of speech court cases in early America, leading some writers to believe the original scope of the free speech right is unknowable. But that is incorrect, because many other kinds of evidence are available.

The Founders considered freedom of speech to be a fundamental natural right. They valued it both as an expression of one's nature and because, they believed, when responsibly used, it elevated and improved government and society.[63] Thus, free speech included freedom from prior restraint: One did not have to obtain any official permission to speak.

The British essayist and playwright Joseph Addison summarized the English law of free speech by saying that speech was protected if it was truthful, in good taste, and with due submission (respect) and innocent of malice. The right did not include speech that was treasonous, blasphemous,[64] seditious (stirring up violence), slanderous, or within certain categories of lewdness.[65] The Articles of War imposed severe punishments on soldiers and associated personnel who spread false alarms; engaged in traitorous, profane, or disrespectful speech; or incited

---

[62] Article I, Section 6, Clause 1. On the Speech and Debate Clause, see Section 4.6.

[63] George Buchanan, the influential 16th-century predecessor of John Locke, had written: "[F]reedom of speaking and comparing thoughts removes obscurities, explains difficult points, corroborates points on which there is doubt, and can close the mouth of the perverse and teach the weak." George Buchanan, De Jure Regni Apud Scotos (1579) (my translation of the Latin text).

[64] See Section 9.7.2.

[65] See Section 9.7.2.

sedition or mutiny.[66]

On the other hand, there was heightened protection for expression, even when slanderous, by witnesses in court proceedings. Lawyers were privileged from anything they might say in court, other than irrelevancies and their own deliberate lies.

The law of slander or "unwritten scandal" permitted a person who thought he had been defamed to seek an award of money damages against the speaker. If the state was the party aggrieved, it also could proceed by criminal action. There was a separate branch of English law that remedied slander against the nobility—the law of *scandalum magnatum* (defamation of magnates)—but the Constitution's proscription on titles of nobility rendered it inapplicable in America.

Well-established rules prevented the law of slander from unduly restricting freedom of speech. In a suit for slander, a plaintiff had to show that the defendant had said what he did with "improper motive"—that is, with deliberate intent to harm the plaintiff. If this was not shown, the action was dismissed. Truth was a defense. Furthermore, the complained-of comments had to be "scandalous." This meant the defendant had to have alleged facts about the plaintiff, usually about his private life, that exposed the plaintiff to public contempt.

If the state brought a criminal prosecution for slander, the state could not charge a felony. The defendant was entitled to a trial by jury, and the jury could release the defendant even if clearly guilty. The jury was not permitted to convict an innocent defendant.

The First Amendment permitted Congress to pass laws against treasonous, seditious, defamatory, or blasphemous speech within the geographical areas subject to its jurisdiction, such as federal territories and enclaves. The First Amendment did not restrict the actions of the states.

9.7.2 Freedom of the Press

The First Amendment barred Congress from "abridging" freedom of the press. This meant that Congress could not, within the understood

---

[66] The Continental Congress's principal Articles of War are in 5 J. Cont. Cong. 788–807 (Sep. 20, 1776), amended in 7 *id.* 264–66 (Apr. 14, 1777) and again in 9 *id.* 476–77 (Jun. 18, 1777).

scope of press freedom, reduce it in any way.[67]

While "speech" meant direct person-to-person talk, "the press" meant communication through a medium. The law treated communication through a medium somewhat differently from in-person communication because the medium gave communication greater potential durability and power and allowed the author to remain anonymous.

Most people in the founding generation thought of freedom of the press (which they usually called "liberty of the press") as a fundamental natural right, although some classified it as a privilege. Whether they labeled it a right or a privilege, both the British and Americans considered freedom of the press to be of inestimable importance. In his influential book on the English Constitution, Jean Louis DeLolme identified freedom of the press as a vital part of the people's reserved censorial power—the power retained by the people to correct the government when it veered from its proper path.[68] Through a free press, writers could motivate electors and shame public officials into doing the right thing. When necessary, authors could help the people coordinate armed resistance to domestic tyranny. One 18th-century essayist wrote that through freedom of the press,

> An unknown author may act the splendid part in which the Grecian orators, and even the Roman emperors, were ambitious to shine; and an anonymous pamphlet may open the eyes of the nation.[69]

A moderate Anti-Federalist writing under the penname of the Federal Farmer called a free press "the channel of communication as to mercantile and public affairs." The Continental Congress stated in letter written by John Dickinson that freedom of the press promoted "truth,

---

[67] This seems to preclude congressional limits on fundraising for publishing political views. Such "campaign finance" restrictions are justified (incorrectly; see Section 6.8.1) under the Times, Places, and Manner Clause (Article I, Section 4, Clause 1). But even if that Clause authorized them initially, it could not do so after ratification of the First Amendment.

[68] The censorial power is discussed in Section 1.3.1.

[69] Anonymous, *Thoughts on the Liberty of the Press*, The Town and Country Magazine 74 (Feb. 1789).

science, morality, and arts in general," diffused "liberal sentiments on the administration of Government," helped communicate "thoughts between subjects," and promoted "union among them." Taking into account several changes in the meaning of language, we can translate Dickinson's statement as meaning that freedom of the press promoted truth, knowledge, morality, the fine arts and technology; that it spread toleration in political affairs; and that it helped communicate thoughts among citizens and promoted union among them.

Comments like these tell us that freedom of the press was to be guaranteed not only for political discourse, but also for discussion of business, artistic, technological, educational, and scientific topics.

As suggested above, freedom of the press was not solely for professional publishers; it protected anyone who communicated responsibly through a medium. It protected the authors, financiers, and printers of newspaper articles, broadsides (single large sheets), pamphlets, and books. From the Founders' point of view, the modern political committee that distributes a flyer or funds a broadcast advertisement is taking advantage of freedom of the press. So is the company advertising its product through the media.

Modern laws often compel people sponsoring political advertising to publicly disclose their names. But to the founding generation, author privacy was a central part of freedom of the press. Most political essays and pamphlets were published either without attribution or, like the essays in *The Federalist*, were signed with a pseudonym. Author privacy was zealously defended. Newspaper editors did not dare reveal the name of a contributor to government officials or to anyone else without that contributor's prior consent.

The most important reason for protecting author privacy was to encourage people, including powerless people, to contribute to the flow of ideas without fear of retaliation.

Of course, when used irresponsibly, the press could cause great damage. A spoken comment was heard only by those in the immediate vicinity and, once spoken, dissipated into air. But the printed page could spread rumors, lies, and defamatory comments throughout the country with great speed and permanence. The risks had induced even John Milton (1608-1674),[70] a strong advocate of freedom of the press, to argue

---

[70] The poet of *Paradise Lost*, and a leading Puritan political figure.

that books should include the names of the author and printer, or at least the printer—and that the publication of unacknowledged "libelous or mischievous" books should be punishable by death![71]

Except in cases of treason, Anglo-American governments refused to go as far as Milton. But for many years, anyone seeking to publish a book in England had to submit it first to the censor, who would decide whether to license it. In 1694, Parliament allowed the licensing statute to expire, and prior restraints on publications ended.

Even after the end of licensing, the scope of press freedom still was limited to prevent abuse. The most serious abuse was high treason, a capital crime. Another was sedition—that is, stirring up violence. In England and the states, the law also punished "lewdness:" pornography and associated activities.

It is unclear how much authority the First Amendment left Congress to address lewdness in the capital district and the federal territories. In England, the common law courts and ecclesiastical courts had divided jurisdiction over the subject, but in America there was no religious establishment, and therefore no ecclesiastical jurisdiction. The jurisdiction remaining probably was broad enough to allow Congress to punish (1) displays destructive of public morality, such as public nudity and obscene theater productions, (2) pornography targeted at the young, and (3) under the law of libel, obscene writings directed against a particular victim. Moreover, a judge could require any pornographer to post bail against potential later violations of public morality.

Also outside the sphere of press freedom was written defamation, called *libel* or *written scandal.* The law of libel was designed to protect reputation and prevent duels and other violence that might arise in absence of a legal remedy. Libel was defined as

> a malicious Defamation, expressed either in Printing or Writing or by Signs, Pictures, &c.[72] tending either to blacken the Memory of one who is dead, or the Reputation of one who is alive, and thereby exposing him to public Hatred, Contempt and

---

[71] In *New York Times v. Sullivan,* 376 U.S. 254, 279 n.19 (1964), the court cited Milton in support of a holding that largely stripped from public officials the protection of defamation law. Milton would have been outraged.

[72] "&c." means "etc."

Ridicule, and may be as well against a private Man as against a Magistrate.[73]

Private parties vindicated their good name by civil lawsuits. When an author defamed or incited a rebellion against a magistrate, however, the case was one of *seditious libel*, and a criminal prosecution might ensue.[74] Moreover, before adoption of the Fifth Amendment Due Process Clause, a legislative chamber could take action against a private citizen for "breach of privilege" if the citizen had defamed a lawmaker for actions taken during his legislative duties.[75]

Under the law of libel, an author also could be punished for blasphemy, which was seen as defaming the reputation of God or religion. Established law punished "all Blasphemies against God, as denying his Being or Providence," including "prophane Scoffing at the Holy Scriptures, or exposing any Part thereof to Contempt or Ridicule."[76] It also punished "contumelious Reproaches of Jesus Christ,"[77] although whether the last survived adoption of the First Amendment's Religion Clauses is open to doubt. During the ratification era, Oliver Ellsworth, a federal convention delegate, leading ratification advocate, and later third chief justice of the Supreme Court, strongly endorsed enforcement of anti-blasphemy law. [78]

---

[73] Anonymous, Digest Concerning the Law of Libels 1 (1760).

[74] In England, under some circumstances one could be convicted of seditious libel even for printing the truth. This was to encourage those with knowledge of wrongful conduct to inform the public prosecutor rather than to disseminate a charge that, if the writer was wrong, might prove false and unfairly damaging.

[75] *E.g.*, the case of Gunning Bedford, Sr. and the Continental Congress, referenced in Section 4.6, footnote 32.

[76] 3 Matthew Bacon ("A Gentleman of the Middle Temple"), A New Abridgment of the Law 38 (5 vols.) (1736–66).

[77] *Id.*

[78] Ellsworth wrote:

> But while I assert the right of religious liberty; I would not deny that the civil power has a right, in some cases, to interfere in matters of religion. It has a right to prohibit and punish gross immoralities and impieties; because the open practice of these is of evil example and public detriment. For this reason,

There is a common view that during the Founding era the only protection granted to freedom of the press was freedom from licensing—that is, from "prior restraint." In fact, however, freedom of the press also included extensive protections for authors of material already published.[79] Thus, in America, truth was an absolute defense to any action for libel. In America, as in England, trial was by jury, and the jury had the discretion to release a guilty printer or writer. As historian Catherine Macaulay Graham remarked, juries were not required to "take the law from the mouth of the judge." But the jury could not exercise the opposite prerogative and convict an innocent defendant.

In prosecutions for seditious libel, the defendant could not be charged with a felony—only a misdemeanor. The alleged libel had to have been scandalous and malicious. The requirement of malice was not met if the item was published as an honest jest. Such restrictions rendered on prosecutions for seditious libel extremely rare.[80]

9.7.3 Speech and Press Summary

After adoption of the First Amendment, Congress could not impose prior restraints of any kind on speech or the press—as the scope of those rights was then defined. Within the District of Columbia and the Territories, Congress could punish expression outside the recognized scope of those rights so long as Congress retained the legal protections considered inherent in those rights, such as trial by jury and the defenses of truth and absence of malice.

The Sedition Act of 1798, passed during the administration of John Adams, often is cited as the quintessential violation of the Free Speech and Free Press Clauses. In fact, however, the Sedition Act preserved the traditional protections for allegedly seditious speech, and thus did not

---

I heartily approve of our laws against drunkenness, profane swearing, blasphemy, and professed atheism.

14 Documentary History, p. 450.

[79] DeLolme made the same point in abbreviated form. DeLolme, pp. 202–04.

[80] But they did occur. In 1786, a Massachusetts judge named William Whiting wrote an article that helped incite Shays' Rebellion. He was indicted, prosecuted, fined and sentenced to prison (although the prison term was suspended). This apparently was deemed consistent with the state constitution's free press clause.

violate the First Amendment as then understood. But the law did violate the Ninth and Tenth Amendments by purporting to regulate speech and the press outside federal jurisdiction and within the territorial boundaries of the states.[81]

9.8 The First Amendment Assembly and Petition Clauses

The First Amendment states in part: "Congress shall make no law . . . prohibiting . . . the right of the people peaceably to assemble, and to petition the Government for a redress of grievances."

Like the rest of the First Amendment, this language was directed at Congress rather than other branches of the federal government. Congress was prohibited from "abridging" freedom of speech and the press. But it was barred only from "prohibiting" peaceful assembly or petitioning. This verb change suggests that Congress enjoyed more latitude in regulating petitions and peaceful assemblies than in regulating speech or the press.

Presumably, Congress could impose some restrictions on petitions and assemblies if otherwise authorized under its enumerated powers. For example, Congress might specify that petitions in the capital district could be presented only on weekdays, or that assemblies must form in parks and town squares rather than in the middle of public streets.

Because "speech" was in-person communication, the right to assemble was considered inherent in the right to free speech. Some Founders questioned whether it was necessary to enumerate it separately.

The rule that free speech not be "abridged" imposed inherent limits on how far Congress could go in regulating assembly. A law specifying that assemblies in the capital district could be held only in a single location one day each month doubtless would abridge the right to free speech. It would be for the courts to determine the boundaries between permissible and impermissible regulation.

The right to assemble was commonly described as the right to consult together for the common good—that is, for the benefit of those

---

[81] It is an open question whether the law of the founding era or modern Supreme Court free speech jurisprudence is more protective of freedom of speech. The Founders' law offered less protection for irreligious, defamatory, and sexually laden expression, but more for commercial advertising and for truthful, good-faith discussion of public issues.

consulting. Contemporaneous dictionaries tell us that people consulted together if they jointly undertook inquiries and investigations, deliberated among themselves, or planned a course of action. The right of political association was, therefore, inherent in the founding generation's concept of peaceful assembly. Congress could regulate political associations within federal territories and enclaves so long as it did not prohibit associations or regulate them so heavily that free speech was abridged.

To what extent could Congress regulate an assembly's execution of its planned course of action? The right of assembly did not include assembling to commit illegal acts. Assembly for such purposes was punishable even if illegal acts had not actually been committed. If the contemplated course of action was a petition or other communication, it was protected by the First Amendment.

However, the right of assembly did not include the power to bind government officials by instructions. Officials could regard, or not regard, petitions as they saw fit.

The right to petition also was connected closely to other First Amendment freedoms. DeLolme considered the right to petition, like freedom of the press, to be part of the people's reserved censorial power.[82]

The law immunized petitions to the legislature from suits for libel. In this respect, petitioners enjoyed protection akin to that granted legislators under the Speech and Debate Clause.[83] In England, a law restricted petitions to no more than twenty signers unless the sponsors previously had obtained judicial authorization to obtain more names. Another English law limited the number of people who could physically present a single petition to a government official or body at one time. St. George Tucker, an early constitutional commentator closely connected with key Founders, says that these rules did not apply in America, although his statement, published in 1803, is too late to constitute authoritative evidence on the views of the Ratifiers.[84]

A congressional ban on petitions with no more than twenty signers probably would have violated the First Amendment's freedom of the

---

[82] DeLolme, p. 201.

[83] Section 4.3.

[84] Section 2.8.

press guarantee. But limiting the number of people who could physically present a petition might have been valid as a reasonable regulation rather than a forbidden "prohibition", since it did not abridge speech and was designed to prevent tumults and other violence.

9.9 The Second and Third Amendments: Health, Hearth, and Home

The Second Amendment stated:

A well regulated Militia, being necessary to the security of a free State, the right of the people to keep and bear Arms, shall not be infringed.

The activity prohibited was to "infringe." As defined in 18th-century dictionaries, the word comprehended violation of a contract or destruction or even mere hindering.[85] Thus, reducing in any way the right to keep and bear arms—as that right was then understood—breached the Second Amendment. In this way, the approach of the Second Amendment paralleled that of the First Amendment's Speech and Press Clauses.[86]

Like the First Amendment, the Second Amendment protected certain natural rights. These included the right to defend oneself and one's home against the lawless and against invaders, and the right of armed resistance to domestic tyrants.[87] Additionally, widespread owner-

---

[85] *E.g.*, the 1782 edition of Samuel Johnson's dictionary: "1. To violate; to break laws or contracts. 2. To destroy; to hinder." The definition in the first American edition of Perry's dictionary (1788) was "to violate, destroy, hinder." The meaning of "infringe" that refers to violating a law or contract, suggests that the word could include a merely partial invasion since total breach is not necessary to violate a contract.

[86] See Section 9.5.

[87] On the right of citizens to armed resistance, see DeLolme, pp. 215–16; 1 William Blackstone, Commentaries *140 (referring to "the right of having and using arms for self-preservation and defence"). Justice Stephen Breyer, dissenting in *McDonald v. Chicago*, 561 U.S. 742, 915–16 (2010), argued that Blackstone's remark was intended only against the Crown, not against Parliament. This overlooks the fact that, unlike the English Bill or Rights, the U.S. Bill of Rights

ship of, and competence with, arms would deter the government from threatening liberty. In the words of Jean Louis DeLolme:

> The Power of the People is not when they strike, but when they keep in awe. It is when they can overthrow every thing [sic], that they never need to move; and Manlius [a Roman consul] included all in four words, when he said to the People of Rome, *Ostendite bellum, pacem habebis* ["Look toward war, and you shall have peace"].[88]

The Second Amendment served purposes besides buttressing the natural right of self-defense and the reserved power of armed resistance. By guaranteeing continuation of state militias, it strengthened state power in the state-federal balance. By protecting the militia, the Amendment promoted citizen involvement in government military affairs, just as the jury system promoted citizen involvement in judicial affairs. Likewise, by protecting the militia, the Second Amendment reduced the need for federal standing armies. The Founders believed that standing armies would encourage federal officials to undertake needless military adventures abroad. They also believed although in time of war an army was vital to the preservation of liberty, in time of peace it could prove destructive to liberty.

The purpose of the Second Amendment suggests that the word "arms" should be interpreted rather broadly to include a range of military and self-defense weapons—a conclusion strengthened by a contemporaneous rule of construction directed to the interpretation of "arms."[89]

The Third Amendment was targeted at one particular standing-army abuse with which Americans were painfully familiar—the billeting of troops with homeowners and families. The Third Amendment reflected

---

applied to the legislature as well as the executive. See also Section 9.3.4 (making the same point about the Fifth Amendment Due Process Clause).

[88] DeLolme, p. 219. Thus, a modern writer certainly erred when she wrote that the Second Amendment, "merely prevents the federal government from disarming the members of the National Guard." Angela Rodday Holden, The Meaning of the Constitution 63 (1987).

[89] *Armorum appellatione non solum scuta et gladii et galeae, sed et fustes et lapides continentur.* ("By the name 'arms' are included not only shields and swords and helmets, but also cudgels and stones.").

several traditional legal rules about the home,[90] and, more generally the legal maxim, *Qui sentit commodum, sentire debet et onus*, which was discussed above in conjunction with the Takings Clause of the Fifth Amendment.[91]

The Third Amendment encouraged the government to procure barracks at the expense of all taxpayers, rather than to foist the cost of maintaining troops on only a portion of the population.

9.10 Protections for the Accused—Treason, Habeas Corpus, and the Fourth, Fifth, Sixth and Eighth Amendments

Some provisions in the Constitution protected those accused or convicted of crimes by entrenching privileges granted by English common law. The value of these guarantees relied on the competence, honesty, and discretion of the judiciary.

9.10.1 The Treason Clauses

English law recognized several categories of treason, including waging war against the king, conspiring to assassinate him or his queen, and counterfeiting. The Framers limited treason to one category: "levying War against [the United States], or in adhering to their Enemies, giving them Aid and Comfort."[92] The meaning of "Comfort" in this context was "support" or assistance." The Framers consciously modeled this language on a section of the Treason Act of 1351, which codified and limited the common law of treason.[93]

Thus, in America, one could not be convicted of treason unless he was aiding an insurrection or assisting an armed force warring upon the United States. The war could be declared or undeclared. It could be an invasion by pirates or terrorists from nations with which the United States was formally at peace.

The Framers added a rule of evidence: "No Person shall be convicted of Treason unless on the Testimony of two Witnesses to the same overt

---

[90] *Domus sua est unicuique tutissimum refugium* ("One's home is the safest refuge for each person") and "Every man's house is his castle."

[91] Section 9.3.3.

[92] Article III, Section 3, Clause 1.

[93] 25 Edw. iii, c.2.

Act, or on Confession in open Court."⁹⁴ The requirement of confession "in open court" was designed to minimize the chances of confession under torture or other duress.

In order for a person to be convicted of treason, that person had to be one who "owed allegiance" to the United States. A person owed allegiance to the United States if he was "abiding in" any state "and deriving protection from the laws of same." This included not only American citizens, but "all persons passing through, visiting, or mak[ing] a temporary stay" in an American state—at least if their presence was legitimate.⁹⁵ Such persons sometimes were called "members" of states.⁹⁶ The category was equivalent to the term "subject" in British law.⁹⁷

Thus, individuals such as foreign combatants, invaders, and spies, while they might be prosecuted for war crimes, could not be convicted of treason to the United States.

Congress's enumerated power to "declare the Punishment of Treason" was subject to the qualification that, "no Attainder of Treason shall work Corruption of Blood, or Forfeiture except during the Life of the Person attainted."⁹⁸ Laws against treason could require that a traitor forfeit his land and personal property, but could not disinherit the traitors' family. This limitation on congressional power paralleled similar protection previously adopted in England.⁹⁹

9.10.2 The Privilege of the Writ of Habeas Corpus

A writ is an order from a magistrate, usually a judge, to a person ordering that person to do, or refrain from doing, something. In Anglo-

---

⁹⁴ Article III, Section 3, Clause 1.

⁹⁵ 5 J. Cont. Cong. 475 (Jun. 24, 1776); cf. id. at 693 (Aug. 21, 1776) (persons present but not in allegiance).

⁹⁶ *E.g.,* Art. Confed. art. IX ("managing all affairs with the Indians, not members of any of the States"); Noah Webster, *A Collection of Essays and Fugitiv* [*sic*] *Writings* 152 (1790).

⁹⁷ In accordance with the maxim, *Protectio trahit subjectionem, & subjectio protectionem* ("Protection brings with it subject-status, and subject-status brings protection").

⁹⁸ Article III, Section 3, Clause 2.

⁹⁹ On attainder and corruption of blood and Parliamentary limitations on the latter, see Section 3.11.

American legal practice, writs customarily were written in Latin and were known by their first few words.

The Anglo-American legal system included a procedure by which an individual in custody or a person acting on behalf of an individual in custody could ask a judge to examine whether the prisoner was being lawfully held. If the judge thought the petition alleged facts tending to show that the imprisonment was illegal, the judge would issue to the captor the writ *habeas corpus ad subjiciendum*—that is, "You may have the body for submitting." The writ directed the captor to show up in court with the prisoner at a designated time and justify why he was holding the prisoner. The writ could be directed either to a public jailor or to a captor who was a private party.

Habeas corpus was used to vindicate the natural right of liberty, but the writ itself was a privilege rather than a right because it was a procedure created by government.

Not everyone was entitled to petition for a writ of habeas corpus. Under English law, one had to be a subject of the king. The term "subject" included not only a country's citizens, but also aliens in "allegiance" to the Crown—that is, those who voluntarily and legally entered the country and put themselves under protection of its laws. An alien captured fighting or spying for an enemy was not in allegiance, and therefore was not entitled to petition for habeas corpus.[100]

One of the most celebrated habeas corpus cases during the Founding era was *Somersett v. Stewart* (1772). In that case, the Court of King's Bench—led by Chief Justice Lord Mansfield[101]—freed James Somersett, an African slave brought by his master from Virginia (which recognized slavery) to England (which did not). Somersett was an African, but he had made himself a British subject for habeas purposes. This was because during a brief escape from captivity, he had sought to remain in England under the protection of English laws.

---

[100] *Boumediene v. Bush,* 553 U.S. 723 (2008) held that captured alien combatants could obtain writs of habeas corpus. The court examined Founding-era cases on the subject, but misconstrued them—in part because in one of those cases the court granted the prisoner his freedom, but on grounds other than habeas corpus. However, the Supreme Court was correct in concluding that a subject's right to habeas corpus was not limited to domestic territories, but "followed King's ministers."

[101] See Section 1.4.

The court freed Somersett on the grounds that slavery was not part of the law of England, and that any slave in England who sought the protection of English laws was free.

The federal government's power to wage war carried with it the incidental power to suspend the writ of habeas corpus. However, the Constitution included a provision, called the Suspension Clause, that limited the suspension power. The Suspension Clause stated that, "The Privilege of the Writ of Habeas Corpus shall not be suspended, unless when in Cases of Rebellion or Invasion the public Safety may require it."[102] Thus, suspension was authorized in cases of defensive, but not offensive, war.

In the first instance, it was for Congress to decide whether a disturbance counted as a rebellion or invasion and whether public safety was compromised sufficiently to justify suspension. But the Suspension Clause did not say "whenever Congress *shall think* the public Safety may require it."[103] It said "whenever the public Safety may require it." Thus, the courts could review a congressional decision to determine whether or not that decision was grounded in fact.

As we have seen, in English law any subject could claim habeas corpus. Although some contemporaneous American habeas statutes protected only citizens, the federal constitutional right was defined by English common law, not by state law. It therefore extended to non-citizens in "allegiance" to the United States. A court or legislature could not narrow the common law right without violating the Suspension Clause; nor could a court broaden it, because that would invade powers assigned by the Constitution to the legislature or executive.

The Suspension Clause did not apply to presidential or other executive suspensions of the writ. However, executive suspensions were limited in scope to the present theater of war.[104]

---

[102] Article I, Section 9, Clause 2.

[103] *Compare* Article I, Section 9, Clause 1 ("as any of the States now existing *shall think* proper"); Article II, Section 3 ("[The President] shall ... recommend to their Consideration such Measures *as he shall judge* necessary and expedient"); Article V ("The Congress, whenever two thirds of both Houses *shall deem it* necessary"). (Italics added).

[104] Section 7.8.

9.10.3 Trial by Jury

Juries were an old and treasured institution in Anglo-American law. They served two principal purposes. First, they enlisted ordinary citizens in the business of government, injecting both democratic governance and practical experience into the court system. Second, they helped protect citizens against government abuse—that is, they operated as a buffer between officialdom and the accused, thereby reducing the likelihood of official persecution. Juries played the same sort of role in civil affairs that citizen militias played in military affairs.

The unamended Constitution specified that one accused of a crime (except by impeachment) was entitled to a trial by jury. If the crime was allegedly committed within a state, the trial would have to be within that state. If the crime was not committed within a state, then trial would be "at such Place or Places as the Congress may by Law have directed."[105]

During the ratification debates, Anti-Federalists attacked the Constitution's jury guarantee as insufficient. For example, they observed that some of the states were quite large: A person charged with a crime in Pittsburgh could be summoned to Philadelphia for trial. They observed also that a prosecutor could pack a jury with biased persons, as sometimes had occurred in England. They pointed out that Article III empowered the Supreme Court to review on appeal issues of fact as well as law,[106] so the Court would not have to defer to a jury's factual finding, as Anglo-American courts traditionally had done.

Several parts of the Bill of Rights were designed to respond to these objections. The Sixth Amendment required that any federal criminal trial be held in the same judicial district of a state where the crime was committed, "which district shall have been previously ascertained by law." That amendment further required that each jury be "impartial"—a guarantee the judges would have to enforce. The Seventh Amendment prescribed that "no fact tried by a jury, shall be otherwise re-examined in any Court of the United States, than according to the rules of common law." This ensured that federal appellate courts were bound by juries' factual findings of juries in almost every case.

At the Virginia ratifying convention, when discussing the Consti-

---

[105] Article III, Section 2, Clause 3.

[106] Article III, Section 2, Clause 2.

tution's use of the word "jury," James Madison referred to a standard by which legal documents (including the Constitution) were interpreted: "[W]here a technical word was used, all the incidents belonging to it necessarily attended it."[107] In other words, the jury guarantees carried with them the central features of the common law jury. The specific example Madison offered was a party's established right to challenge potential jurors.[108] Other crucial features of civilian jury trial (besides the right to challenge) were that there be twelve jurors and that their verdict had to be unanimous.[109]

Madison's original draft for a bill of rights stipulated that trial juries consist "of freeholders of the vicinage, with the requisite of unanimity for conviction, of the right of challenge, and other accustomed requisites." However, Congress dropped that language, implying that while the Constitution protected the central or "necessary" features of jury trial, Congress could alter features that were merely customary.

9.10.4 Searches and Seizures

English law required that before a law enforcement officer could search property, the officer first had to swear to a magistrate that he had good reason to believe ("probable cause") that evidence of crime was on the premises. The premises had to be named with specificity, and the magistrate had to be sufficiently convinced to issue a warrant. Similarly, a law enforcement officer desiring to arrest a person not caught in the act of crime needed to identify the person to the magistrate under oath and convince the magistrate to issue a warrant.

When governing the American colonies, British officials sometimes disregarded these procedures. Parliament authorized officers looking for

---

[107] 10 Documentary History, p. 1409 (confirming a similar comment by Edmund Randolph).

[108] At common law, a party could challenge potential jurors for cause or, in capital cases, raise a peremptory challenge (without cause). Since Madison was responding to George Mason's argument that peremptory challenges might not be permitted in federal court, Madison probably was implying that both kinds of challenges were part of the jury system.

[109] Some English statutes governing certain cases provided for juries of six members. Juries of other sizes heard special inquests and military trials. But the common law trial jury always consisted of twelve.

contraband to proceed under "general warrants"—warrants with descriptions of places and contraband so general as to authorize trawling operations. The Fourth Amendment responded to abuses by requiring that searches and seizures be "reasonable" in the opinion of the presiding magistrate. The Fourth Amendment limited warrants to those that were supported by probable cause and that "particularly describ[ed] the place to be searched, and the persons or things to be seized."

9.10.5   Due Process—Cross-Reference

The Fifth Amendment requirement of "due process of law" is treated in Section 9.3.2.

9.10.6   Other Pre-Conviction Safeguards

The Fifth, Sixth, and Eighth Amendments guaranteed other common law protections for criminal defendants. The Fifth Amendment recognized the right of a defendant to be formally accused of any serious federal crime by a grand jury rather than by an information (a formal criminal charge) filed by a prosecutor. The accusation might be initiated by the prosecutor and approved by the grand jury (indictment) or initiated by the grand jury itself (presentment). The advocates of the Constitution represented that the "necessary incidents"[110] of juries at common law would have to be honored in federal court. One of those incidents was that the number of grand jurors, which was usually twenty-four, never be less than twelve. Another was that at least a majority had to vote to indict—but never fewer than twelve, no matter what the size of the grand jury.

The Fifth Amendment imposed a bar against "double jeopardy"—that is, it protected persons from being prosecuted to the end of trial for the same crime twice.[111] It also prevented the authorities from coercing criminal defendants into testifying against themselves: the privilege against self-incrimination. Before that privilege was fully established in England, defendants sometimes were tortured or otherwise pressured

---

[110] An incident is something customarily or necessarily connected to a larger item. See the discussion of incidental powers in Section 5.5.

[111] In accordance with the legal dictum, *Nemo debet bis puniri pro uno delicto* ("No one should be punished twice for one wrong").

into confessing alleged crimes.[112]

Besides expanding trial by jury, the Sixth Amendment required that criminal trials be speedy and public. This was to guard against procedures that had been used by some European courts—particularly ecclesiastical courts—of holding prisoners for a long time and then trying them secretly.[113]

The Sixth Amendment entitled a criminal defendant to hear the witnesses against him in open court, and it enabled him to compel testimony from witnesses who he believed could help his case.

The Sixth Amendment also entitled the defendant to be represented by an attorney, thereby repudiating the one-time English rule that defendants in capital cases had to speak for themselves. Nothing in the Sixth Amendment required the government to pay for the defendant's attorney.[114]

Discussion of the extent to which the Fifth and Sixth Amendments—and, indeed, the remainder of the Bill of Rights—applied to military personnel and captured enemy combatants appears below.[115]

The Eighth Amendment inserted into the Constitution the provision from the English Bill of Rights that bail for an accused person could not be "excessive." This meant that bail should not be set at an amount greater than necessary to secure the appearance of the accused in court. This provision, like several others, relied on the wisdom and competence of the judiciary for interpretation.

---

[112] Hence the development of the maxims, *Nemo tenetur armare adversarium contra se* ("No one is bound to arm his adversary against himself") and *Nemo tenetur seipsum accusare* ("No one is bound to accuse himself").

[113] In England, secret trials had developed a particularly bad reputation during the 16th century, when conducted by the Court of Star Chamber. By the Founding era, the practice of secret trials had ceased. DeLolme observed in his book on the English constitution: "For the farther prevention of abuses, it is the invariable usage, that the trial be public." DeLolme, p. 131.

[114] The Supreme Court invented this refinement in *Gideon v. Wainwright*, 372 U.S. 335 (1963), during the court's most activist period. However desirable this rule may be, it was not part of the Sixth Amendment as the ratifiers understood it.

[115] Sections 9.12.1 and 9.12.2.

9.10.7 Post-Conviction Proceedings

In addition to limiting the level of bail, the Eighth Amendment specified that "excessive fines" should not be "imposed, nor cruel and unusual punishments inflicted." This language was copied from the English Bill of Rights of 1689. While the English Bill of Rights was binding on the executive and judicial branches of government rather than on Parliament, Eighth Amendment limited all branches of the federal government.

The "excessive fines" and "cruel and unusual punishments" provisions did not apply to pre-conviction proceedings, so unlike the Fifth Amendment privilege against self-incrimination, they were not designed to prevent torture before trial. They were designed to assure that punishment after trial was proportionate to the severity of the offense. (Proportionality of punishment was a topic in which educated members of the founding generation were much interested.)

The phrase "cruel and unusual" seems to have had a single meaning. A cruel and unusual punishment was one that involved torture—such as the rack, or drawing and quartering—or was grossly disproportionate to the offense. Among the punishments not considered cruel and unusual were whipping (if limited so as not to cause permanent injury), time in the pillory or stocks, branding the convict with a small mark to record the conviction, and—for serious crimes—a quick death, as by hanging.[116]

An excessive fine was monetary punishment that was either out of proportion to the seriousness of the offense or so high that the defendant would have to sell the implements of his trade in order to pay it. This provision may have been directed at civil as well as criminal fines.

9.11 The Seventh Amendment: Protecting the Common Law Jury

The Seventh Amendment was drafted to respond to two specific Anti-Federalist criticisms, both embodied in resolutions adopted by some of the state ratifying conventions. One criticism was that, although the Constitution protected jury trial for federal criminal cases, it did not contain a like guarantee for federal civil cases. The other criticism was that the clause giving the Supreme Court "appellate Jurisdiction, both as

---

[116] The Second Continental Congress prescribed both whipping and death as punishments for certain crimes committed in the military. 3 J. Cont. Cong. 331–33, 378 & 381–82 (1775).

to Law and Fact"[117] could render jury trial largely worthless in both criminal and civil cases, because the Court could overturn a jury's factual findings. In traditional English common law, appeals courts could not overturn a jury finding that had evidence to support it.

The lack of protection for civil juries and the discretion given the Supreme Court over jury verdicts led some Anti-Federalists to argue that adoption of the Constitution might encourage the central government to abandon common law rules in favor of a Roman law system, such as prevailed on the continent of Europe. European countries used panels of judges instead of civil juries, and appellate judges had wide discretion to overturn the factual findings of the trial judges.

The Seventh Amendment thus protected trial by jury in civil cases "where the value in controversy shall exceed twenty dollars." It rescinded the power of the Supreme Court to freely set aside jury findings, restoring the traditional common law rule instead.

9.12 Application of the Bill of Rights to Military Personnel

9.12.1 American Military Personnel

The Constitution gave Congress the power to "make Rules for the Government and Regulation of the land and naval Forces"[118] and for "governing such Part of [the Militia] as may be employed in the Service of the United States."[119] It granted the President authority to act as "Commander in Chief of the Army and Navy of the United States, and of the Militia of the several States, when called into the actual Service of the United States."[120] We shall now examine the extent to which the first eight amendments of Bill of Rights protected military personnel against those congressional and presidential powers.

The literal text applies most of the Bill of Rights to military personnel, for there was no general exception for soldiers. The Fifth Amendment did contain a single specific exception for military personnel: It

---

[117] Article III, Section 2, Clause 2.

[118] Article I, Section 8, Clause 14.

[119] Article I, Section 8, Clause 16.

[120] Article II, Section 2, Clause 1.

guaranteed grand jury indictment for those accused of serious crimes "except in cases arising in the land or naval forces, or in the Militia, when in actual service in time of War or public danger." The exception ended with a semi-colon and was followed by unconditional protection of other rights. This single exception gives force to the conclusion that the rest of the Bill applied to military personnel, for under prevailing rules of construction, an exception was read narrowly and strengthened the general rule outside the exception.[121] In other words, the specific exception for the military in one part of the Bill of Rights suggested that the military was not excepted from other parts.

There are some other reasons for believing that the military enjoyed the protection of most of the Bill of Rights. They are as follows:

- The First Amendment, unlike other amendments, protected against congressional action, but not against presidential action. One likely reason is that the President needed the prerogative of curtailing rights of speech and assembly for military personnel.[122]
- There would have been no reason for denying a soldier serving away from home the protection the Bill of Rights offered against billeting troops on this family, seizing his property without compensation, or denying him a trial by jury in a civil case.
- The Fourth Amendment standard of reasonable searches was sufficiently malleable to be adapted to military needs.
- The transcript of the Virginia ratifying convention suggests that one reason for seeking protection from cruel and unusual punishment was to shield militiamen on active duty from abusive practices.

Possibly the most difficult Bill of Rights question pertaining to the military is whether the Sixth Amendment guarantee of trial by jury applied to courts martial. Some argue that it makes no sense for a soldier denied grand jury indictment to be granted jury trial. They contend that

---

[121] "[E]xception strengthens the force of a law in cases not excepted." (Commonly attributed to Sir Francis Bacon).

[122] An additional reason is that the President might have to negotiate treaties that impacted freedom of religion. See Sections 7.9.2 & 9.5.

Founding-era practice was not to try military personnel by jury. The Sixth Amendment spoke of trials within "the State and district wherein the crime shall have been committed," but military trials might well be held in foreign land or U.S. territories outside of any state.

Because the Sixth Amendment required that an accused be granted a trial by jury "[i]n all criminal prosecutions," without explicit exception for military cases, those contending for a military exception are, in effect, arguing for application of the rule of equitable construction to conform the language to the intent behind it.[123] There are at least two problems with this position. The first is the evidence, already mentioned, that most of the Bill of Rights was to be applied to military personnel. The second is that applying a military exception to jury trial would suggest that the exception also applied to rights mentioned later in the Sixth Amendment:

> To be informed of the nature and cause of the accusation; to be confronted with the witnesses against him; to have compulsory process for obtaining witnesses in his favor, and to have the Assistance of Counsel for his defense.

But there is no obvious reason why soldiers should be denied those rights.

More importantly, the Founding-era doctrine of equitable construction was employed only when the words of a document, through oversight or other mishap, were at odds with the makers' clear intent. So those claiming such an exception should be able to point to clear evidence that the Founders wanted to except soldiers from jury trial. To date, no scholar has done so. Indeed, the historical record shows no Founding-era consensus on the role of juries in military cases. The direct predecessors of the Fifth and Sixth Amendment—state constitutional provisions and ratifying convention recommendations—vary on the point. Some provisions did not exempt solders from either the grand jury or the trial jury right. Others denied the grand jury right but not the trial jury right. Still others guaranteed the grand jury right but not the trial jury right. Some denied solders both kinds of jury. Given these variations in conspicuous public documents, the most logical inference is that the structure in the language of the Sixth Amendment was adopted know-

---

[123] On equitable construction, see Section 2.7.

ingly and deliberately.

The trial jury right in Article III of the unamended Constitution offers some additional insight.[124] Article III did not guarantee a grand jury for anyone, military or not. But it did guarantee a trial jury for "all Crimes, except in Cases of Impeachment." According to the rule that exceptions were interpreted narrowly to strengthen the text outside the exceptions, the impeachment exception strongly implies that the jury trial really did apply to all other crimes—including those committed by soldiers. Additionally, Article III empowered Congress to fix the place of trial for crimes committed outside state boundaries—thereby making provision for many military crimes.

Thus, the weight of the evidence is that the Constitution did recognize trial by jury for military personnel. But prior usage suggests the rules for a military jury could be different than for a common law jury. In the Continental Congress's Articles of War—based on the British Articles of War—Congress required that serious crimes be tried by a president of the court and twelve other officers. Conviction in most cases could be by a mere majority vote, although death sentences required the vote of two-thirds and confirmation by Congress or (later) by the general officer in charge.[125]

9.12.2 Captured Enemy Personnel

At least some parts of the Bill of Rights protected non-citizens. For example, the Fifth Amendment specifically required a grand jury indictment for any "person," and the Sixth prescribed a trial jury to the

---

[124] Article III, Section 2, Clause 3:

> The Trial of all Crimes, except in Cases of Impeachment, shall be by Jury; and such Trial shall be held in the State where the said Crimes shall have been committed; but when not committed within any State, the Trial shall be at such Place or Places as the Congress may by Law have directed.

[125] The Continental Congress's principal Articles of War are in 5 J. Cont. Cong. 788–807 (Sep. 20, 1776), amended in 7 *id.* 264–66 (Apr. 14, 1777) and again in 9 *id.* 476–77 (Jun. 18, 1777). Later amendments permitted reduction of the panel from thirteen to as low as five members, but only in extraordinary circumstances. 30 *id.* 316–22 (May 31, 1786).

"accused." Neither provision contained any requirement of citizenship. Thus, a resident alien accused of crime was entitled to both rights.

We have seen that the Sixth Amendment right to trial by jury extended, in modified form, to American military personnel. But the Fifth Amendment specifically excepted them from the grand jury requirement. A difficult question is whether the same rules applicable to American military personnel also applied to captured enemy aliens accused of war crimes, such as spying. The grand jury question is particularly challenging because the text had no specific exclusion for enemy soldiers, as it did for American soldiers.

Yet it is inherently implausible that the drafters and Ratifiers of the Bill of Rights intended to allow enemy combatants to claim grand jury indictment and civilian-style jury trial when those rights were denied to American soldiers. British practice had been to try such persons, without prior indictment, by the same court martial procedure used for British soldiers.[126] In an August 1776 resolution, the Continental Congress specifically adopted that practice—deciding that persons who were not "members" of any state (i.e., not in allegiance to a state and therefore not subject to the law of treason)[127] and were accused of spying would be tried by a court martial, with a potential sentence of death.[128]

Moreover, Americans did, in fact, follow that procedure in such cases.[129] The most famous example was the case of Major John André, a British subject caught spying during the Revolutionary War. Without grand jury indictment, General Washington ordered a military tribunal of fifteen (two more than required) to try him. The tribunal sentenced André to death, and the sentence was carried out. Although the case was controversial in some respects, no one suggested that André was entitled

---

[126] *E.g.*, 1 William Hawkins, A Treatise of Pleas of the Crown 51 (1787) (stating that enemy hostiles are to be treated by martial law, not by the law applicable to citizens).

[127] Section 9.10.1.

[128] 5 J. Cont. Cong. 693 (Aug. 21, 1776).

[129] The André case is referenced in J. Cont. Cong. 918 (Oct. 12, 1780). Other instances of the general understanding that enemy troops violating the law of war were subject to court martial—appear at 7 *id.* 210 (Mar. 21, 1777) (James Molesworth); 12 *id.* 1125–29 (Nov. 12, 1778) (John Connolly—although eventually he was tried as a POW, 14 *id.* 825–26 (Jul. 14, 1779]).

to a grand jury. As noted earlier, the size of the panels required for courts martial did provide the accused with a form of trial by jury.[130]

In view of this evidence, the Fifth Amendment grand jury provision may be one place in the Constitution calling for equitable construction[131] to square the text with the intent of the makers. During World War II, the Supreme Court so construed the Fifth Amendment in a famous case involving German saboteurs.[132] In two other parts of the case, however, the court erred. One of the saboteurs was an American citizen, and as such he was entitled to be formally charged for treason and given the benefit of a grand jury, a right the court denied. Moreover, the court erred in holding that the Sixth Amendment did not grant military personnel some form of jury trial. It should have ruled either that the composition of the tribunal met the Sixth Amendment requirement or that the Amendment had been violated.

9.13 What About Unenumerated Rights?

Many judges and commentators have argued that the Founders expected the courts to strike down laws that violated rights not specifically enumerated in the Constitution. Each writer seems to have his own list of rights worthy of this protection.

The evidence supporting the unenumerated rights theory is thin: It includes a much-disputed 17th-century remark by legal scholar Edward Coke,[133] a 1789 equitable construction case decided by a South Carolina court,[134] and a gratuitous and contested comment by an idiosyncratic Supreme Court justice issued several years after the ratification.[135] Very

---

[130] Section 9.12.1.

[131] Section 2.7.

[132] *Ex Parte Quirin*, 317 U.S. 1 (1942).

[133] Dr. Bonham's Case (C.P. 1610) 8 Co. Rep. 107a, 77 Eng. Rep. 638.

[134] *Ham v. McClaws*, 1 S.C.L. (1 Bay) 93 (S.Ct. Ct. Com. Pl. 1789). On equitable construction, see Section 2.7.

[135] In *Calder v. Bull*, 3 U.S. (3 Dall.) 386 (1798), Justice Samuel Chase argued that a statute might be invalid if it violated natural law. However, comments issued that long after ratification are not good evidence of the Constitution's original legal force, especially when contested, as this statement was by Justice James

little evidence comes from the debates over the Constitution. On the contrary, the widespread demand for a Bill of Rights suggests that most people believed that courts would protect directly only rights enumerated in the federal or state constitutions.

Several provisions in the Constitution are said to protect unenumerated rights: the Privileges and Immunities Clause,[136] the Fifth Amendment Due Process Clause, and the Ninth Amendment.[137] However, the purpose of the Privileges and Immunities Clause was not to protect what the Founders considered natural rights, but rather to guarantee access by visiting out-of-staters to whatever benefits a host state had decided to grant its local citizens.[138] The Due Process Clause merely required government to follow pre-established rules when proceeding against a person civilly or criminally.[139] This might serve to protect other rights, but did so only incidentally: If pre-established rules required a jury trial, for example, then Due Process required a jury trial.

As for the Ninth Amendment, the conclusion that it protected "rights" as we understand them is based largely on what appears to be a plain reading of that Amendment: "It means what it says," as some modern commentators are fond of asserting. Unfortunately, due to intervening changes in the English language, they misunderstand what the Amendment really said. The Amendment's purpose was to protect personal freedom by reinforcing the Constitution's limits on federal power rather than by carving out discrete rights in the modern sense.[140]

The best case for judicial protection of unenumerated rights is the case least made. The Necessary and Proper Cause requires that federal laws enacted pursuant to Congress's incidental powers be "proper." There is good evidence that this meant that Congress had to act consist-

---

Iredell. See Section 2.8. In 1804, Chase was impeached (although not convicted) for his unprofessional conduct on the bench.

[136] Article IV, Section 2, Clause 1.

[137] Also cited are two provisions in the Fourteenth Amendment: its Due Process and Privileges or Immunities Clauses. That Amendment was adopted in 1868, and therefore was not part of the original Constitution.

[138] Section 3.10.2.

[139] Section 9.3.4.

[140] Section 10.2.

ently with duties of public trust.[141] By this interpretation, a law adopted under the Necessary and Proper Clause would be "improper," and therefore void, if it classified people in a way that was utterly without reasonable basis, or was bare special interest legislation, or violated another provision of the Constitution. If a court invalidated such a law, this would have the incidental effect of protecting the people's unenumerated rights.

---

[141] Section 5.5.

CHAPTER TEN

The Ninth and Tenth Amendments

10.1 Review of Some Founding-era Concepts

This chapter discusses two provisions added to the Bill of Rights to clarify how the Constitution should be read. Understanding how those two provisions worked requires a review of the Founders' ideas on natural law, natural rights, and the role of government.[1]

According to prevailing natural law theory, people originally were in a state of nature with one another. When in a state of nature, each person possessed many rights. In this context, the Founding-era meaning of "right" was a broad, and now largely archaic, one: It meant any ability or power. Some of these rights were benign, such as the right to defend oneself, trade for goods, and raise a family. Other rights were harmful, such as the right (power) to war on others.

Now, according to the state-of-nature story, people eventually realized that the harmful rights/powers hurt not only others, but themselves as well. If anyone had the unfettered right to attack anyone else, this endangered one's innocent rights. A person could lose his rights, property, family, or life at any time. Accordingly, the people transferred some

---

[1] See also Chapter One.

of their rights/powers to a central authority: government. Rights that could be properly transferred to government were called *alienable rights*.

Which alienable rights were conveyed to government varied with the society. Government exercised those conveyed rights/powers to protect people from common enemies and from each other.

However, some rights could never be justly transferred. The people always retained them. They were called *inalienable* or *unalienable* rights. ("Alienate" was, and is, a common legal term for "transfer away.") Examples of unalienable rights were self-defense, freedom of conscience, and the right to property.

In most societies, the people retained more than unalienable rights such as self-defense, conscience, and property. They also retained thousands of mundane personal choices: when to get up in the morning, where to shop and what to buy at what price, whether to wear a hat—and if so, what color hat. Today, we might call such choices "rights" in casual conversation ("I have a right to dress as I please"), but the Founders called them rights even in constitutional discourse.

By the Declaration of Independence (the theory was), the American people withdrew the rights/powers they had conferred upon the government of Great Britain. They then bestowed rights/powers on their new state governments. The exact powers conferred on each state government depended on the terms of that state's constitution. The state governments, in turn, ceded authority over foreign relations and a few other subjects to the Continental Congress. The Articles of Confederation, ratified in 1781, formalized this arrangement.

By adopting the U.S. Constitution, the people granted a new set of rights/powers to the federal government and its officers and departments, limiting state powers in the process. Those rights/powers not granted remained either in the state governments or with the people, according to the mixture prescribed in each state's constitution. Thus, through the medium of the Constitution, the American people transferred some rights/powers, such as most authority over foreign commerce, from the state governments to the federal government. They terminated the Confederation Congress (if, indeed, anything was left of it) and transferred nearly all its powers to the new federal government. They withheld from state governments certain powers entirely, such as the power to enact ex post facto laws.

10.2 The Ninth Amendment

When ratifying the Constitution, the people restricted their grants of power to the federal government with internal, quasi-external, and external limitations.[2] But as Anti-Federalists pointed out, the Constitution explicitly said very little about preserving either specific unalienable rights or treasured privileges[3] previously granted by British law. Anti-Federalists therefore argued that the Constitution should be amended to add a bill of rights protecting expressly both natural rights such as freedom of conscience, and traditional privileges such as trial by jury in civil cases. Federalists responded that because the power of the federal government was circumscribed, the rights people had against it were infinite, so a longer list of exceptions would necessarily be incomplete. An incomplete list of retained rights could encourage those in control of the government to contend that the federal government had all rights/powers outside of those excepted.[4]

For example: The enumerated powers of Congress did not include authority to regulate local businesses.[5] Managing local businesses free from federal control was, a right/power that, depending on each state's constitution, was either retained by the people or qualified by a grant to state government. If the U.S. Constitution were amended to protect newspapers from federal censorship, Congress might later claim—presumably relying on its implied powers—that it could regulate other sorts of local businesses. In essence, Congress might say, "Look, if the Founders thought we couldn't use the Necessary and Proper[6] or General Welfare Clauses[7] to regulate local businesses, then why did they bother to insert a specific provision to protect newspapers? Clearly, they protected newspapers because they recognized we could otherwise regulate local businesses."

---

[2] These terms are explained in Section 5.2.

[3] See Section 3.10.2 for the difference between privileges and natural rights.

[4] They could base this contention on several legal maxims, including *Inclusio unius est exclusio alterius* ("The designation of one is the exclusion of the other") and "Exception strengthens the force of a law in cases not excepted."

[5] This statement seems quaint today.

[6] Article I, Section 8, Clause 18.

[7] Article I, Section 8, Clause 1.

Although this argument was first advanced by the Federalists, the Anti-Federalists soon turned it against them. Anti-Federalists contended that the new government might abuse its General Welfare and Necessary and Proper powers.[8] Patrick Henry pointed out in the Virginia ratifying convention that the English Crown notoriously had relied on theories of "implication" (such as that incorporated in the Necessary and Proper Clause) to augment its own authority. Other Anti-Federalists reminded the public how English courts, particularly the Court of Exchequer, had used similarly creative theories to enlarge their jurisdictions. So to reassure almost everyone, several of the ratifying conventions proposing a bill of rights asked for clarifying language stating, in effect: "The Constitution has a list of exceptions to federal power, but don't forget that federal powers are limited in other ways as well." The Virginia ratifying convention's proposal was as follows:

> . . . those clauses which declare that Congress shall not exercise certain powers, be not interpreted, in any manner whatsoever, to extend the powers of Congress; but that they be construed either as making exceptions to the specified powers where this shall be the case, or otherwise, as inserted merely for greater caution.[9]

The conventions in New York, North Carolina, and later Rhode Island, all proposed similar or identical language.[10]

James Madison was elected to the House of Representatives in the First Congress. At the opening congressional session in 1789, Madison proposed a bill of rights including the following amendment:

---

[8] Indeed, such abuse is exactly what happened in the 20th century—with both the Necessary and Proper and the General Welfare Clauses.

[9] In accordance with the legal maxim, *Abundans cautela non nocet* ("Overflowing caution doesn't hurt").

[10] North Carolina tracked Virginia's language. New York and Rhode Island resolved:

> And that those Clauses in the said Constitution, which declare, that Congress shall not have or exercise certain Powers, do not imply that Congress is entitled to any Powers not given by the said Constitution; but such Clauses are to be construed either as exceptions to certain specified Powers, or as inserted merely for greater Caution.

The exceptions here or elsewhere in the constitution, made in favor of particular rights, shall not be so construed as to diminish the just importance of other rights retained by the people; or as to enlarge the powers delegated by the constitution; but either as actual limitations of such powers, or as inserted merely for greater caution.

After further editing, this language became the present Ninth Amendment:

The enumeration in the Constitution, of certain rights, shall not be construed to deny or disparage others retained by the people.[11]

The Virginia ratifying convention's proposal had used the word "powers." Madison's proposal had used both "rights" and "powers." The final version of the Ninth Amendment referred to "rights." This difference has confused modern commentators, apparently because they are not aware that in this context the two words were interchangeable.[12] In Congress, Madison explained that the purpose of the amendment was to protect against "implication, that those rights which were not singled out, were intended to be assigned into the hands of the General Govern-

---

[11] Some have argued that Congress's decision to drop the second half of Madison's proposal shows that the Ninth Amendment was only about protecting rights, not limiting federal powers. Because rights and powers were considered the opposite sides of the same coin, the more likely reason is that Congress saw the second half as repetitive. The latter reason is the only one consistent with the demands of the ratifying conventions.

[12] *E.g.*, Angela Rodday Holden, The Meaning of the Constitution 81 (1987) ("This amendment is designed to protect all the basic human rights that are not specifically covered by another provision of the Constitution"). Note the word, "basic," which is not in the amendment. If you believe the amendment protects "basic" rights, you have to explain which ones qualify. This inevitably results in a political, not a constitutional, selection. See also Leonard W. Levy, Original Intent and the Framers' Constitution 281 (1988) (displaying similar confusion when discussing letters from Hardin Burnley to James Madison and from Madison to George Washington).

ment." (Today, we would speak of assigning a "power" to the government, not a "right.")[13]

A few months later, when the Virginia legislature was debating the Bill of Rights, Edmund Randolph opposed the Ninth Amendment because, he said, it would have been more efficient to focus on restricting the relatively few powers granted rather than protecting the indefinite number of rights retained. But in a letter to George Washington, Madison wrote that he could "see not the force of this distinction" because restricting granted powers and protecting enumerated rights amounted to exactly the same thing.[14]

That the Ninth Amendment was a rule of construction was shown by its central verb: "construed." It told the reader how to construe the Constitution. In effect, it said, "The Constitution has a list of exceptions to federal power, but don't forget that federal powers are limited—and thus people's rights are preserved—in other ways as well." The Ninth Amendment did not add exceptions to the enumerated powers; rather, it pointed to the limits within the Constitution's grants of power. Whenever a court enforced those limitations, it enforced the Ninth Amendment.[15]

The First Congress placed the Ninth Amendment after the last item in the expanded list of exceptions—that is, after what is now the Eighth Amendment. This was because in 18th-century legal drafting practice rules of construction generally followed substantive provisions. The only amendment placed after the Ninth was the Tenth, another rule of construction.[16]

---

[13] Madison usually was careful to use "rights" to mean what the people retained and "powers" to mean what was granted to government. But he sometimes interchanged the words, as others did.

[14] Madison's letter also implied that Randolph had a point: It would have been easier to concentrate on what was granted than what was retained. But Madison said he didn't think it was worth jeopardizing the entire Constitution to accommodate that point.

[15] In this sense, some commentators are correct to point out that the Ninth Amendment helped to protect the states by emphasizing limits on the federal power. But that is only an incidental effect of its primary purpose of protecting the people.

[16] In Madison's original proposal, there was a third rule of construction located in the same place, one that affirmed separation of powers among legislative, executive, and judicial branches.

10.3 The Tenth Amendment

The Tenth Amendment also originated in the ratification debates. Like the Ninth, it arose in response to Anti-Federalist fears that the new government might become all-powerful and oppress the states and the people. One concern was the same that gave rise to the Ninth Amendment: that the General Welfare Clause and the Necessary and Proper Clause could be interpreted too broadly. But there was another purpose unique to the Tenth Amendment. Anti-Federalists wished to forestall future claims that the central government possessed inherent powers in addition to those enumerated.

This was a realistic concern. Throughout the period when Congress had only a few powers delegated by the states (1775-89), advocates of a strong central government had argued that, in addition to whatever powers the states had yielded, Congress also enjoyed a reservoir of authority inherent in national sovereignty. Sometimes, they claimed Congress had received inherent sovereign powers from the British Crown.[17] Sometimes, they claimed Congress enjoyed this authority by reason of its status as agent for foreign affairs.

The fullest exposition of the theory of "inherent sovereign authority" appeared in James Wilson's *Considerations on the Bank of North America*. Wilson's purpose in composing this paper was to justify the Confederation Congress's decision to charter a national bank. Anti-Federalists suspected (correctly, as later events showed)[18] that devotees of centralized government might raise the same arguments after the Constitution was ratified. Anti-Federalists therefore sought an amendment affirming that the central government had no powers beyond those enumerated in the Constitution.

Federalists, including an unabashed James Wilson, assured the people that the Anti-Federalists were worrying unnecessarily. After all, the Constitution carefully enumerated the government's powers—and the

---

[17] The many problems with this theory are examined in Robert G. Natelson, *The False Doctrine of Implied Sovereign Authority*, 24 Federalist Soc'y Rev. 346 (2023).

[18] Not only did Wilson make this argument at the federal convention, Farrand-Supp., p. 95 (notes of Robert Lansing), but advocates used it to justify creation of another national bank in 1791, after the Constitution was approved, but before the Tenth Amendment was ratified. Despite the clear wording of the Tenth Amendment, the argument sometimes resurfaces today. See Section 3.2.

inclusio unius[19] maxim would render the enumeration exclusive. If a power was not on the list, it wouldn't exist.

Anti-Federalists were unwilling to rely on the assurances of people like Wilson. They wanted the limits spelled out in clear words. As Patrick Henry told the Virginia ratifying convention:

> If we trust our dearest rights to implication, we shall be in a very unhappy situation.... The first thing that [we] thought of was a bill of rights. We were not satisfied with your constructive, argumentative rights.

Bargains between the Constitution's proponents and leading political moderates resulted in several ratification conventions proposing amendments to reinforce the *inclusio unius* reading of the enumerated powers. The initial proposal came from the Massachusetts ratifying convention. It provided "that all powers not expressly delegated to Congress are reserved to the several states, to be by them exercised." Former Governor Sam Adams explained it this way:

> It... gives assurance that, if any law made by the federal government shall be extended beyond the power granted by the proposed Constitution... it will be an error, and adjudged by the courts of law to be void.

There were two problems with the Massachusetts proposal. First, it would have reserved all powers not *expressly* granted. The word "expressly" was ambiguous in the 18th century: It could mean either "clearly" or "in words rather than implied."[20] If it meant the latter, the proposal would essentially repeal the "necessary" component of the Necessary and Proper Clause.[21] The second problem was that, by reserving rights only to

---

[19] *Inclusio unius est exclusio alterius*—"The inclusion of one is the exclusion of the other."

[20] *E.g.*, Nathan Bailey, A Universal Etymological English Dictionary (unpaginated) (1783) (giving as definitions of "express" the words "clear," "plain," and "manifest"); Thomas Sheridan, A Complete Dictionary of the English Language (unpaginated) (1789) ("plain" and "apparent"); William Perry, Royal Standard English Dictionary (1st American ed., 1788) ("in direct terms" and "plainly").

[21] On the Necessary and Proper Clause, see Section 5.5.

the states, the proposal did not account for the fact that in all or most states, the people had retained rights/powers they had not granted their state governments.

The subsequent conventions of South Carolina and New Hampshire retained the word "expressly." Later state conventions, however, resolved the first problem by either omitting "expressly" (Virginia, North Carolina) or substituting "clearly" (New York[22] and Rhode Island).[23] But none of the conventions solved the second problem. Even Madison's proposal in the First Congress, which omitted both "expressly" and "clearly," protected only the reserved powers of states. However, during the congressional drafting process the words "or to the people" were added:

> The powers not delegated to the United States by the Constitution, nor prohibited by it to the States, are reserved to the States respectively, or to the people.

This final version spoke in terms of "powers" being reserved as well as delegated—reflecting once again the interchangeability of those two words in this context.

To summarize: The Ninth and Tenth Amendments were both rules of construction without substantive force of their own. The words "rights" and "powers" in the two provisions were essentially interchangeable. The Ninth Amendment reminded the reader that although the Constitution created exceptions to some federal powers, it limited federal powers in other ways, too. The Ninth Amendment implicitly acknowledged that the federal government had implied, incidental powers, but warned the reader not to construe them too broadly. The Tenth Amendment embodied a similar caution about construing powers too broadly. The Tenth Amendment also reminded the reader that the *inclusio unius* maxim applied to the Constitution's enumerated powers, and expressly excluded the theory that the federal government enjoyed unenumerated powers arising from inherent sovereign authority.

---

[22] The New York convention rejected a proposal for an amendment limiting Congress to powers "expressly given," 22 Documentary History, p. 2089, in favor of one adopting the phrase "clearly delegated." 23 *Id.*, p. 2326.

[23] 26 *Id.* 997.

CHAPTER ELEVEN

Removal from Office

The Constitution created four methods by which government officials could be removed from office. They were as follows:

- Members of Congress, the President, and the Vice President could be defeated for re-election. The Constitution imposed no limits or standards on the will of the voters.
- Two thirds of the members of either chamber of Congress could expel a colleague from that chamber.[1] Again, the Constitution prescribed no limits or standards for the exercise of congressional discretion.
- The Senate could convict an officer of "Treason, Bribery, or other high Crimes and Misdemeanors"[2] after the House of Representatives had issued articles of impeachment[3] and the Senate had tried him. This procedure could be used against the

---

[1] Article I, Section 5, Clause 2.

[2] Article II, Section 4.

[3] Article II, Section 4.

President, Vice President, and judicial and executive officers, but not against Members of Congress.
- The President, as manager of the executive branch, could fire a subordinate employee. Although the Constitution did not itemize this procedure explicitly, it was inherent in the text.[4]

11.1 Removal Following Impeachment and Trial

The Constitution provided that an officer could be impeached and removed for either treason or bribery. It also provided that treason was limited to (1) making war against the United States or (2) giving aid and comfort to the enemies of the United States.[5] The definition of treason was adopted from a venerable British statute.[6]

The Constitution further specified that removal could follow Senate conviction for "other high Crimes and Misdemeanors."[7] We know from the Founding-era record that the adjective "high" modifies "Misdemeanors" as well as "Crimes."

For a very long time, commentators argued about, and speculated on, the meaning of the phrase "high Misdemeanors." During the first congressional impeachment hearings of President Donald J. Trump, a congressional panel of four law professors each defined "high Misdemeanor" differently. Contributing to the uncertainty was that the grounds for impeachment in Britain had varied over the centuries, and one could read the history in different ways. In earlier editions of this book, I contended, based on fairly good evidence, that "high Misdemeanor" meant "breach of public trust"—that is, breach of fiduciary duty.

None of us was correct. As is true of so much constitutional interpretation, the correct answer lay in 18th-century English and American law books, which almost no one had thought to consult.

In 18th century law, the phrase "high Misdemeanor" was a very common legal term with a specific meaning.[8] Imagine four concentric

---

[4] Section 11.2.

[5] Article III, Section 3. Clause 1.

[6] Section 9.10.1.

[7] Article II, Section 4.

[8] See the bibliography to this chapter.

circles. The outermost circle contains all crimes—also called in the 18th century, "misdemeanors" and "offenses." The next smaller circle contains only the more serious misdemeanors, known as "high misdemeanors," "great misdemeanors," or "misprisions." The next smaller circle contains only those high misdemeanors known as "felonies" or "high crimes." They included murder, arson, rape, burglary, and some other offenses. Felonies were, in theory (although often not in practice), punishable by death—usually by hanging. The innermost circle is the most serious felony of all: treason. It was punishable by particularly ghoulish forms of death, although by the 18th century, the sentence was almost invariably reduced to hanging.

Although all serious crimes were high misdemeanors, in common speech the term "high misdemeanors" applied to those serious crimes that did not merit death—that is, those crimes within the second-largest circle but not within the two inner circles. Examples of high misdemeanors included attempted murder, receipt of stolen goods, assault not resulting in death, and bribery.

The Constitution's list of grounds for impeachment—"Treason, Bribery, or other high Crimes and Misdemeanors"—began with a high crime ("Treason"), proceeded to a high misdemeanor ("Bribery"), and then added general words covering offenses in both categories: "other high Crimes" and "other . . . [high] . . . Misdemeanors."

Thus, the Constitution authorized impeachment only for commission of grave crimes—offenses typically meriting jail time.

The document further provided that:

> Judgment in Cases of Impeachment shall not extend further than to removal from Office, and disqualification to hold and enjoy any Office of honor, Trust or Profit under the United States: but the Party convicted shall nevertheless be liable and subject to Indictment, Trial, Judgment and Punishment, according to Law.[9]

In other words, an officer impeached and removed from office was not, by that fact alone, subject to fines, imprisonment, or other punishments. He would have to be prosecuted criminally first.

---

[9] Article I, Section 3, Clause 7.

A controversial question is whether an officer could be prosecuted criminally before impeachment and removal. Other than in the case of the President, there seems to be no bar to this. It can be inferred from contemporaneous practice, however, that before the President could be prosecuted by federal officials, he would have to be removed, since any other approach would impair the unity of the federal executive power.[10] There did not seem to be any bar to prosecution by state officials under state law.

The provision that punishment not extend further than "removal from Office, and disqualification to hold and enjoy any Office of honor, Trust or Profit under the United States"[11] prevented impeachment from being used to inflict criminal punishments, as had occurred in Britain.

11.2 Removal of Executive Officers by the President

Because impeachment-and-conviction was reserved for serious crimes, it is unlikely that the Founders intended it to be the only way to remove an employee serving in the executive branch. The President would need power to dismiss federal employees for other causes if he was to have any hope of serving effectively as commander-in-chief[12] or ensuring "that the Laws be faithfully executed."[13]

The first session of the First Congress engaged in a high-toned debate on whether the President unilaterally could remove other executive officers.[14] The debaters explored three possible interpretations of the constitutional language: (1) Officers were removable only through impeachment and conviction; (2) officers could be removed by the President alone; or (3) officers could be removed by the President alone if appointed (pursuant to law) by the President alone, but if the Senate had approved the appointment, the Senate had to concur in the dismissal.

---

[10] *Cf.* DeLolme, p. 76 (explaining why a sitting King could not be arraigned before judges).

[11] Article I, Section 3, Clause 7.

[12] Article II, Section 2, Clause 1.

[13] Article II, Section 3.

[14] Section 2.5 explains why records from the first have special value.

Ultimately, Congress decided that the second alternative was correct.[15]

The position that officers were to serve indefinitely until impeached was clearly untenable. The Constitution specified that only judges, not executive branch officials, were to serve "during good Behaviour."[16] This implied that executive branch officials were subject to a different rule from judges.

Moreover, a proposed interpretation was, as Madison said, "triable by its consequences."[17] The impeachment process was slow and cumbersome, and relying exclusively on it was an impossible way of managing hundreds (soon to be thousands) of federal employees. Furthermore, impeachment required a serious offense. A President trying to manage the executive branch effectively—"tak[ing] Care that the Laws be faithfully executed"[18]—often would have to dismiss people for other reasons.

As a result of such considerations, few in the First Congress concluded that executive branch officials could be fired only by impeachment and trial. The more difficult choice was between the second and third interpretations.

An initial step toward a solution was recognizing, as most members of the First Congress did, that the removal power was incidental to the appointment power. In other words, whoever had the power to appoint had the power to remove. That led to the next question: "If the Senate concurred in an appointment, who actually made the appointment—the President alone, or the President-and-Senate?"

Article II, Section 2 was a series of power-grants from the people to the President.[19] Clause 2 of that section stated that the President "shall nominate, and by and with the Advice and Consent of the Senate, shall appoint . . . all other Officers of the United States. . . ."[20] This sentence

---

[15] Most of the Framers in Congress—including James Madison—agreed with this decision.

[16] Article III, Section 1.

[17] Sir Edward Coke propounded the maxim: *Interpretatio talis in ambiguis semper fienda est, ut evitetur inconveniens et absurdum* (An interpretation of ambiguous circumstances should must be rendered in a way that inconveniency and absurdity are avoided).

[18] Article II, Section 3.

[19] Section 7.5.1 and 7.5.2.

[20] Article II, Section 2, Clause 2.

suggested that it was the President who appointed. Senatorial consent was merely what lawyers call a "condition precedent" to the appointment. On the other hand, wording later in the same Clause of the Constitution stated that "the Congress may by Law vest the Appointment of such inferior Officers, as [Congress] think proper, in the President alone, in the Courts of Law, or in the Heads of Departments." This language suggested that when Congress did not pass such a law, the appointment was not "in the President alone." If so, then it had to be in the President-and-Senate. There appeared, therefore, to be a conflict between the earlier and later provisions in the same Clause.

This is where rules of construction prove their worth. Two rules break the tie in favor of the earlier provision—that is, in favor of the view that the President alone appoints. One rule of construction held that in grants (other things being equal), earlier language trumped inconsistent later language. The later language was considered "repugnant" to the earlier, and to the extent it was inconsistent with the earlier language, it was disregarded.[21]

The second rule of construction was that more specific language trumped more general or vague language.[22] In this case, the earlier provision in Article II, Section 2, Clause 2 was more specific. It prescribed that "he [the President] shall appoint . . . all . . . Officers," while the later passage said that Congress could vest an appointment power "in the President alone." Thus, the former passage declared directly that the President "shall appoint," while the second only implied (it did not state) that in the absence of congressional authorization, the appointment was a joint one. Hence, the first passage should control. And if the President appointed and removal was incidental to appointment, then the President could remove.

As it happens, there is evidence outside the text that the Ratifiers would have considered the President's nomination as an appointment even if the Senate had not yet concurred. In the records of the Continental Congress, an officer's designation of a subordinate was regularly called an "appointment." If Congress had to approve the appointment,

---

[21] *E.g.*, 2 William Blackstone, Commentaries *381 ("[I]n a deed, if there be two clauses so totally repugnant to each other, that they cannot stand together, the first shall be received and the latter rejected.").

[22] *Generalibus specialia derogant* and *Generalia sunt praeponenda singularibus.*

that process was called "confirmation."[23]

Another argument used to support the conclusion that the President may freely remove executive branch officers is based on the view that the first sentence of Article II does not merely designate the President but also grants him a broad "executive Power." I have not relied on this argument because I believe that interpretation of the first sentence of Article II is incorrect. See Section 7.2.[24]

---

[23] *E.g.*, 4 J. Cont. Cong. 110 (Feb. 5, 1776; 7 *id.* 332 (May 6, 1777); 10 *id.* 178 (Feb. 17, 1778). These are only a few of many examples. On the other hand, the Confederation Congress, sometimes granted the power to appoint and remove separately. *E.g.*, 28 J. Cont. Cong. 21–22 (Jan. 27, 1785) (outlining powers of "Secretary at War"); *id.* 141 (Mar. 11, 1785) (outlining power of ministers abroad).

[24] James Madison so argued, claiming that removal was incidental to "The executive Power."

CHAPTER TWELVE

Ratification and Amendment

12.1 Ratification

Article VII specified how the Constitution would come into effect:

> The Ratification of the Conventions of nine States, shall be sufficient for the Establishment of this Constitution between the States so ratifying the Same.

Thus, the Constitution was to be approved not by the state legislatures, but by special delegates elected by the people, meeting in conventions in each state. Recall that an Anglo-American tradition had arisen of making significant governmental changes in convocations called together for that purpose—"convention parliaments" in England, and state and interstate ("federal") conventions in America.[1] (In 1780, Massachusetts had gone even further along the road toward popular sovereignty by ratifying its state constitution by referendum.)

At the Constitutional Convention, some commissioners pointed out that conventions probably would be more favorable to the Constitution

---

[1] Section 1.4.

than the state legislatures. There also were more fundamental reasons for preferring the state convention route. The Articles of Confederation had been approved only by the state legislatures, so the Articles did not have the direct sanction of the people. The Constitution, on the other hand, was to be an instrument by which the people granted power to the new government directly.[2] James Madison was reported as observing:

> The people were in fact, the fountain of all power, and by resorting to them, all difficulties were to be got over. They could alter constitutions as they pleased. It was a principle in the [English and state] Bills of rights, that first principles might be resorted to.[3]

The Framers designed the ratification procedure to require the approval of nine of the 13 states to ratify. This was a two-thirds majority among the states and a common margin under the Articles for major decisions. Additionally, as shown by contemporaneous population estimates and by the initial allocation of the House of Representatives, even the smallest nine states would represent a majority of the people.[4] Of course, in theory the estimate could have over-counted the free (non-slave) population in the nine smallest states.[5] If so, the problem also was merely theoretical, since everyone knew that ratification by the nine smallest states alone was not sufficient to get the government running. Furthermore, the Framers knew that approval by Pennsylvania, the second most populous state, was highly probable. If any eight others joined her, then the ratifying conventions certainly would represent a majority of the people.[6]

---

[2] Section 3.1.

[3] 2 Farrand, p. 476.

[4] Approval by only the nine smallest states would represent thirty-three (a bare majority) of the sixty-five Representatives in the First Congress.

[5] The apportionment rule by which a slave was counted as three-fifths of a free person skewed congressional allocation somewhat. This might have been a problem if slave states were uniformly more or less populous than free states. But this was not the case.

[6] In theory, nine ratifying conventions might approve by narrow margins while four rejected it by huge margins, resulting in ratification by an overall delegate

12.2 Amendment

The Framers sought to assure that successful amendments were supported by supermajorities of the people and in all, or almost all, regions of the country. Article V, which outlined the amendment procedures, therefore required multiple steps in order to amend—all of them difficult.

Article V provided roles in the amendment process for Congress, for the state legislatures, for a federal convention, and for state conventions. When acting under Article V, these entities received their power directly from the U.S. Constitution. An entity receiving its power directly from the Constitution is said to perform a "federal function."[7]

12.2.1 Methods of Amending the Constitution

Article V allowed four possible procedures for amending.[8] The first began with two-thirds of the House and two-thirds of the Senate proposing an amendment. The reason for allowing Congress to initiate amendments was that Congress, by working regularly with the mechanism of government, would be likely to perceive any need for reform.[9] Article V's language ("shall deem it necessary") communicated that the decision to propose an amendment was within the absolute discretion of Congress. The President had no role in this decision.

Congress also would decide whether the proposed amendment should be ratified by state legislatures or conventions. If Congress selected state legislatures, Congress sent its proposal to them. If three-quarters of the legislatures ratified it, the amendment became part of the Constitution. Thus, the first amendment procedure required congressional proposal and state legislative ratification.

The second procedure was the same as the first, except that Congress

---

minority. But this possibility was exceedingly remote. Ultimately, 1064 of the 1641 delegates who voted on the Constitution voted for it—65 percent. If the delegates to the Vermont convention are added, the figure is 67 percent.

[7] See Section 1.3.5.

[8] As of the time of publication, only the first two procedures have been used. The Twenty-First Amendment was adopted by the second procedure, and all the rest by the first.

[9] 2 Farrand, p. 558 (Madison) (quoting Alexander Hamilton).

opted to send its proposed amendment to state ratifying conventions elected by the people and organized under state legislative direction. If three-fourths of the conventions agreed, the amendment would become part of the Constitution.

The third and fourth procedures required state legislatures to apply to Congress for a "Convention for proposing Amendments." If two-thirds of state legislatures applied on the same subject or subjects, Congress was to call the convention. If the convention proposed one or more amendments, then Congress would decide whether ratification would be by state legislatures (third procedure) or state conventions (fourth procedure). Approval by three-fourths of the state legislatures or conventions was needed for ratification.

12.2.2 Conventions for Proposing Amendments

Recent scholarship has clarified the nature, composition, and role of conventions for proposing amendments. This author has played a role in that scholarship. The Bibliography for this chapter provides citations to studies and sources.

The Constitution's Framers wrote the convention for proposing amendments into Article V to enable the people, acting through their state legislatures, to amend without congressional consent. The convention method could be used for any reason, but its principal purpose was to allow the public to curb Congress if it exceeded or abused its power. This was thoroughly explained during the ratification debates.

Numerous Founding-era records tell us that a convention for proposing amendments was to be a "convention of the states."[10] This was a familiar institution: Before 1776, there had been over 20 conventions among colonies and from 1776 through 1787 there were 11 more among states. Most of these gatherings were partial (regional), but at least five were general. A general convention was one to which all states, or at least states from all regions, had been invited.[11]

---

[10] This is one of the most well-attested propositions in the Founding-era record and has been confirmed by the U.S. Supreme Court, so it is astounding that some people still deny it. For the sources see the bibliography to this chapter.

[11] Some commentators have assumed the word "general" referred to broad subject matter. In fact, it referred only to the number of states invited. The general conventions were the Albany Congress of 1754, the Stamp Act Congress

A convention for proposing amendments, like a state convention for ratifying a proposed amendment, drew its power directly from the Constitution. Just as common incidents and understandings inhered in the Constitution's use of the word "jury,"[12] common incidents and understandings attached to the multi-state convention. Applications could be conditional or time-limited, they could be rescinded, and they remained valid until rescinded or expired or until the convention was called.[13]

Legislative applications might specify that the convention be empowered to consider all possible amendments, as did a 1789 New York application. But earlier interstate conventions generally were limited to one or more subjects, and the Founders assumed that most amendment conventions would be similarly limited. Convention authority was restricted to the scope of the applications and the resulting call. The convention probably could not be limited to merely voting up or down an amendment of prescribed wording, since that was contrary to the understanding of the nature of a "Convention[s] for proposing."

When two-thirds of the states applied for a convention addressing one or more matching subjects, Congress was required to issue a call designating time, place, and subject. Because the Framers provided for amendments conventions as a device to check Congress and because interstate convention procedure was fixed by custom, Congress's role in the procedure was minimal. Congress had no authority to mandate how the states chose their delegates or how many to choose, or to dictate convention rules. As an agent for the states during this procedure, Congress was obliged to treat all states equally.

---

of 1765, the First Continental Congress of 1774, the Philadelphia Price Convention of 1780, the Annapolis Convention of 1786, and the Constitutional Convention of 1787. (Until the word "congress" became irrevocably fixed as the name of the federal legislature, it was a synonym for a multi-government convention.)

Since the founding, two general conventions of states have been held (1861 and 2017), and at least nine regional conventions. *List of Conventions of States and Colonies in American History*, https://articlevinfocenter.com/list-conventions-states-colonies-american-history/. All conventions of states follow similar protocols.

[12] See Section 1.4.

[13] The end-point for rescission was either achievement of the two-thirds threshold or issuance of the call—probably the former.

Each state legislature would send to the convention a "committee" consisting of one or more "commissioners." Each state legislature would be responsible for choosing, paying, commissioning, and instructing those commissioners. The convention would adopt its own rules and elect its own officers. In the absence of a convention rule to the contrary, the rule of decision was that prevailing throughout the Anglo-American world: a majority of those voting.[14] In this case, "those voting" were the represented states, based on one state/one vote.

Because the convention's power was limited by the applications and call, any recommendations outside the scope of the applications were, as in the case of those issued by the 1786 Annapolis Convention, purely recommendations. They were not ratifiable proposed amendments.

12.2.3 Additional Amendment Rules

Whichever entity proposed an amendment—Congress or a convention—could incorporate a time limit for ratification. The limit almost certainly could not be extended without proposing a fresh amendment.

Founding-era law and practice imply that a state's ratification, like its application, lasted either until revoked or until the requisite number of states had acted—whichever occurred first. That is why some states' ratifications of the Twenty-Seventh Amendment endured for two centuries.[15]

Article V reserved three provisions as unamendable—two temporarily and one permanently. These provisions could be altered only by amending the amendment process or by scrapping the entire Constitution.

Prior to 1808, no amendment could change the provision[16] preventing Congress from banning either state-approved (1) immigration of free persons or (2) importation of slaves. Likewise, before 1808 no amendment could change the provision[17] apportioning direct taxes among states in rough approximation to their respective populations.

The permanent restriction on amendment was that "no State, with-

---

[14] Section 1.4.

[15] On the Twenty-Seventh Amendment, see Section 9.1 and Chapter Thirteen.

[16] Article I, Section 9, Clause 1.

[17] The restriction on Congress is in Article I, Section 9, Clause 4.

out its Consent, shall be deprived of its equal Suffrage in the Senate." In effect, this required unanimity among the states to change the rule allocating the same number of Senators to each state. It did not prevent an amendment altering the number of Senators each state was entitled to elect. An ordinary amendment could, for example, reduce the number of Senators from each state to one or increase it to three or four.

CHAPTER THIRTEEN

Conclusion

The United States Constitution sometimes is called "the world's oldest written national constitution." This is inaccurate, because there were several earlier ones: Sweden's Instrument of Government (1634) and two English charters from the era of Oliver Cromwell: the Instrument of Government (1653) and the Humble Petition and Advice (1657).

Sometimes, the U.S. Constitution is labeled "the world's oldest written national Constitution still in effect." But in no realistic sense is the original Constitution still fully in effect, even as formally amended.

The original Constitution lasted a good long time. For nearly a century and a half, the Supreme Court generally applied it in good faith and, for the most part, consistently with the original understanding. Only two leading cases were, in my view, clear exceptions: *Chisholm v. Georgia*[1] and *Dred Scott v. Sandford*,[2] both quickly overruled by constitutional amendment.

---

[1] 2 U.S. (2 Dall.) 419 (1793) (allowing unwilling states to be sued in federal court).

[2] 60 U.S. 393 (1857) (ruling that African-Americans could never be citizens of the United States on the basis of an inaccurate portrayal of Founding-era events and views).

238 : The Original Constitution

Otherwise, despite dramatic changes in social and technological conditions—and a great Civil War—the American people amended the Constitution only rarely. Moreover, the few amendments they did ratify were broadly consistent with the visions of the leading Founders. The Eleventh Amendment (1795) merely reaffirmed the prevailing understanding of the Ratifiers by reversing *Chisholm v. Georgia*.[3] The Twelfth Amendment (1804) affirmed the original understanding of the Vice President's qualifications, and refined the original Constitution's method of electing the President and Vice President. The Thirteenth Amendment (1865) was more radical: It abolished slavery. But this alteration was consistent with Founding-era natural law views and the dominant expectation that slavery was headed for extinction.

The Fourteenth Amendment (1868) restored the original understanding by correcting the Supreme Court's erroneous holding in *Dred Scott v. Sandford* (1857). It also imposed new rules on the states—but they were the same rules of fiduciary governance that influenced most of the Founders: respect for treasured privileges and immunities, due process, and equal protection. The Fifteenth Amendment (1870) prohibited states from denying the vote on the basis of race—a principle already honored in some states when the Constitution was written.

The Thirteenth, Fourteenth, and Fifteenth Amendments also granted new enumerated powers to Congress. These powers were limited to ensuring that the amendments were enforced. As construed for several decades, they altered the constitutional balance only in limited respects.

Then there was no amendment at all for another 43 years. During that period, the Supreme Court continued to approach constitutional questions in the spirit of the Founding. When the Court did err, the mistake often arose from efforts to preserve the constitutional balance.[4]

Since 1913, there have been 12 additional amendments. Six of these

---

[3] Section 3.4.

[4] For example, the court construed the Coinage Clause too narrowly, but corrected this with a counterbalancing construction of the Necessary and Proper Clause. The Legal Tender Cases, 79 U.S. 457 (1870) (upholding legal-tender paper money). Some argue that the Fourteenth Amendment was construed too narrowly in the Slaughter House Cases, 83 U.S. (16 Wall.) 36 (1873) (sharply limiting state obligations under the Amendment), and many contend that it was construed too narrowly in *Plessy v. Ferguson*, 163 U.S. 537 (1896) (holding that "separate but equal" segregation did not offend the Fourteenth Amendment).

were extrapolations of Founding-era principles. The Founders might well have anticipated the Nineteenth Amendment (1920), which extended the vote to women in states that did not yet grant it. At the Founding, women already were voting in New Jersey and, informally, in some other states, and the Framers had written the Constitution in a gender-neutral way.[5]

The Twentieth Amendment (1933)[6] and the Twenty-Fifth (1967)[7] were Article II administrative reforms comparable to those of the Twelfth (1804). The Twenty-First (1933) reversed the Eighteenth (Prohibition, ratified in 1919) and restored control of alcoholic beverages to the state governments, where the Founders had placed it. The Twenty-Second (1951) constitutionalized the presidential two-term tradition established by George Washington. The Twenty-Seventh (1992) was the original "second amendment," conceived in 1789 by James Madison and proposed the same year.

The other six 20th-century alterations had more significant effects, although some are overstated. The Sixteenth Amendment (1913) did not, as is widely believed, grant Congress power to adopt an income tax; Congress always had that power, and sometimes had used it. Rather, the Sixteenth Amendment ended the Constitution's requirement that income tax revenue be apportioned by state. When, two decades later, Congress began to overrun the traditional limits on federal spending, the Sixteenth Amendment facilitated the process.

The Seventeenth Amendment (1913) provided that the people, rather than the state legislatures, would elect United States Senators. Advocates justified the change by an appeal to Founding-era values, and it was consistent with the Founding-era value of independence among branches of government.[8] There were additional arguments for the change as well, and some analysts believe it may have strengthened the federal balance by

---

[5] Section 4.4.

[6] Containing administrative details pertaining to the President, Vice President, and Congress.

[7] Containing more administrative details about the presidential succession. The Twenty-Fifth and, to some extent the Twentieth, Amendments responded to long-standing problems arising from deficiencies in Article II, the weakest of the Constitution's Articles.

[8] Section 1.3.5.

unbundling state and federal issues. Others argue that the Seventeenth Amendment impaired the constitutional balance by weakening the voice of state governments and facilitating the growth of the federal government.

It may be that the arguments on both sides are overstated: Empirical studies of the impact of the amendment have found only marginal effects.[9]

Striking more directly at Founding-era values than either the Sixteenth or Seventeenth Amendments was the Eighteenth (1919), which established national prohibition of alcoholic beverages. This was a direct attack on federalism. Not only did it work a major transfer of police power from the states to the central government, it also involved federal agencies in the traditional state function of routine law enforcement. Although soon repealed by the Twenty-First (1933), the Eighteenth inured Americans to federal policing.

Three additional amendments, while uncontroversial today, cut at Founding-era values—in particular the principle of independence. The Founders believed that decision makers in a republic should be financially and personally independent, but all three enfranchised citizens who, to a disproportionate extent, were heavily dependent on others. The Twenty-Third Amendment (1961) admitted the District of Columbia—heavily populated with government employees—to presidential elections. The Twenty-Fourth (1964) compelled states to enfranchise people unable or unwilling to pay taxes. The Twenty-Sixth (1971) required states to enfranchise eighteen-, nineteen-, and twenty-year-olds—an age group once largely self-supporting, but now mostly dependent on parents and such government benefits as subsidized tuition.

Yet the constitutional system was altered less by direct amendment than by politicians and judges. One of the Constitution's chief purposes was to restrain federal officeholders, but after 1933, those officeholders

---

[9] See Robert G. Natelson, *Understanding the Constitution: The 17th Amendment and the Direct Election of Senators*, https://i2i.org/understanding-the-constitution-the-17th-amendment-and-direct-election-of-senators/. For most of the first two decades after the amendment's ratification, federal spending as a share of Gross Domestic Product *declined*.

broke much of that restraint.[10] They were able to do so in part because the judiciary failed to check sufficiently the power of Congress and the President. Successive opinions by the Supreme Court (1) largely repealed the constitutional limits on the Taxing and Spending,[11] Commerce,[12] and Enclave[13] Powers;[14] (2) discarded the Founding-era rule that fiduciary power could not be delegated, (3) resurrected the dead doctrine of "inherent sovereign authority,"[15] (4) weakened the Contracts Clause,[16] and (5) approved presidential decisions to incarcerate, even execute, American citizens without benefit of habeas corpus, grand jury indict-

---

[10] There were precedents during the Civil War and World War I, but they were short-lived. For a description of the change, see *1937–1944: How the Supreme Court Re-wrote the Constitution—the Complete Series*, https://i2i.org/1937-1944-complete-series/.

[11] *Helvering v. Davis*, 310 U.S. 619 (1937); *Charles C. Steward Machine Co. v. Davis*, 310 U.S. 548 (1937); *United States v. Butler*, 297 U.S. 1 (1936). The method by which the court concluded that Congress could spend on virtually anything was typical of its disingenuous methods during that era. First, *Butler* merely stated this conclusion as gratuitous dicta, irrelevant to the holding. Then *Helvering* and *Steward Machine* pretended it was settled law.

[12] *United States v. Darby Lumber*, 312 U.S. 100 (1941) (enabling Congress to regulate manufacturing under the Commerce Power); *Wickard v. Filburn*, 317 U.S. 111 (1942) (enabling Congress to regulate agriculture under the Commerce Power); *United States v. South-Eastern Underwriters Ass'n*, 322 U.S. 533 (1944) (enabling Congress to regulate insurance under the Commerce Power). *South-Eastern Underwriters* illustrates the disingenuous methodology of the time, featuring, for example, footnotes that do not support the text.

[13] *Collins v. Yosemite Park*, 304 U.S. 518 (1938).

[14] One gets a peek into the conscious nature of the court's surrender in Barry Cushman, Rethinking the New Deal Court: The Structure of a Constitutional Revolution (1998). See *id.* 208–24, in which Cushman discusses the decision to abdicate responsibility to police the boundaries of the Commerce Power.

[15] *United States v. Curtiss-Wright*, 299 U.S. 304 (1936). For the doctrine, see Section 3.2.

[16] *Home Bldg & Loan Assn v. Blaisdell*, 290 U.S. 398 (1934). This case was followed by several in which the court tried to retreat from *Blaisdell*. Robert G. Natelson, *How the Contracts Clause Was gutted—and How SCOTUS' early efforts to correct this have been ignored*, https://i2i.org/how-the-contracts-clause-was-gutted-and-how-the-supreme-courts-early-efforts-to-correct-the-situation-have-been-ignored/ (2013).

ment, or jury trial.¹⁷ State officials also failed to employ their checks on federal overreaching, opting to accept federal grant-in-aid programs and neglecting the state application and convention procedure of Article V.

As the Supreme Court permitted federal officials to break loose, it increasingly boxed in the states. The court ceased using the Fourteenth Amendment Due Process Clause to overturn state economic regulations, but it deployed its "dormant commerce clause" doctrine to the same purpose. It also began intrusive review of many other kinds of state laws. As early as 1931, the court began to apply its version of the Bill of Rights to the states.¹⁸ In the ensuing years, the court supervised how state governments treated religion, speech, assembly and the press; how they tried the accused and punished the convicted; how they regulated defamation, education, health, social services, family law, and land use; and even how state legislatures and local governments were structured.

As a result, the Constitution was transformed into a system in which federal politicians do almost anything they choose and in which a massive bureaucracy enjoys nearly unlimited claims against citizens. In 2012, the Supreme Court held that Congress may tax people for not purchasing government-approved health insurance.¹⁹ Many found that decision stunning, but it was nowhere near as significant as the Court's tacit holding that Congress has regulatory authority to micromanage the personal health care decisions of every person in the country. The latter ruling was all the more breathtaking for being essentially uncontested.

And not long before this writing, came the extraordinary news that federal officials had been undermining the speech and press protections of the First Amendment by pressuring social media platforms and the nation's largest bookseller into exercising direct censorship of views those

---

[17] *Korematsu v. United States*, 323 U.S. 214 (1944) (approving the relocation of American citizens of Japanese descent to concentration camps); Ex Parte Quirin, 317 U.S. 1 (1942) (approving execution of an American citizen by a secret military tribunal).

[18] *Stromberg v. California*, 283 U.S. 359 (1931). Earlier statements to this effect, *e.g.*, in *Gitlow v. New York*, 268 U.S. 652 (1925), were dicta. A property takings case decided in the 1890s sometimes is described as applying the Fifth Amendment to the states, but it actually made no mention of the Fifth Amendment. *Chicago, Burlington & Quincy R.R. v. Chicago*, 166 U.S. 226 (1897).

[19] Nat'l Fed. of Independent *Business v. Sebelius*, 567 U.S. 519 (2012).

officials opposed.

The tattered remains of the original Constitution do persist: in periodic elections, heavily biased toward incumbents—in a handful of individual rights, distorted and sporadically enforced—in a residual judicial respect for state governments.[20] Yet this is quite different from the Constitution "We the People" ratified and amended.

Whether "We the People" really want our Constitution back is for us to decide.

---

[20] *Id.*; *Printz v. United States*, 521 U.S. 898 (1997); *New York v. United States*, 505 U.S. 144 (1992).

BIBLIOGRAPHY

General Sources

There are many useful sources on the original Constitution. This bibliography lists a selection of primary and secondary sources—which include my research articles, on which part of this book is based. The list of works by other authors is necessarily selective. The titles of articles are *italicized* and titles of books are in LARGE AND SMALL CAPITALS.

Sources Relevant Across Chapters

The following materials supplement all, or many, of the chapter topics:

Founding-era Sources

During the 1787 convention the Framers consulted a variety of sources, including the first volume of John Adams' A DEFENCE OF THE CONSTITUTIONS OF GOVERNMENT OF THE UNITED STATES OF AMERICA (1787), which is an encyclopedia of republican governments; J.L. DeLolme's THE CONSTITUTION OF ENGLAND (reissued in 2007 by Liberty Fund), Baron Montesquieu's THE SPIRIT OF THE LAWS; Emer de Vattel's THE LAW OF NATIONS; and William Blackstone's COMMENTARIES ON THE LAWS OF ENGLAND.

The standard reference work for the proceedings of the convention is THE RECORDS OF THE FEDERAL CONVENTION OF 1787 (Max Farrand ed., 1937). The SUPPLEMENT TO MAX FARRAND'S THE

246 : THE ORIGINAL CONSTITUTION

RECORDS OF THE FEDERAL CONVENTION OF 1787 (James H. Hutson, ed. 1987) reproduces later-discovered material, such as John Dickinson's convention notes.

For the ratification debates, THE DOCUMENTARY HISTORY OF THE RATIFICATION OF THE CONSTITUTION AND THE BILL OF RIGHTS (Merrill Jensen et al. eds., 1976 - present) provides complete coverage. It has superseded the formerly standard source, THE DEBATES IN THE SEVERAL STATE CONVENTIONS ON THE ADOPTION OF THE FEDERAL CONSTITUTION (Jonathan Elliot, 2d ed. 1836). Shorter collections of ratification-era material include (1) ALEXANDER HAMILTON, JAMES MADISON & JOHN JAY, THE FEDERALIST, of which multiple editions are available, (2) COLLEEN A. SHEEHAN & GARY L. MCDOWELL, FRIENDS OF THE CONSTITUTION: WRITINGS OF THE "OTHER" FEDERALISTS: 1787-88 (1998), and (3) THE COMPLETE ANTI-FEDERALIST (Herbert J. Storing, ed. 1981).

THE FOUNDERS' CONSTITUTION (Philip B. Kurland & Ralph Lerner, eds. 1986), online at https://press-pubs.uchicago.edu/founders/, is a five-volume collection of background materials for every clause of the Constitution and the Bill of Rights.

THE DOCUMENTARY HISTORY OF THE FIRST FEDERAL CONGRESS OF THE UNITED STATES OF AMERICA, sponsored by the National Historical Publications and Records Commission and George Washington University, includes the diary of Senator William Maclay, an important source of information about proceedings in the Senate, which were then closed to the general public.

Leading Modern Sources

THE HERITAGE GUIDE TO THE CONSTITUTION (to which your author contributes) discusses, clause by constitutional clause, both original meaning and modern jurisprudence. THE OXFORD GUIDE TO THE SUPREME COURT (Kermit L. Hall, ed., 2d ed., 2005) contains constitutional entries in a manner similar to the Heritage Guide, but it is a much larger book, and is dedicated primarily to the Supreme Court.

Jack N. Rakove, ORIGINAL MEANINGS (1996) is an excellent work by America's one of America's best politically liberal constitutional historians. See also Akhil Reed Amar, AMERICA'S CONSTITUTION: A BIOGRAPHY (2005), written by one of America's most highly regarded law professors—who also leans liberal.

Chapter One: History, Structure, and Preamble

History

My general discussion of how to use sources in recreating the Constitution's original legal force is *A Bibliography for Researching Original Understanding*, http://constitution.i2i.org/files/2013/11/Originalist-Bibliography-2013-1113.pdf. For law books in early America, see W. Hamilton Bryson, CENSUS OF COMMON LAW BOOKS IN COLONIAL VIRGINIA (1978); HERBERT A. JOHNSON, IMPORTED 18TH CENTURY LAW TREATISES IN AMERICAN LIBRARIES 1700-1799 (1978); and EDWIN WOLF II, THE BOOK CULTURE OF A COLONIAL AMERICAN CITY: PHILADELPHIA BOOKS, BOOKMEN, AND BOOKSELLERS (1988).

Valuable databases include The Gale Company's *Eighteenth Century Collections Online*, Proquest's *House of Commons Parliamentary Papers*, Evans' *Early American Imprints: Series I*, and JSTOR (all by subscription only); and the publicly available databases *Google Books*, *British History Online*, and the Library of Congress's *American Memory*.

Two surveys of the entire period from the beginning of pre-Revolutionary unrest through the ratification are Gordon Wood, THE CREATION OF THE AMERICAN REPUBLIC: 1776-1787 (1969) and Edmund S. Morgan, THE BIRTH OF THE REPUBLIC: 1763-89 (3d ed. 1992).

Focusing on the intellectual origins of the Revolution is TREVOR COLBOURN, THE LAMP OF EXPERIENCE: WHIG HISTORY AND THE INTELLECTUAL ORIGINS OF THE AMERICAN REVOLUTION (1965) (reissued by Liberty Fund, 1998). Other standard works include two by Bernard Bailyn: THE ORIGINS OF AMERICAN POLITICS (1969) and THE IDEOLOGICAL ORIGINS OF THE AMERICAN REVOLUTION (1967).

Readers wishing to explore these ideas through original sources can consult leading pamphlets from the pre-Revolutionary era, particularly James Otis, *The Rights of the British Colonies Asserted and Proved* (3d ed. 1766); Daniel Dulany, *Considerations on the Propriety of Imposing Taxes on the British Colonies* (1766); John Dickinson, *Letters from a Farmer in Pennsylvania* (1767-68) and James Wilson, *Considerations on the Nature and the Extent of the Legislative Authority of the British Parliament* (1774) (most of which are on the Internet) and John Adams, THE REVOLUTIONARY WRITINGS OF JOHN ADAMS (C. Bradley Thompson ed.) (Liberty Fund 2000).

For histories of the Revolution and the period leading up to it by members of the founding generation themselves, see David Ramsey, THE HISTORY OF THE AMERICAN REVOLUTION (1789) (Lester H. Cohen, ed., 1990 reprint) and Mercy Otis Warren, HISTORY OF THE RISE, PROGRESS AND TERMINATION OF THE AMERICAN REVOLUTION (1805). Ramsey served as Chairman of the Confederation Congress for a time, and thus presided in absence of the president. Mrs. Warren was both a leading Anti-Federalist and the sister of James Otis, one of the most prominent pre-revolutionary pamphleteers.

For works focusing more specifically on the origins of the Constitution, see those by Forrest McDonald, particularly NOVUS ORDO SECLORUM (1985) and Charles Warren, THE MAKING OF THE CONSTITUTION (1928).

If one were to pick two Founders most representative of American moderate opinion at the time the Constitution was ratified, one might well choose John Dickinson and Edmund Randolph. My article, *The Constitutional Contributions of John Dickinson*, 108 Penn. State L. Rev. 415 (2003), examines Dickinson's career, contributions, and political thought. The best biography of Dickinson is Milton E. Flower, JOHN DICKINSON: CONSERVATIVE REVOLUTIONARY (1983). Randolph's life is treated in John J. Reardon, EDMUND RANDOLPH: A BIOGRAPHY (1974).

Fiduciary Government/Public Trust

Several of articles that I authored or co-authored discuss the Founders' ideas of public trust: *The Constitution and the Public Trust*, 52 Buffalo L. Rev. 1077 (2004); *Judicial Review of Special Interest Spending: The General Welfare Clause and the Fiduciary Law of the Founders*, 11 Tex. Rev. L. & Pol. 239 (2007); and Gary Lawson, Guy I. Seidman & Robert G. Natelson, *The Fiduciary Foundations of Federal Equal Protection*, 94 B.U. L. Rev. 415 (2014). A co-authored book is Gary Lawson, Geoffrey Miller, Robert G. Natelson & Guy I. Seidman, THE ORIGINS OF THE NECESSARY AND PROPER CLAUSE (2010). My article, *The Government as Fiduciary: Lessons from the Reign of the Emperor Trajan*, 35 Richmond L. Rev. 191 (2001), is not about the Founding, but it surveys the fiduciary practices of the Roman Emperor most admired during the Founding era.

Some writers have assumed that the Constitution made no grants to the U.S. government as such. I think this is clearly incorrect. See Robert G. Natelson, *More News on the Powers Reserved Exclusively to the States*, 20 Federalist Soc'y Rev. 92, 95-96 (2019).

On "federal functions" see Robert G. Natelson, *Federal Functions: Execution of Powers the Constitution Grants to Persons and Entities Outside the Federal Government*, 23 U. Penn. J. Const. L. 193 (2021).

Further explaining the view that the permissible extent of congressional delegation depends on the power being delegated is Robert G. Natelson, *How Much Power May Congress Delegate to Federal Agencies?* https://i2i.org/how-much-power-may-congress-delegate-to-federal-agencies/.

For an article suggesting that Congress could delegate some responsibilities to just one house, see Seth Barrett Tillman, *A Textualist Defense of Article I, Section 7, Clause 3: Why Hollingsworth v. Virginia Was Rightly Decided, and Why INS v. Chadha Was Wrongly Reasoned*, 83 Tex. L. Rev. 1265 (2005).

Other Founding-era Values

A compelling survey of the Founders' values that focusses on rebutting mistaken claims about what they did, and did not believe, is Thomas G. West's VINDICATING THE FOUNDERS: RACE, SEX, CLASS, AND JUSTICE IN THE ORIGINS OF AMERICA (1997). My article, *A Reminder: The Constitutional Values of Sympathy and Independence*, 91 Ky. L.J. 353 (2003), examines two of the Founders' core principles often overlooked in modern discussions of the Constitution.

Chapter Two: Interpreting the Constitution

Readers wishing to wander in the thicket of competing modern theories of constitutional interpretation are welcome to sample the book entitled INTERPRETING THE CONSTITUTION: THE DEBATE OVER ORIGINAL INTENT (Jack N. Rakove ed. 1990). Randy E. Barnett, *Underlying Principles*, 24 Const. Comm. 405 (2007), contains a short discussion of how originalists and living constitutionists apply the Framers' underlying principles.

On applying the Founders' own interpretative methods to the Founders' document, see John O. McGinnis & Michael B. Rappaport, *Original Methods Originalism: A New Theory of Interpretation and the Case Against Construction*, 103 Nw. U. L. Rev. 751 (2009).

Largely due to the influence of a mistaken article published in the Harvard Law Review decades ago, many constitutional writers have been under the impression that Founding-era judges and lawyers considered only the text of a legal document—that is, the "original public meaning"—and not the subjective understanding behind the document. I corrected this in *The Founders' Hermeneutic: The Real Original Understanding of Original Intent*, 68 Ohio St. L.J. 1239 (2007). But for an article disagreeing, see John O. McGinnis & Michael P. Rappaport, *Unifying Original Intent and Original Public Meaning*, 113 Nw. U. L. Rev. 1371 (2019). I elaborated the case for subjective understanding in *Applying the Founders' Originalism*, 26 Federalist Soc'y Rev. 117 (2025).

Understanding the Founders requires familiarity with the Greco-Roman classical tradition. See Carl J. Richard, THE FOUNDERS AND THE CLASSICS: GREECE, ROME, AND THE AMERICAN ENLIGHTENMENT (1994) and Robert G. Natelson, *Why Constitutional Lawyers Need to Know Latin*, 19 Federalist Soc'y Rev. 74 (2018). It also requires knowing how the English language has changed. For an example, see Nora Tillman & Seth Barrett Tillman, *A Fragment on Shall and May*, 50 Am. J. Leg. Hist. 453 (2010).

Many 18th-century dictionaries are now available on the Internet. Do not rely solely on Samuel Johnson's famous dictionary, whose definitions can be idiosyncratic and archaic. For tips and observations on how to use 18th-century dictionaries, see George E. Maggs, *A Concise Guide to Using Dictionaries from the Founding Era to Determine the Original Meaning of the Constitution*, 82 Geo. Wash. L. Rev. 358 (2014).

Founding-era rules of construction are listed in T. Branch, PRINCIPIA LEGIS ET AEQUITATIS (1753) (available by subscription in the Gale database, Eighteenth Century Collections Online). A useful, if sometimes difficult, modern article discussing the Founders' use of interpretive rules is Caleb Nelson, *Originalism and Interpretive Conventions*, 70 U. Chi. L. Rev. 519 (2003).

Chapter Three: The States

On federalism, see Raoul Berger, FEDERALISM: THE FOUNDERS' DESIGN (1987). For a view (contrary to mine) in favor of the compact theory, see Kevin R.C. Gutzman, *Edmund Randolph and Virginia Constitutionalism*, 66 Rev. of Politics 469 (2004).

My article, *The Enumerated Powers of States*, 3 Nev. L.J. 469 (2003) collects most of the ratification-era representations by the Constitution's advocates as to the powers that would remain outside the federal sphere.

I reported additional representations in *The Founders Interpret the Constitution: The Division of Federal and State Powers,* 19 Federalist Soc'y Rev. 60 (2018) and *More News on the Powers Reserved Exclusively to the States,* 20 Federalist Soc'y Rev. 92 (2019).

My other articles explaining the Constitution's rules of federalism include *A Republic, Not a Democracy? Initiative, Referendum, and the Constitution's Guarantee Clause,* 80 Tex. L. Rev. 807 (2002); *Statutory Retroactivity: The Founders' View,* 39 Idaho L. Rev. 489 (2003) (discussing the Ex Post Facto Clauses and the Fifth Amendment); *The Original Meaning of the Privileges and Immunities Clause,* 43 Ga. L. Rev. 1117 (2009).

The Constitution, Invasion, Immigration, and the War Powers of States, 13 Brit. J. Am. L. Stud. 1 (2024) (which I co-authored with Andrew T. Hyman) is a detailed examination of reserved state war powers, allegiance, and the meaning of "invasion."

On the difference between treaties and compacts, see David E. Engdahl, *Characterization of Interstate Arrangements: When is a Compact not a Compact?* 64 Mich. L. Rev. 63 (1965).

There is wide scholarly debate about whether the federal judicial power allowed a private party to sue a non-consenting state. The discussion in the text is based principally on my own independent look at the evidence, including the often-overlooked interpretive resolutions of New York and Rhode Island. Caleb Nelson, *Sovereign Immunity as a Doctrine of Personal Jurisdiction,* 115 Harvard L. Rev. 1559 (2002) is one of the newer and better articles on the subject, and one can find other citations in its footnotes.

Chapter Four: The House, the Senate, and the Vice President

This book's discussion of advice and consent is based on my article, *"Advice" in the Constitution's Advice and Consent Clause: New Evidence from Contemporaneous Sources,* 19 Federalist Soc'y Rev. 60 (2018). See also Adam J. White, *Toward the Framers' Understanding of "Advice and Consent": A Historical and Textual Inquiry,* 29 Harvard J.L. & Pub. Pol'y 103, 136-39 (2005).

On the use of the word "emolument," see Robert G. Natelson, *The Original Meaning of "Emoluments" in the Constitution,* 52 Ga. L. Rev. 1 (2017). It collects the evidence and cites other views as well.

For other sources relevant to this chapter, see the list under the heading "Sources Relevant Across Chapters."

Chapter Five: About the Grants of Powers to Congress

The organizational scheme of Article I is discussed in Robert G. Natelson, *The Original Meaning of the Constitution's "Executive Vesting Clause"—Evidence from 18th century Drafting Practice*, 31 Whittier L. Rev. 1 (2009).

On the Origination Clause, see Robert G. Natelson, *The Founders' Origination Clause (And Implications for the Affordable Care Act)*, 38 Harvard J.L. & Pub. Policy 629 (2015).

On the Necessary and Proper Clause, see Gary Lawson, Geoffrey Miller, Robert G. Natelson & Guy Seidman, THE ORIGINS OF THE NECESSARY AND PROPER CLAUSE (Cambridge Univ. Press 2010). See also my own articles, *Tempering the Commerce Power*, 68 Mont. L. Rev. 95 (2007); *The Agency Law Origins of the Necessary and Proper Clause*, 55 Case Western Res. L. Rev. 243 (2004); and *More News on the Powers Reserved Exclusively to the States*, 20 Federalist Soc'y Rev. 92 (2019). The last of these addresses the claim that the Necessary and Proper Clause recognizes unenumerated congressional powers.

Chapter Six: The Authority of Congress

The discussion of Congress's power under the Taxation Clause relies on my articles, *Judicial Review of Special Interest Spending: The General Welfare Clause and the Fiduciary Law of the Founders*, 11 Tex. Rev. L. & Pol. 239 (2007); *The General Welfare Clause and the Public Trust: An Essay in Original Understanding*, 52 U. Kan. L. Rev. 1 (2003); and *What the Constitution Means by "Duties, Imposts, and Excises"—and Taxes (Direct or Otherwise)*, 66 Case Western Res. L. Rev. 297 (2015). I collected Founding-era direct tax statutes in *More Evidence that "Direct Taxes" include Levies on Wealth and Income*, https://reason.com/volokh/2024/07/19/more-evidence-that-direct-taxes-include-levies-on-wealth-and-income/.

Some writers have claimed that the Commerce Power was intended to encompass authority over the entire economy or even over all human interactions. As shown in Richard A. Epstein, *The Proper Scope of the Commerce Power*, 73 Va. L. Rev. 1387 (1987), the Constitution's text does not support this hypothesis. Neither do studies of how the founding generation used the word "commerce" or the phrase "regulate commerce." Randy E. Barnett, *The Original Meaning of the Commerce Clause*, 68 U. Chi. L. Rev. 101 (2001); Randy E. Barnett, *New Evidence of the*

Original Meaning of the Commerce Clause, 55 Ark. L. Rev. 847 (2003); Calvin H. Johnson, *The Panda's Thumb: The Modest and Mercantilist Original Meaning of the Commerce Clause*, 13 Wm. & Mary Bill of Rts. J. 1 (2004); Robert G. Natelson & David Kopel, *Commerce in the Commerce Clause*, 109 Mich. L. Rev. First Impressions 55 (2010); Robert G. Natelson, *The Legal Meaning of "Commerce" In the Commerce Clause*, 80 St. John's L. Rev. 789 (2006) and *The Meaning of 'Regulate Commerce' to the Constitution's Ratifiers*, 23 Federalist Soc'y Rev. 307 (2022).

This chapter also relies on my articles *The Original Meaning of the Indian Commerce Clause*, 85 Denver U. L. Rev. 201 (2007); *The Original Understanding of the Indian Commerce Clause: An Update*, 23 Federalist Soc'y Rev. 209 (2022); *Paper Money and the Original Understanding of the Coinage Clause*, 31 Harvard J.L. & Pub. Pol. 1017 (2008); and *Federal Land Retention and the Constitution's Property Clause: The Original Understanding*, 76 U. Colo. L. Rev. 327 (2005).

For the view (agreed with in this book) that there is no general spending power in the Taxation Clause and also for the view (contested in this book) that the Property Clause included an unrestricted spending power, see David E. Engdahl, *The Basis of the Spending Power*, 18 Seattle L. Rev. 215 (1995).

The material on the Times, Places and Manner Clause is based on my article, *The Original Scope of the Congressional Power to Regulate Elections*, 13 U. Pa. J. Const. L. 1 (2010).

Chapter Seven: The Executive

In my view, the "vesting clause" thesis has been put to rest by Curtis A. Bradley & Martin S. Flaherty, *Executive Power Essentialism and Foreign Affairs*, 102 Mich. L. Rev. 545 (2004), which exhaustively examines the records from the federal convention and the ratification debates, and by my own article, *The Original Meaning of the Constitution's "Executive Vesting Clause"—Evidence from 18th century Drafting Practice*, 31 Whittier L. Rev. 1 (2009).

Arguments to the contrary include Charles C. Thach, Jr., THE CREATION OF THE PRESIDENCY, 1775-1789 (reissued by Liberty Fund in 2007) and Steven G. Calabresi and Saikrishna B. Prakash, *The President's Power to Execute the Laws*, 104 Yale L.J. 541 (1994). In the latter article, see also the conclusion that the executive was to be unitary rather than plural—seems clearly correct.

Readers interested in commissions and instructions to colonial governors should consult ROYAL INSTRUCTIONS TO BRITISH COLONIAL GOVERNORS 1670-1776 (Leonard Woods Labaree ed., 1935) and Anthony Stokes, A VIEW OF THE CONSTITUTION OF THE BRITISH COLONIES (1783). The latter work is available online from Google Books.

The text mentions several Article II drafting defects. For another, see Robert J. Reinstein, *Recognition: A Case Study on the Original Understanding of Executive Power*, 45 U. Rich. L. Rev. 801 (2011).

Finally, Robert G. Natelson, *The Origins and Meaning of "Vacancies that May Happen During the Recess" in the Constitution's Recess Appointments Clause*, 37 Harvard J. of L. & Pub. Pol'y 199 (2014) is a comprehensive review of the Founding-era meanings of "the Recess" and "may happen."

Chapter Eight: The Judicial Branch

This chapter draws on my article, *The Original Meaning of the Constitution's "Executive Vesting Clause"—Evidence from 18th century Drafting Practice*, 31 Whittier L. Rev. 1 (2009).

Scholarship has fully debunked the once-common opinion that the Founders did not contemplate judicial review. See Randy E. Barnett, *The Original Meaning of the Judicial Power*, 12 Sup. Ct. Econ. Rev. 115 (2004) and William Michael Treanor, *Judicial Review Before Marbury*, 58 Stanford L. Rev. 455 (2005).

Chapter Nine: The Bill of Rights and other External Limitations on Federal Powers

A documentary collection devoted specifically to the Bill of Rights is Bernard Schwartz, THE BILL OF RIGHTS: A DOCUMENTARY HISTORY (2 vols.) (1971). Moreover, THE DOCUMENTARY HISTORY OF THE RATIFICATION OF THE CONSTITUTION has been expanded to include five volumes on the Bill of Rights, of which three have been published as of the date of this edition.

First Amendment

There is little reliable writing on the original force of the Free Speech, Press, Assembly, and Petition Clauses. The best-known book on the subject is Leonard W. Levy's LEGACY OF SUPPRESSION (1960), which, among other defects, exaggerated Founding-era restrictions on speech—a fault he corrected somewhat in his EMERGENCE OF A FREE PRESS (1985).

My first effort to fill the gap (other than earlier editions of this book) is Robert G. Natelson, *Does "The Freedom of the Press" Include a Right to Anonymity? The Original Understanding*, 9 N.Y.U. J. of Law & Liberty 160 (2015).

There is a great deal of writing on the Religion Clauses, but much of it is not historically accurate. My principal contribution is *The Original Meaning of the Establishment Clause*, 14 Wm. & Mary Bill Rights J. 73 (2005).

A collection of documents pertaining to government and religion is THE SACRED RIGHTS OF CONSCIENCE (Daniel L. Dreisbach & Mark David Hall eds. 2009). Useful articles include Paul Horwitz, *Religious Tests in the Mirror: The Constitutional Law and Constitutional Etiquette of Religion in Judicial Nominations*, 15 Wm. & Mary Bill Rts. J. 75 (2006); Noah Feldman, *The Intellectual Origins of the Establishment Clause*, 77 N.Y.U. L. Rev. 346 (2002); and Michael W. McConnell, *The Origins and Understanding of the Free Exercise of Religion*, 103 Harvard L. Rev. 1409 (1990). Two helpful books are Philip Hamburger, SEPARATION OF CHURCH AND STATE (2004) and Daniel L. Dreisbach, THOMAS JEFFERSON AND THE WALL OF SEPARATION BETWEEN CHURCH AND STATE (2002).

As noted in the text, the Supreme Court's Free Speech jurisprudence is a creation of the 20th century, with almost no connection with the actual meaning of the Free Speech Clause. For a short and celebratory description of that development, see Geoffrey R. Stone, *Free Speech in the Twenty-First Century: Ten Lessons from the Twentieth Century*, 38 Pepperdine L. Rev. 273 (2009).

Second Amendment

Although I have followed a different line of argument to the conclusion that the Second Amendment created an individual, as well as a state, right, the leading book on the subject is probably Stephen P. Halbrook,

THE FOUNDERS' SECOND AMENDMENT: ORIGINS OF THE RIGHT TO BEAR ARMS (2008).

My colleague at the Independence Institute, Dave Kopel, is America's leading Second Amendment scholar. His summary of British efforts to disarm Americans before the Revolution explains why the Second Amendment is worded as it is. David B. Kopel, *How the British Gun Control Program Precipitated the American Revolution*, 6 Charleston L. Rev. 283 (2012).

Fifth and Sixth Amendments

Two worthwhile pieces on the Takings Clause are William Michael Treanor, *The Original Understanding of the Takings Clause and the Political Process*, 95 Columbia L. Rev. 782 (1995) and Matthew P. Harrington, *"Public Uses" and the Original Understanding of the So-Called "Takings Clause,"* 53 Hastings L.J. 1245 (2002).

I examined the question of whether the Constitution granted an eminent domain power in *Did the Constitution Grant the Federal Government Eminent Domain Power? Using Eighteenth Century Law to Answer Constitutional Questions*, 19 Federalist Soc'y Rev. 88 (2018). On both the Takings and Due Process Clauses, see Robert G. Natelson, *Statutory Retroactivity: The Founders' View*, 39 Idaho L. Rev. 489 (2003).

Several writers have made brave attempts to prove that the Founders believed Due Process of Law to include a range of procedural and substantive protections. Two examples are Rodney L. Mott, DUE PROCESS OF LAW, pp. 87-142 (1926) and Frederick Mark Gedicks, *An Originalist Defense of Substantive Due Process: Magna Carta, Higher-Law Constitutionalism, and the Fifth Amendment*, 58 Emory L.J. 585 (2009). Others, while agreeing that the Founders had a narrow view of due process, suggest that the concept expanded significantly in time for ratification of the Fourteenth Amendment's Due Process Clause in 1868. A review of the cases cited for that position, however, shows that (other than dicta in the Dred Scott case) they were simply applications of the "no retroactivity" principle to legislatures. The idea that the due process guarantee imposed broad limits on the ability of legislatures to restrict individual rights does not seem to have been promulgated widely until the late nineteenth century.

The dispute over the extent to which the Bill of Rights applies to military personnel is captured in two contending articles in Harvard Law Review: Gordon D. Henderson, *Courts-Martial and the Constitution: The Original Understanding*, 71 Harvard L. Rev. 293 (1957) and Frederick

Bernays Wiener, *Courts-Martial and the Bill of Rights: The Original Practice*, 72 Harvard L. Rev. 1 & 266 (1958). However, both articles assume that military personnel had no right to trial by jury.

Eighth Amendment

Treatments of the Eighth Amendment are David F. Forte, *Cruel and Unusual Punishment* in THE HERITAGE GUIDE TO THE CONSTITUTION (2d ed. 2014); Calvin R. Massey, *The Excessive Fines Clause and Punitive Damages: Some Lessons from History*, 40 Vanderbilt L. Rev. 1233 (1987); and Nicholas M. McLean, *Livelihood, Ability to Pay, and the Original Meaning of the Excessive Fines Clause*, 40 Hastings Const. L.Q. 833 (2013). Laurence Claus, *The Antidiscrimination Eighth Amendment*, 28 Harvard J.L. & Pub. Pol. 119 (2004) ascribes a different meaning from the one I have adopted in the text.

Chapter Ten: The Ninth and Tenth Amendments

For a range of views on the Ninth Amendment, see Randy E. Barnett, RIGHTS RETAINED BY THE PEOPLE: THE HISTORY AND MEANING OF THE NINTH AMENDMENT (1990). In general, treatments of the amendment fail to recognize that in 18th-century discourse, the words "rights" and "powers" were often synonyms. Calvin Massey's engaging book, SILENT RIGHTS (1995), takes a while to arrive to that realization, and when it does, its argument that the Ninth Amendment was intended as more than rule of construction almost vanishes. But it is one of the best surveys of the Founding-era record on the subject.

I examined the practical effect the Tenth Amendment was supposed to have in *The Enumerated Powers of States*, 3 Nev. L.J. 469 (2003) and in three articles for Federalist Society Review: *The Founders Interpret the Constitution: The Division of Federal and State Powers*, 19 Federalist Soc'y. Rev. 60 (2018); *More News on the Powers Reserved Exclusively to the States*, 20 Federalist Soc'y. Rev. 92 (2019); and *The Meaning of "Regulate Commerce" to the Constitution's Ratifiers*, 23 Federalist Soc'y Rev. 307 (2022).

Chapter Eleven: Removal from Office

See Robert G. Natelson, *New Evidence on the Constitution's Impeachment Standard: "high . . . Misdemeanors" Means Serious Crimes*, 21 Federalist Soc'y

Rev. 24 (2020). This supersedes the discussion of "high misdemeanors" in Raoul Berger, IMPEACHMENT: THE CONSTITUTIONAL PROBLEMS (1973).

Readers interested in the history of impeachment can consult the anonymous work by "A Barrister at Law" entitled THE LAW OF PARLIAMENTARY IMPEACHMENTS (1788), appearing in the Eighteenth Century Collections Online database (by subscription only). Also in that database is William Petyt, JUS PARLIAMENTARIUM: OR THE ANTIENT POWER, JURISDICTION, RIGHTS, LIBERTIES, AND PRIVILEGES OF THE MOST HIGH COURT OF PARLIAMENT (1741). British History Online, https://www.british-history.ac.uk/ offers many of the Parliamentary journals with articles of impeachment.

The debate in the First Congress on presidential removal of executive branch officials appears in the first volume of the ANNALS OF CONGRESS (Joseph Gales, Sr., ed. 1834), available at:

https://www.congress.gov/annals-of-congress/volume-1.pdf.

Chapter Twelve: Ratification and Amendment

The copious evidence that an amendments convention is a convention of the states is collected in Robert G. Natelson, *Is the Constitution's Convention for Proposing Amendments a "Mystery"? Overlooked Evidence in the Narrative of Uncertainty*, 104 Marquette L. Rev. 1 (2020), supplemented by *List of Additional Founding-era Descriptions of an Article V Convention as a "Convention of States*," https://articlevinfocenter.com/list-of-additional-founding-era-descriptions-of-an-article-v-convention-as-a-convention-of-states/.

My publications on the amendment process include THE LAW OF ARTICLE V: STATE INITIATION OF CONSTITUTIONAL AMENDMENTS (Apis Books, 2d ed. 2020); *Counting to Two Thirds: How Close Are We to A Convention for Proposing Amendments to the Constitution?* 19 Federalist Soc'y Rev. 50 (2018); *Founding-era Conventions and the Meaning of the Constitution's "Convention for Proposing Amendments"*, 65 Fla. L. Rev. 615 (2013); *The Article V Convention Process and the Restoration of Federalism*, 36 Harvard J. L. & Pub. Pol. 955 (2013); and *Proposing Constitutional Amendments by Convention: Rules Governing the Process*, 78 Tenn. L. Rev. 693 (2011). See also the Article V Information Center, https://articlevinfocenter.com/, which I moderate.

Other useful articles on the amendment process are Henry P. Monaghan, *We the People[s], Original Understanding, and Constitutional Amendment*, 96 Columbia L. Rev. 121 (1996); Michael B. Rappaport, *The Constitutionality of a Limited Convention: An Originalist Analysis*, 28 Const. Comment. 53 (2012); and Michael Stern, *Reopening the Constitutional Road to Reform: Toward a Safeguarded Article V Convention*, 78 Tenn. L. Rev. 765 (2011).

Chapter Thirteen: Conclusion

Two books mentioned above—The HERITAGE GUIDE and Professor Amar's AMERICAN CONSTITUTION—offer the reader contrasting views of modern constitutional law.

My view of the change in constitutional interpretation during the late 1930s and early 1940s is found in the series of essays, *1937-1944: How the Supreme Court Re-wrote the Constitution–the Complete Series*, https://i2i.org/1937-1944-complete-series/. See also Robert G. Natelson & David Kopel, *Health Insurance is not "Commerce"*, Nat'l L. J. (May 28, 2011).

APPENDIX

The Constitution of the United States as of December 15, 1791

(Article and Section numbers appear in the original and capitalization is as in original, including oversights. Clause numbers have been added.)

***

We the People of the United States, in Order to form a more perfect Union, establish Justice, insure domestic Tranquility, provide for the common defence, promote the general Welfare, and secure the Blessings of Liberty to ourselves and our Posterity, do ordain and establish this Constitution for the United States of America.

ARTICLE I

Section 1.

All legislative Powers herein granted shall be vested in a Congress of the United States, which shall consist of a Senate and House of Representatives.

Section 2.

[1] The House of Representatives shall be composed of Members chosen every second Year by the People of the several States, and the Electors in each State shall have the Qualifications requisite for Electors of the most numerous Branch of the State Legislature.

[2] No person shall be a Representative who shall not have attained to the Age of twenty five Years, and been seven Years a Citizen of the United States, and who shall not, when elected, be an Inhabitant of that State in which he shall be chosen.

[3] Representatives and direct Taxes shall be apportioned among the several States which may be included within this Union, according to their respective Numbers, which shall be determined by adding to the whole Number of free Persons, including those bound to Service for a Term of Years, and excluding Indians not taxed, three-fifths of all other Persons. The actual Enumeration shall be made within three Years after the first Meeting of the Congress of the United States, and within every subsequent Term of ten Years in such Manner as they shall by Law direct. The Number of Representatives shall not exceed one for every thirty Thousand, but each State shall have at Least one Representative; and until such enumeration shall be made, the State of New Hampshire shall be entitled to chuse three, Massachusetts eight, Rhode Island and Providence Plantations one, Connecticut five, New York six, New Jersey four, Pennsylvania eight, Delaware one, Maryland six, Virginia ten, North Carolina five, South Carolina five, and Georgia three.

[4] When vacancies happen in the Representation from any State, the Executive Authority thereof shall issue Writs of Election to fill such Vacancies.

[5] The House of Representatives shall chuse their Speaker and other Officers; and shall have the sole Power of Impeachment.

Section 3.

[1] The Senate of the United States shall be composed of two Senators from each State, chosen by the Legislature thereof, for six Years; and each Senator shall have one Vote.

[2] Immediately after they shall be assembled in Consequence of the first Election, they shall be divided as equally as may be into three Classes. The Seats of the Senators of the first Class shall be vacated at the

Expiration of the second Year, of the second Class at the Expiration of the fourth Year, and of the third Class at the Expiration of the sixth Year, so that one third may be chosen every second Year; and if Vacancies happen by Resignation, or otherwise, during the Recess of the Legislature of any State, the Executive thereof may make temporary Appointments until the next Meeting of the Legislature, which shall then fill such Vacancies.

[3] No person shall be a Senator who shall not have attained to the Age of thirty years, and been nine Years a Citizen of the United States, and who shall not, when elected, be an Inhabitant of that State for which he shall be chosen.

[4] The Vice President of the United States shall be President of the Senate, but shall have no Vote, unless they be equally divided.

[5] The Senate shall chuse their other Officers, and also a President pro tempore, in the Absence of the Vice President, or when he shall exercise the Office of President of the United States.

[6] The Senate shall have the sole Power to try all Impeachments. When sitting for that Purpose, they shall be on Oath or Affirmation. When the President of the United States is tried, the Chief Justice shall preside: and no Person shall be convicted without the Concurrence of two thirds of the Members present.

[7] Judgment in Cases of Impeachment shall not extend further than to removal from Office, and disqualification to hold and enjoy any Office of honor, Trust or Profit under the United States: but the Party convicted shall nevertheless be liable and subject to Indictment, Trial, Judgment and Punishment, according to Law.

Section 4.

[1] The Times, Places and Manner of holding Elections for Senators and Representatives, shall be prescribed in each State by the Legislature thereof; but the Congress may at any time by Law make or alter such Regulations, except as to the Places of choosing Senators.

[2] The Congress shall assemble at least once in every Year, and such Meeting shall be on the first Monday in December, unless they shall by Law appoint a different Day.

Section 5.

[1] Each House shall be the Judge of the Elections, Returns, and Qualifications of its own Members, and a Majority of each shall constitute a Quorum to do Business; but a smaller Number may adjourn from day to day, and may be authorized to compel the Attendance of absent Members, in such Manner, and under such Penalties as each House may provide.

[2] Each House may determine the Rules of its Proceedings, punish its Members for disorderly Behaviour, and, with the Concurrence of two thirds, expel a Member.

[3] Each House shall keep a Journal of its Proceedings, and from time to time publish the same, excepting such Parts as may in their Judgment require Secrecy; and the Yeas and Nays of the Members of either House on any question shall, at the Desire of one fifth of those present, be entered on the Journal.

[4] Neither House, during the Session of Congress, shall, without the Consent of the other, adjourn for more than three days, nor to any other Place than that in which the two Houses shall be sitting.

Section 6.

[1] The Senators and Representatives shall receive a Compensation for their Services, to be ascertained by Law, and paid out of the Treasury of the United States. They shall in all Cases, except Treason, Felony and Breach of the Peace, be privileged from Arrest during their Attendance at the Session of their Respective Houses, and in going to and from the same; and for any Speech or Debate in either House, they shall not be questioned in any other Place.

[2] No Senator or Representative shall, during the Time for which he was elected, be appointed to any civil Office under the Authority of the United States, which shall have been created, or the Emoluments whereof shall have been encreased during such time; and no Person holding any Office under the United States, shall be a Member of either House during his Continuance in Office.

Section 7.

[1] All Bills for raising Revenue shall originate in the House of Representatives; but the Senate may propose or concur with Amendments as

on other Bills.

[2] Every Bill which shall have passed the House of Representatives and the Senate, shall, before it become a Law, be presented to the President of the United States; If he approve he shall sign it, but if not he shall return it, with his Objections to that House in which it shall have originated, who shall enter the Objections at large on their Journal, and proceed to reconsider it. If after such Reconsideration two thirds of that House shall agree to pass the Bill, it shall be sent, together with the Objections, to the other House, by which it shall likewise be reconsidered, and if approved by two thirds of that House, it shall become a Law. But in all such Cases the Votes of both Houses shall be determined by yeas and Nays, and the Names of the Persons voting for and against the Bill shall be entered on the Journal of each House respectively. If any Bill shall not be returned by the President within ten Days (Sundays excepted) after it shall have been presented to him, the Same shall be a Law, in like Manner as if he had signed it, unless the Congress by their Adjournment prevent its Return, in which Case it shall not be a Law.

[3] Every Order, Resolution, or Vote to which the Concurrence of the Senate and House of Representatives may be necessary (except on a question of adjournment) shall be presented to the President of the United States; and before the Same shall take Effect, shall be approved by him, or being disapproved by him, shall be repassed by two thirds of the Senate and House of Representatives, according to the Rules and Limitations prescribed in the Case of a Bill.

Section 8.

[1] The Congress shall have Power

To lay and collect Taxes, Duties, Imposts and Excises, to pay the Debts and provide for the Common Defence and general Welfare of the United States; but all Duties, Imposts and Excises shall be uniform throughout the United States;

[2] To borrow Money on the credit of the United States;

[3] To regulate Commerce with foreign Nations, and among the several States, and with the Indian Tribes;

[4] To establish an uniform Rule of Naturalization, and uniform Laws on the subject of Bankruptcies throughout the United States;

[5] To coin Money, regulate the Value thereof, and of foreign Coin,

and fix the Standard of Weights and Measures;

[6] To provide for the Punishment of counterfeiting the Securities and current Coin of the United States;

[7] To establish Post Offices and post Roads;

[8] To promote the Progress of Science and useful Arts, by securing for limited Times to Authors and Inventors the exclusive Right to their respective Writings and Discoveries;

[9] To constitute tribunals inferior to the supreme Court;

[10] To define and punish Piracies and Felonies committed on the High Seas, and Offenses against the Law of Nations;

[11] To declare War, grant Letters of Marque and Reprisal, and make Rules concerning Captures on Land and Water;

[12] To raise and support Armies, but no Appropriation of Money to that Use shall be for a longer Term than two Years;

[13] To provide and maintain a Navy;

[14] To make Rules for the Government and Regulation of the land and naval Forces;

[15] To provide for calling forth the Militia to execute the Laws of the Union, suppress Insurrections and repel Invasions;

[16] To provide for organizing, arming, and disciplining, the Militia, and for governing such Part of them as may be employed in the Service of the United States, reserving to the States respectively, the Appointment of the Officers, and the Authority of training the Militia according to the discipline prescribed by Congress;

[17] To exercise exclusive Legislation in all Cases whatsoever, over such District (not exceeding ten Miles square) as may, by Cession of particular States, and the Acceptance of Congress, become the Seat of the Government of the United States, and to exercise like Authority over all Places purchased by the Consent of the Legislature of the State in which the Same shall be, for the Erection of Forts, Magazines, Arsenals, dock-Yards, and other needful Buildings;—And

[18] To make all Laws which shall be necessary and proper for carrying into Execution the foregoing Powers, and all other Powers vested by this Constitution in the Government of the United States, or in any Department or Officer thereof.

Section 9.

[1] The Migration or Importation of such Persons as any of the

States now existing shall think proper to admit, shall not be prohibited by the Congress prior to the Year one thousand eight hundred and eight, but a Tax or duty may be imposed on such Importation, not exceeding ten dollars for each Person.

[2] The Privilege of the Writ of Habeas Corpus shall not be suspended, unless when in Cases of Rebellion or Invasion the public Safety may require it.

[3] No Bill of Attainder or ex post facto Law shall be passed.

[4] No Capitation, or other direct, Tax shall be laid, unless in Proportion to the Census or Enumeration herein before directed to be taken.

[5] No Tax or Duty shall be laid on Articles exported from any State.

[6] No Preference shall be given by any Regulation of Commerce or Revenue to the Ports of one State over those of another: nor shall Vessels bound to, or from, one State, be obliged to enter, clear, or pay Duties in another.

[7] No Money shall be drawn from the Treasury, but in Consequence of Appropriations made by Law; and a regular Statement and Account of the Receipts and Expenditures of all public Money shall be published from time to time.

[8] No Title of Nobility shall be granted by the United States: and no Person holding any Office of Profit or Trust under them, shall, without the Consent of the Congress, accept of any present, Emolument, Office, or Title of any kind whatever from any King, Prince, or foreign State.

Section 10.

[1] No State shall enter into any Treaty, Alliance, or Confederation; grant Letters of Marque and Reprisal; coin Money; emit Bills of Credit; make any Thing but gold and silver Coin a Tender in Payment of Debts; pass any Bill of Attainder, ex post facto Law, or Law impairing the Obligation of Contracts, or grant any Title of Nobility.

[2] No State shall, without the Consent of the Congress, lay any Imposts or Duties on Imports or Exports, except what may be absolutely necessary for executing it's inspection Laws: and the net Produce of all Duties and Imposts, laid by any State on Imports or Exports, shall be for the Use of the Treasury of the United States; and all such Laws shall be subject to the Revision and Controul of the Congress.

[3] No State shall, without the Consent of Congress, lay any Duty of

Tonnage, keep Troops, or Ships of War in time of Peace, enter into any Agreement or Compact with another State, or with a foreign Power, or engage in War, unless actually invaded, or in such imminent Danger as will not admit of delay.

ARTICLE II

Section 1.

[1] The executive Power shall be vested in a President of the United States of America. He shall hold his Office during the Term of four Years, and, together with the Vice President, chosen for the same Term, be elected, as follows:

[2] Each State shall appoint, in such Manner as the Legislature thereof may direct, a Number of Electors, equal to the whole Number of Senators and Representatives to which the State may be entitled in the Congress: but no Senator or Representative, or Person holding an Office of Trust or Profit under the United States, shall be appointed an Elector.

[3] The Electors shall meet in their respective States, and vote by Ballot for two Persons, of whom one at least shall not be an Inhabitant of the same State with themselves. And they shall make a List of all the Persons voted for, and of the Number of Votes for each; which List they shall sign and certify, and transmit sealed to the Seat of the Government of the United States, directed to the President of the Senate. The President of the Senate shall, in the Presence of the Senate and House of Representatives, open all the Certificates, and the Votes shall then be counted. The Person having the greatest Number of Votes shall be the President, if such Number be a Majority of the whole Number of Electors appointed; and if there be more than one who have such Majority, and have an equal Number of Votes, then the House of Representatives shall immediately chuse by Ballot one of them for President; and if no Person have a Majority, then from the five highest on the List the said House shall in like Manner chuse the President. But in chusing the President, the Votes shall be taken by States, the Representation from each State having one Vote; a quorum for this Purpose shall consist of a Member or Members from two thirds of the States, and a Majority of all the States shall be necessary to a Choice. In every Case, after the Choice of the President, the Person having the greatest Number of Votes of the

Electors shall be the Vice President. But if there should remain two or more who have equal Votes, the Senate shall chuse from them by Ballot the Vice President.

[4] The Congress may determine the Time of chusing the Electors, and the Day on which they shall give their Votes; which Day shall be the same throughout the United States.

[5] No Person except a natural born Citizen, or a Citizen of the United States, at the time of the Adoption of this Constitution, shall be eligible to the Office of President; neither shall any Person be eligible to that Office who shall not have attained to the Age of thirty five Years, and been fourteen Years a Resident within the United States.

[6] In Case of the Removal of the President from Office, or of his Death, Resignation, or Inability to discharge the Powers and Duties of the said Office, the Same shall devolve on the Vice President, and the Congress may by Law provide for the Case of Removal, Death, Resignation, or Inability, both of the President and Vice President, declaring what Officer shall then act as President, and such Officer shall act accordingly, until the Disability be removed, or a President shall be elected.

[7] The President shall, at stated Times, receive for his Services, a Compensation, which shall neither be encreased nor diminished during the Period for which he shall have been elected, and he shall not receive within that Period any other Emolument from the United States, or any of them.

[8] Before he enter on the Execution of His Office, he shall take the following Oath or Affirmation:—"I do solemnly swear (or affirm) that I will faithfully execute the Office of President of the United States, and will to the best of my Ability, preserve, protect and defend the Constitution of the United States."

Section 2.

[1] The President shall be Commander in Chief of the Army and Navy of the United States, and of the Militia of the several States, when called into the actual Service of the United States; he may require the Opinion, in writing, of the principal Officer in each of the executive Departments, upon any Subject relating to the Duties of their respective Offices, and he shall have Power to grant Reprieves and Pardons for

Offenses against the United States, except in Cases of Impeachment.

[2] He shall have Power, by and with the Advice and Consent of the Senate, to make Treaties, provided two thirds of the Senators present concur; and he shall nominate, and by and with the Advice and Consent of the Senate, shall appoint Ambassadors, other public Ministers and Consuls, Judges of the Supreme Court, and all other Officers of the United States, whose Appointments are not herein otherwise provided for, and which shall be established by Law: but the Congress may by Law vest the Appointment of such inferior Officers, as they think proper, in the President alone, in the Courts of Law, or in the Heads of Departments.

[3] The President shall have Power to fill up all Vacancies that may happen during the Recess of the Senate, by granting Commissions which shall expire at the End of their next Session.

Section 3.

He shall from time to time give to the Congress Information of the State of the Union, and recommend to their Consideration such Measures as he shall judge necessary and expedient; he may, on extraordinary Occasions, convene both Houses, or either of them, and in Case of Disagreement between them, with Respect to the Time of Adjournment, he may adjourn them to such Time as he shall think proper; he shall receive Ambassadors and other public Ministers; he shall take Care that the Laws be faithfully executed, and shall Commission all the Officers of the United States.

Section 4.

The President, Vice President and all civil Officers of the United States, shall be removed from Office on Impeachment for, and Conviction of, Treason, Bribery, or other high Crimes and Misdemeanors.

ARTICLE III

Section 1.

The judicial Power of the United States, shall be vested in one supreme Court, and in such inferior Courts as the Congress may from time to time ordain and establish. The Judges, both of the supreme and inferior Courts, shall hold their Offices during good Behaviour, and shall, at stated Times, receive for their Services, a Compensation, which shall not be diminished during their Continuance in Office.

Section 2.

[1] The judicial Power shall extend to all Cases, in Law and Equity, arising under this Constitution, the Laws of the United States, and Treaties made, or which shall be made, under their Authority,—to all Cases affecting Ambassadors, other public Ministers and Consuls;—to all Cases of admiralty and maritime Jurisdiction;—to Controversies to which the United States shall be a Party;—to Controversies between two or more States;—between a State and Citizens of another State;—between citizens of different States,—between citizens of the same State claiming Lands under Grants of different States, and between a State, or the Citizens thereof, and foreign States, Citizens or Subjects.

[2] In all Cases affecting Ambassadors, other public Ministers and Consuls, and those in which a State shall be Party, the supreme Court shall have original Jurisdiction. In all the other Cases before mentioned, the supreme Court shall have appellate Jurisdiction, both as to Law and Fact, with such Exceptions, and under such Regulations as the Congress shall make.

[3] The Trial of all Crimes, except in Cases of Impeachment, shall be by Jury; and such Trial shall be held in the State where the said Crimes shall have been committed; but when not committed within any State, the Trial shall be at such Place or Places as the Congress may by Law have directed.

Section 3.

[1] Treason against the United States, shall consist only in levying War against them, or in adhering to their Enemies, giving them Aid and Comfort. No Person shall be convicted of Treason unless on the Testimony of two Witnesses to the same overt Act, or on Confession in open Court.

[2] The Congress shall have Power to declare the Punishment of Treason, but no Attainder of Treason shall work Corruption of Blood, or Forfeiture except during the Life of the Person attainted.

ARTICLE IV

Section 1.

Full Faith and Credit shall be given in each State to the public Acts, Records, and judicial Proceedings of every other State And the Congress may by general Laws prescribe the Manner in which such Acts, Records and Proceedings shall be proved, and the Effect thereof.

Section 2.

[1] The Citizens of each State shall be entitled to all Privileges and Immunities of Citizens in the several States.

[2] A Person charged in any State with Treason, Felony, or other Crime, who shall flee from Justice, and found in another State, shall on Demand of the executive Authority of the State from which he fled, be delivered up to be removed to the State having Jurisdiction of the Crime.

[3] No Person held to Service of Labour in one State, under the Laws thereof, escaping into another, shall, in Consequence of any Law or Regulation therein, be discharged from such Service or Labour, but shall be delivered upon Claim of the Party to whom such Service or Labour may be due.

Section 3.

[1] New States may be admitted by the Congress into this Union; but no new State shall be formed or erected within the Jurisdiction of any other State; nor any State be formed by the Junction of two or more States, or Parts of States, without the Consent of the Legislatures of the States concerned as well as of the Congress.

[2] The Congress shall have Power to dispose of and make all needful Rules and Regulations respecting the Territory or other Property belonging to the United States; and nothing in this Constitution shall be so construed as to Prejudice any Claims of the United States, or of any particular State.

Section 4.

The United States shall guarantee to every State in this Union a Republican Form of Government, and shall protect each of them against Invasion; and on Application of the Legislature, or of the Executive (when the Legislature cannot be convened) against domestic Violence.

ARTICLE V

The Congress, whenever two thirds of both Houses shall deem it necessary, shall propose Amendments to this Constitution, or, on the Application of the Legislatures of two thirds of the several States, shall call a Convention for proposing Amendments, which, in either Case, shall be valid to all Intents and Purposes, as Part of this Constitution, when ratified by the Legislatures of three fourths of the several States, or by Convention in three fourths thereof, as the one or the other Mode of Ratification may be proposed by the Congress; Provided that no Amendment which may be made prior to the Year One thousand eight hundred and eight shall in any Manner affect the first and fourth Clauses in the Ninth Section of the first Article; and that no State, without its Consent, shall be deprived of its equal Suffrage in the Senate.

ARTICLE VI

[1] All Debts contracted and Engagements entered into, before the Adoption of this Constitution, shall be as valid against the United States under this Constitution, as under the Confederation.

[2] This Constitution, and the Laws of the United States which shall be made in Pursuance thereof; and all Treaties made, or which shall be made, under the Authority of the United States, shall be the supreme Law of the Land; and the Judges in every State shall be bound thereby, any Thing in the Constitution or Laws of any State to the Contrary notwithstanding.

[3] The Senators and Representatives before mentioned, and the Members of the several State Legislatures, and all executive and judicial Officers, both of the United States and of the several States, shall be bound by Oath or Affirmation, to support this Constitution; but no religious Test shall ever be required as a Qualification to any Office or public Trust under the United States.

ARTICLE VII

The Ratification of the Conventions of nine States, shall be sufficient for the Establishment of this Constitution between the States so ratifying the Same.

Done in Convention by the Unanimous Consent of the States present, the Seventeenth Day of September in the Year of our Lord one thousand seven hundred and Eighty seven and of the Independence of the United States of America the Twelfth
   In Witness whereof We have hereunto subscribed our Names,

   [Thirty-nine signatures follow.]

* * *

Articles in Addition to, and in Amendment of, the Constitution of the United States

Amendment I

   Congress shall make no law respecting an establishment of religion, or prohibiting the free exercise thereof; or abridging the freedom of speech, or of the press; or the right of the people peaceably to assemble, and to petition the Government for a redress of grievances.

Amendment II

   A well regulated Militia, being necessary to the security of a free State, the right of the people to keep and bear Arms, shall not be infringed.

Amendment III

   No Soldier shall, in time of peace be quartered in any house, without the consent of the Owner, nor in time of war, but in a manner to be prescribed by law.

Amendment IV

   The right of the people to be secure in their persons, houses, papers, and effects, against unreasonable searches and seizures, shall not be violated, and no Warrants shall issue, but upon probable cause, supported by Oath or affirmation, and particularly describing the place to be searched, and the persons or things to be seized.

Amendment V

No person shall be held to answer for a capital, or otherwise infamous crime, unless on a presentment or indictment of a Grand Jury, except in cases arising in the land or naval forces, or in the Militia, when in actual service in time of War or public danger; nor shall any person be subject for the same offence to be twice put in jeopardy of life or limb; nor shall be compelled in any criminal case to be a witness against himself, nor be deprived of life, liberty, or property, without due process of law; nor shall private property be taken for public use, without just compensation.

Amendment VI

In all criminal prosecutions, the accused shall enjoy the right to a speedy and public trial, by an impartial jury of the State and district wherein the crime shall have been committed, which district shall have been previously ascertained by law, and to be informed of the nature and cause of the accusation; to be confronted with the witnesses against him; to have compulsory process for obtaining witnesses in his favor, and to have the Assistance of Counsel for his defense.

Amendment VII

In Suits at common law, where the value in controversy shall exceed twenty dollars, the right of trial by jury shall be preserved, and no fact tried by a jury shall be otherwise re-examined in any Court of the United States, than according to the rules of the common law.

Amendment VIII

Excessive bail shall not be required, nor excessive fines imposed, nor cruel and unusual punishments inflicted.

Amendment IX

The enumeration in the Constitution, of certain rights, shall not be construed to deny or disparage others retained by the people.

Amendment X

The powers not delegated to the United States by the Constitution, nor prohibited by it to the States, are reserved to the States respectively, or to the people.

* * *

Note on the Eleventh Amendment. In 1795—four years after the Bill of Rights was ratified—the Eleventh Amendment was added to the Constitution. It did not change the document substantively, but affirmed the dominant Founding-era understanding and corrected the Supreme Court's decision in *Chisholm v. Georgia*, 2 U.S. 419 (1793). The Eleventh Amendment reads as follows:

> The Judicial power of the United States shall not be construed to extend to any suit in law or equity, commenced or prosecuted against one of the United States by Citizens of another State, or by Citizens or Subjects of any Foreign State.

Note on the Twelfth Amendment. Congress proposed the Twelfth Amendment on December 9, 1803 and it was declared ratified on September 25, 1804. It was the last amendment in whose adoption the Founders played a role.

The amendment confirmed the earlier understanding that the qualifications of the Vice President were the same as for the President. It reformed somewhat the presidential election procedure, but did not change the essential roles of the state legislatures, the Electoral College, or Congress. The Twelfth Amendment reads as follows:

> The Electors shall meet in their respective states, and vote by ballot for President and Vice-President, one of whom, at least, shall not be an inhabitant of the same state with themselves; they shall name in their ballots the person voted for as President, and in distinct ballots the person voted for as Vice-President, and

they shall make distinct lists of all persons voted for as President, and of all persons voted for as Vice-President, and of the number of votes for each, which lists they shall sign and certify, and transmit sealed to the seat of the government of the United States, directed to the President of the Senate;—the President of the Senate shall, in the presence of the Senate and House of Representatives, open all the certificates and the votes shall then be counted;—the person having the greatest number of votes for President, shall be the President, if such number be a majority of the whole number of Electors appointed; and if no person have such majority, then from the persons having the highest numbers not exceeding three on the list of those voted for as President, the House of Representatives shall choose immediately, by ballot, the President. But in choosing the President, the votes shall be taken by states, the representation from each state having one vote; a quorum for this purpose shall consist of a member or members from two-thirds of the states, and a majority of all the states shall be necessary to a choice. And if the House of Representatives shall not choose a President whenever the right of choice shall devolve upon them, before the fourth day of March next following, then the Vice-President shall act as President, as in the case of the death or other constitutional disability of the President.—The person having the greatest number of votes as Vice-President, shall be the Vice-President, if such number be a majority of the whole number of Electors appointed, and if no person have a majority, then from the two highest numbers on the list, the Senate shall choose the Vice-President; a quorum for the purpose shall consist of two-thirds of the whole number of Senators, and a majority of the whole number shall be necessary to a choice. But no person constitutionally ineligible to the office of President shall be eligible to that of Vice-President of the United States.

INDEX

"abridge", definition, 184
abridge, 182
Abundans cautela non nocet, 28
Accessorius sequitur naturam sui principalis, 85
Adams, John, 11, 131
Adams, Sam, 218
Addison, Joseph, 183
admiralty, 153
advice and consent
 defined, 73, 74
advise, definition, 141
agent, definition, 32
agriculture, 104, 110
alienable rights, 212
allegiance, 195
ambassadors, 142, 154
Ambassadors Clause, 142
amendment process, 231
American Revolution, 3, 106, 144, 256
anachronism (as interpretive mistake), 33
Anglo-American constitutional tradition, 2
Anglo-American law, 2, 20, 42, 153, 198
Animus hominis est anima scripti, 27
Annapolis Convention, 4, 233, 234

Anti-Federalists
 defined, v
 dislike of Senate, 75
 values, 7
appellate jurisdiction, defined, 154
Apportionment Clause, 162, 180
Apportionment Clauses, 167
apportionment, legislative, 60
Appropriations Clause, 93, 170
Arabs, 36
Aristotle, 26
Armies Clause, 81, 94, 95, 108
Armorum appellatione non solum scuta et gladii et galeae, sed et fustes et lapides continentur., 193
Article I, organization, 59
Article III, organization, 151
Article IV, 97, 106
Article V, 231
Article V (amendments), 31
Articles of Confederation, vi, 2, 5, 10, 37, 38, 39, 50, 53, 68, 86, 109, 124, 135, 143, 151, 153, 212, 230
 war & foreign affairs power divided, 46
Articles of War, 108, 183, 206

assocation, right to. *See* First
   Amendment
atheism, 133, 168, 182
attainder, defined, 54
attorn, definition, 13
attorney, meaning agent, 13
ballot, definition, 129
Bankruptcy Clause, 99, 101, 115
Bedford, Gunning, Jr., 68
Bedford, Gunning, Sr., 68
Bible, 26
bicameralism, 60
bill of rights
   proposed in Congress, 6
Bill of Rights, 5, 6
   Anti-Federalists argue for, 162
   English, 2
   Federalists argue against, 162
   preamble, 163
   protection of natural rights, 164
   protection of privileges, 165
   ratification, 164
   the gentlemen's agreement, 163
Bill of Rights, New York, 172
bills of attainder, 177
Bills of Attainder, 54
bills of credit, 50
bills of pains and penalties, 177
Blackstone
   William, iii
Blackstone, William, 26
Bond v. United States, 145
Borrowing Clause, 93
Boumediene v. Bush, 196
Bowman v. Middleton, 178
Brennan, William J., Jr., 32
Breyer, Stephen, 32, 192
bribery, 222
Buchanan, George, 14
buildings, 111
Butler v. Craig, 178
Calder v. Bull, 56, 178, 208
call
   to Constitutional Convention, 4
Calvin, John, 14
Calvin's Case, 19
campaign finance laws, 118
Canada, 145

canals, 102
capital district, 40
Captures Clause, 107
cases and controversies, 152
censorial power, 9, 185, 191
census, 119
Chancellor (English), 75
Charles C. Steward Machine Co. v.
   Davis, 241
Charles II, 144
Charta est legatus mentis, 27
Chase, Samuel, 178, 208
Chiafolo v. Washington, 128
Chicago, Burlington & Quincy R.R.
   v. Chicago, 242
Chisholm v. Georgia, 44, 237
Cicero, Marcus Tullius, 14, 26
Civil War, 36
Coinage Clause, 83, 98, 115, 238
Coke
   Edward, 2, 208
Coke, Edward, 30
Coke, Sir Edward, 20, 85, 177, 225
Collins v. Yosemite Park, 112, 241
Comity Clause, 52
Commander in Chief Clause, 140,
   203
Commerce
   division of power, 50
   division of powers, 48
Commerce Clause, 91, 100, 115,
   179, 241
commerce, state power, 41
Commissioning Clause, 148
Commissions Clause, 139
Commonwealth v. Caton, 83
Compact theory of union, 35
compacts, distinguished from
   treaties, 143
concurrent jurisdiction, 40, 45
Confederation Congress, v, vi, 4
confederation, definition, 39
Confrontation Clause. *See* Sixth
   Amendment
Congress
   derivation of word, v
   First Federal, vi

Congress, Confederation, 5, 6, 27, 38, 68, 70, 89, 111, 173, 212, 227
Congress, Continental, 27, 38, 46, 65, 106, 108, 142, 157, 173, 206, 212, 226
Congress, Federal, 6, 16, 17, 34, 89, 163, 216, 224, 233
  discretion, amount of, 87
Congressional Emoluments Clause, 65, 66, 169
Connecticut, 2, 5, 19, 60, 62
conscription (soldiers), 108
constitutional amendments, 120
Constitutional Convention, 11
consuls, 142, 154
consuls, defined, 73
Continental Congress
  first, v
  second, vi
  Second, vi
Contracts Clause, 56, 171, 241
Contracts. obligation of, 56
convention
  constitutional, 4
convention for proposing amendments, 232
Convention for proposing Amendments, 232
Convention, Constitutional, 27
conventions
  intercolonial, 4
  of states, 229
  of the people, 229
conventions of states, 39
corporate charters, 102
corruption of blood, defined, 54
counterfeiting, 98, 109
court martial, 100, 107, 207
criminal law, 100, 104, 109
  federal jurisdiction, 109
Cromwell, Oliver, 98, 237
curative legislation, 177
Cushing, William, 13
Davie, William, 119
debt, 93
decentralized government, 11
Declaration of Independence, 36, 212

declaration of war, 107
declaration of war, purpose, 45
defamation, 67
defensive war, 197
Define and Punish Clause, 109
Delaware, 5, 19, 33, 60
Delegata potestas non potest delegari, 15
delegate, fiduciary duty not to, 17
DeLolme, Jean Louis, 9
DeLolme, Jean-Louis, 10, 21, 185, 191, 193
Democracy (as Founding-era value), 33
democracy, direct, 54
Derivativa potestas non potest esse major primitiva, 85
Designatio Justiciariorum est a Rege, Jurisdictio vero ordinaria a Lege, 157
Dickinson, John, 5, 17, 19, 23, 37, 69, 70, 185
direct tax, 18
diversity jurisdiction, 154
Dobbs v. Jackson Women's Health, 178
Domus sua est unicuique tutissimum refugium., 194
dormant commerce clause (Supreme Court doctrine), 50, 242
double jeopardy, 200
Dred Scott v. Sandford, 237, 238
dual sovereignty, 35
Due Process Clause, 176, 209
Due Process Clause (Fifth Amendment), 55, 68
Due Process Clause, limits, 177
due process of law, 172
due process of law, defined, 176
duties (financial charges), 48
duties, regulatory, 102
Eighteenth Amendment, 239, 240
Eighth Amendment, 201
ejusdem generis, 111
Election Clause
  opposition to, 118
election, presidential, 68

elections
    President, Vice President, 77
    presidential, 126
    presidential, counting electoral votes, 129
    Senate, 71
    Senators, 239
Elections Clause, 115, 116, 118, 127
elections, congressional, 41
elections, presidential, 42
Electoral College, 68, 72, 126, 128
Eleventh Amendment, 34, 44, 154, 238
Ellsworth
    Oliver, 90, 179, 188
Ellsworth, Oliver, 17, 19
eminent domain, 173
emolument, 120
emoluments, 169
Emoluments Clauses, 64
emoluments, defined, 65
Enclave Clause, 50, 81, 87, 109, 110, 115, 184, 241
enclaves, federal, 40
enemy combatants, trial, 207
enumerated powers
    fiduciary nature, 83
    interpretation, 82
    judiciary, 153
    limits, kinds of, 80
    of the President, 125
    president, 133
    President, 134, 138
Enumerated Powers
    congressional, 79
enumerated powers, judiciary, 152
equitable construction, 205, 208
Equitable Construction, 30
Equity, 153
equity (traditional body of law), 57
Errors of Interpretation, 31
Essex Result, 8
Establishment Clause. See First Amendment
Every man's house is his castle., 194
Ex Post Facto Clauses, 171, 177
Ex Post Facto Law, 55

ex post facto laws, 171, 212
Exceptio semper ultima ponenda est, 161
Exception strengthens the force of a law in cases not excepted, 213
Exception strengthens the force of a law in cases not excepted., 204, 206
excessive bail or fines. *See* Eighth Amendment
executive power
    variations on, 125
Executive Vesting Clause, 122
explusion from Congress, 221
export duties, 166
Expressio eorum quae tacite insunt nihil operatur, 86
external limitation, defined, 82
external limitation, definition, 161
extradition, 51
Federal Congress, v
federal courts, 120
federal enclaves, 51
Federal Farmer, 43, 185
federal function
    (modern legal term), 13, 40, 41, 42, 231
federal land, 40, 110, 112, 114
    treaty acquisition, 144
federal territories, 40
Federalism, 11
Federalist Papers, v, 118
Federalists
    defined, iv
    values, 7
fiduciaries, duties, 14
fiduciaries, duties of, 15
fiduciary
    duty not to delegate, 60
fiduciary duties, 165
Fiduciary Government, 12
fiduciary, defined, 14
Fifteenth Amendment, 238
Fifth Amendment, 171, 176, 178, 200, 203, 206, 208, 242
    grand jury, 31
First Amemdment
    "prohibiting", definition, 190

First Amendment, 204
  "speech" and "press" distinguished, 183
  anonymity of author, 186
  assembly, 190
  association, 191
  blasphemous speech, 183
  campaign finance laws, 185
  censorial power, 185
  Establishment Clause, 182
  Free Exercise Clause, 182
  free speech, scope, 183
  freedom of speech, as natural right, 183
  freedom of the press, 184
  instructions, 191
  lewd speech, 183
  overview, 180
  petition, 190
  petition, right to, 9
  pornography, 187
  press licencing, 187
  press, blasphemy, 188
  press, definition, 185
  press, freedom of, 9
  press, libel, 187
  press, prior restraint, 189
  press, seditious libel, 188
  religion clauses, 181
  right of association, 180
  rights often exercised together, 180
  scandalum magnatum, inapplicable in U.S., 184
  Sedition Act of 1798, 189
  slander, 183
  slander, limits on, 184
  speech, freedom of, 9
  treasonous speech, 183
  use of the "people", 37
First Continental Congress, 10, 233
foreign affairs
  division of power under Constitution, 46
foreign affairs power, state, 45
foreign affairs powers, 141
foreign diplomats, 154

Foreign Emoluments Clause, 65, 120, 149, 169
Founders
  common background, 17
  defined, v
founding generation
  defined, v
Fourteenth Amendment, 178, 209, 238
  Due Process Clause, 242
Fourth Amendment, 200, 204
  use of "the people", 37
Framers, 23, 34
  defined, iv
free exercise of religion. See First Amendment
freedom of speech. See First Amendment
freedom of the press. See First Amendment
French (language), 26
Fugitive Slave Clause, 51, 116, 179
Full Faith and Credit Clause, 51, 115
Fundamental Orders of Connecticut, 2
gender, Constitution neutral on, 64
General Welfare Clause, 28, 82, 95, 213
  as a limitation, 92
Generalibus specialia derogant and Generalia sunt praeponenda singularibus, 47
Generalibus specialia derogant, and Generalia sunt praeponenda singularibus., 226
Georgia, 5, 33, 60, 127, 179, 276
Germans, 36
Gerry, Elbridge, v, 5, 6, 102
Gibbons v. Ogden, 101
Gideon v. Wainwright, 201
Gitlow v. New York, 242
Gorham, Nathaniel, 4, 23, 70, 158
Graham, Catherine Macaulay, 65
grand jury, 200
grants
  of powers, 14
Greece, 2

Greece, ancient, 26, 92, 105
Guarantee Clause, 41, 53, 105, 116
Haaland v. Brackeen, 38
habeas corpus, 18, 53, 106, 196, 241
  suspension by President, 141
Habeas Corpus Act, 2
Ham v. McClaws, 31, 172, 178, 208
Hamilton
  Alexander, 57
Hamilton, Alexander, v, 4, 33, 43, 71, 86, 94, 118, 125, 126, 131
  Report on Manfacturers, 95
Helvering v. Davis, 96, 241
Henry I
  charter of, 1
Henry, Patrick, 37, 214, 218
high crimes, defined, 223
high Misdemeanors, 222
Hodel v. Indiana, 104
Holy Roman Empire, 128
Home Bldg & Loan Assn v. Blaisdell, 241
House of Representatives
  in general, 61
  prerogatives, 66, 67
  rule of decision, 68
  size, 63
House of Representatives, qualifications, 63
House of Representatives, term, 62
Humble Petition and Advice
  early English constitution, 2
Humble Petition and Advice (temporary English constitution), 237
Hume, David, 26
immigration
  division of power, 48
immigration, state power, 45, 46
immunity, defined, 52
impartiality
  fiduciary duty of, 16
impartiality, fiduciary duty of, 165
impeachment, 68, 69, 221
  grounds, 222
  punishment, 223
Impeachment Clause, 148

Implied Sovereign Authority, theory of, 38
imposts, 102, 166
inalienable rights, 212
incidental powers, 83, 86
  President, 135
Inclusio unius est exclusio alterius, 29, 218
Inclusio unius est exclusio alterius., 213
Independence (Founding-era value), 16
Indian Commerce Clause, 50, 102
Indians, taxed & not taxed, 167
indictment, 200, 242
Inferior Courts Clause, 155
inherent sovereign authority, 217
initiatives and referenda, 54
Inns of Court, 17
inspection laws, 49
Instrument of Government
  early English constitution, 2
Instrument of Government (Sweden), 237
Instrument of Government (temporary English constitution), 237
Intellectual Property Clause, 52, 81, 99
intent of the makers, 24, 83
intent-based construction, 83
internal limitation, defined, 80
internal limitation, definition, 161
Interpretatio talis in ambiguis semper fienda est, ut evitetur inconveniens et absurdum., 225
interstate comity, 51
invasion, 45
Iredell
  James, 145, 209
Iredell, James, 12, 44
Italian (language), 26
Italians, 36
Jay, John, v, 56, 74, 109
Jefferson, Thomas, 131, 144
Judicial Review, 156
Judicial Vesting Clause, 151

judiciary
  advisory opinions, 152
  enumerated powers, 152, 153
  terms of office, 152
Judiciary
  limitations, 157
jurisdiction stripping, 157
jury
  trial by, 18
jury trial, 155, 158, 162, 208, 242,
  See also Seventh Amendment
  slander suits, 184
Jury trial, 198
jury trial, location, 198
jury trial, military, 206
jury, grand, 208
jus
  meanings of, 8
Kamper v. Hawkins, 31
Kelo v. City of New London, 174
King, Rufus, 23, 43, 70, 158
Kleppe v. New Mexico, 114
Koreans, 36
Korematsu v. United States, 242
land claims, state, 97
Lansing, John, 176
Lansing, John, Jr., 95
Latin (language), 27
Latin language, 26
law (as opposed to equity), 153
law merchant, 97, 102
law merchant, defined, 100
law of the land (due process), 176
Lee, Charles, 155
legal tender, defined, 98
letter of attorney, 13
limitations, kinds of, 161
Livy (Titus Livius), 26
Locke
  John, 183
Locke, John, 3, 7, 26
Louis XIV, 144
Machiavelli, Niccolo, 26
Madison
  James, 216, 230, 239
Madison, James, v, 6, 9, 18, 33, 43,
  49, 66, 81, 86, 91, 99, 131, 143,
  163, 164, 172, 176, 199, 214,
  219, 225, 227
Magna Carta, 1, 3, 157, 173, 176,
  178
mala in se, 109
mala prohibita, 109
Manfield, 1st Earl of (William
  Murray), 19
manner of election, 117
Manner of holding Elections, 117,
  127
Mansfield, 1st Earl of (William
  Murray), 196
manufacturing, 104, 110
Marbury v. Madison, 29, 156, 157
marque and reprisal, 69
Marque and Reprisal, 107
Marshall, John, 29, 36, 43, 86, 101,
  156, 158
martial law, 141
Maryland, 5, 49, 60, 70
Mason, George, v, 5, 49, 91, 144,
  145, 199
Massachusetts, 2, 5, 8, 13, 43, 53,
  60, 64, 98, 134, 135, 154, 157,
  176, 218, 229
Massachusetts Charter of Rights
  and Liberties, 2
Mayflower Compact, 2
McCulloch v. Maryland, 36
McDonald v. Chicago, 192
McDonald, Forrest, 6
Mercer, John Francis, 145
Migration or Importation Clause,
  179
military personnel
  Bill of Rights, 203
Military Regulation Clause, 109
Military Regulations Clause, 108,
  203
military tribunal, 106, 141
militia, 48, 104
Militia Clause (calling forth), 106
Militia Training Clause, 106
Militia, Calling Forth Clause, 81
militia, training, 81
Milton, John, 186
misdemeanor

high, 18
Missouri v. Holland, 145
Monaghan, Henry, 31
money, 69, 98, 101
Money, 50
money bills, 170
Money, paper, 50
Montesquieu, Baron, 26
Morris, Gouverneur, 21, 71, 74, 75, 113
Mutiny Act (Great Britain), 108
Nat'l Fed. of Independent Business v. Sebelius, 85, 242
National Labor Relations Board v. Noel Canning, 139
NATO (North Atlantic Treaty Organization), 39
natural rights, 7, 211
 not privileges or immunities, 52
natural-born citizen, 132
 definition, 132
Naturalization Clause, 80, 115
navigation, 101
navigation, congressional power, 101
Navy Clause, 94, 95, 108
Nazi saboteurs case, 208
Necessary and Expedient Clause, 137
necessary and proper
 as legal term, 18
Necessary and Proper Cause
 unenumerated rights, 209
Necessary and Proper Clause, 29, 94, 101, 103, 107, 108, 114, 137, 146, 213
 in general, 84
 limits, 86
 proper, meaning, 86
needful, 111
needful Buildings, 87
Nemo debet bis puniri pro uno delicto., 200
Nemo tenetur armare adversarium contra se., 201
Nemo tenetur seipsum accusare., 201
Netherlands, 10, 145

New Hampshire, 6, 60, 219
New Jersey, 5, 33, 60, 61, 64, 157, 239
New York, i, v, 4, 6, 33, 43, 56, 60, 95, 119, 134, 154, 157, 171, 172, 214, 219, 233
New York City, 6
New York State Rifle & Pistol Association Inc. v. Bruen, 33
New York Times v. Sullivan, 187
New York v. United States, 243
Nineteenth Amendment, 239
Ninth Amendment, 190, 209, 213
 and treaties, 145
 as rule of construction, 29
 use of "the people", 37
North Carolina, i, v, 6, 12, 28, 49, 60, 119, 145, 179, 214, 219
Northwest Ordinance, 68, 112
Nova constitutio futuris formam imponere debet, non praeteritis, 56
nullification, 35
oath of office, 133, 168
Obamacare (Affordable Care Act), 85, 242
offensive, 197
officers, differences, 148
Oldknow v. Wainright, 19
Opinion Clause, 138
original intent, 25
original jurisdiction, defined, 154
original legal force, 208
original meaning, 24, 25
original public meaning, 24
original understanding, 24, 25
Origination Clause, 68
paper money, 98
pardon, presidential, 137
Parliament, v, 11, 16, 19, 29, 54, 60, 64, 67, 69, 75, 106, 108, 125, 132, 133, 170, 181, 187, 192, 199, 202
Parsons, Theophilus, 8
patents, 53
Pendleton
 Edmund, 37, 156
Pendleton, Edmund, 17, 43

Pennsylvania, 5, 9, 19, 43, 60, 111, 157, 230
Perpich v. Dep't of Defense, 106
petition, 190
Petition of Right, 1
petition, right to. *See* First Amendment
Philadelphia, i, ii, iv, vi, 4, 6, 233
Pinckney, Charles, 107, 152
piracy, 109
Plessy v. Ferguson, 238
Plutarch, 26
police power, 40, 240
Popular Grant theory of union, 35
Port Preference Clause, 103, 166
post road, defined, 99
Postal Clause, 80, 94, 95, 99, 110
power of attorney, 13
powers, meaning of, 8
powers/rights
  when interchangeable, 9
Praetextu liciti non debet admitti illicitum, 85
preamble, 20, 29
presentment, 200
President
  appointment power, 138
  calling Congress into session, 136
  incidental power to instruct, 139
  limits on, 147
  qualifications, 131
  salary, 132
  term of office, 126
  treaties, 141
Presidential Emolument Clause, 133
Presidential Emoluments Clause, 65, 169
presidential succession, 120
press. *See* First Amendment
principal
  employer of fiduciary, 14, 16
Printz v. United States, 243
privilege, 196
privilege, defined, 52
Privileges and Immunities Clause, 25, 52, 116, 209

Property Clause, 106, 112
  as basis for spending, 96
Protectio trahit subjectionem, & subjectio protectione, 195
provide for, 95
proviso, defined, 81
public ministers, 73
public Ministers, 142, 154
public ministers, defined, 73
Public Trust, 12
public use, 175
quam diu se bene gesserit, 152
quasi-external limitation, defined, 81
quasi-external limitation, definition, 161
Qui sentit commodum, sentire debet et onus, 172
Qui sentit commodum, sentire debet et onus., 194
Quirin, ex parte, 208
Randolph, Edmund, 5, 17, 19, 43, 69, 144, 199, 216
Randolph, Peyton, 18
ratification
  by 9 states, 230
  nine state requirement, 37
Ratifiers, 12, 24, 33, 34, 43
  defined, iv
Recess Appointments Clause, 139
Reed, George, 5
reformation (legal remedy), 30
regulating commerce, defined, 100
regulating commerce. meaning, 98
religion, freedom of, 25
removal by President, 224
removal from office, 221
republican government, 10, 53, 170
  definition of, 10
Republican Government, 10
Reserved state powers
  itemization by Federalists, 40
retroactive laws, 170
Revenue bills as tax bills, 69
Rhode Island, i, v, 2, 6, 34, 43, 44, 60, 62, 67, 119, 214, 219
right to counsel. *See* Sixth Amendment

right, meaning of, 7
Roman Catholic Church, 128, 145
Rome, 2, 193
Rome, ancient, 9, 10, 14, 26, 36, 52, 54, 55, 98, 105, 185, 193, 203
rule against grants *in futuro*, 152
rule of law, 170
rules of construction, 226
Rules of Construction, 27
Rutledge
    John, 74
Rutledge, John, 17, 19
salaries, 120, 132
searches and seizures. *See* Fourth Amendment
secession, 35, 36
Second Amendment, 192
    "infringe", defined, 192
    use of "the people", 37
Sedition Act of 1798, 189
seigniorage, 98
self-incrimination, 200
Senate
    election, 71
    equality among states unamendable, 235
    executive powers, 73
    in general, 70
    prerogatives, 72
    qualifications, 71
    revenue bills, 71
    rule of decision, 71
    size, 70
    term, 70
    voting, 71
Seneca, Lucius Annaeus (the Younger), 14
separation of powers, 75
Sergeant, John Dickinson, 68
Seventeenth Amendment, 60, 239
Seventh Amendment, 155, 159, 198, 202
Sherman, Roger, 158, 164, 179
single subject rule, 170
Sixteenth Amendment, 239
Sixth Amendment, 159, 198, 201, 204, 206
Slaughter House Cases, 238

slavery
    believed to be dying out, 179
    slave trade, 179
slaves, 51
social contract theory, 211
Somersett v. Stewart, 196
Somersett, James, 196
sources
    standard and other, iii
South Carolina, 6, 31, 60, 62, 127, 157, 179, 208, 219
sovereign immunity, 42
special limitation, defined, 81
Speech and Debate Clause, 67, 183, 191
speedy trial. *See* Sixth Amendment
spending power, 241
Stamp Act, 181
Stamp Act Congress, v
Stamp Tax, 92
state constitutions, 205
state land claims, 112
state power, congressional veto, 115
State powers, reserved, 40
state powers, reserved, reasons, 40
state sovereignty, limits, 45
Steele, John, 28, 119
strict construction, 84
Stromberg v. California, 242
structure
    of Constitution, 19
Stuart v. Laird, 155
subject, person in allegiance, 195, 196
Substantive Due Process, 178
Supremacy Clause, 29, 57, 146, 159
Supreme Court
    implied sovereign authority theory, 38
Suspension Clause, 106, 141
sympathy (Founding-era value), 61, 63

Tacitus, Cornelius, 26
Take Care Clause, 138, 140
    and treaties, 146
Takings Clause, 172
Takings Clause, scope, 172

tariff, 91
tariffs, 102
tax
  definition, 90
  direct, 91
  direct, defined, 91
  duty, defined, 92
  excise, defined, 92
  indirect, 91
  indirect, defined, 91
  land tax laws, 91
Taxation Clause, 81, 90, 95, 102, 179, 241
taxes, direct, 167
tender laws, 11, 50, 51
Tenth Amendment, 190, 217
  and treaties, 145
  as rule of construction, 29
  use of "the people", 37
Territories and Property Clause, 106, 112
Territories Clause, 102, 106, 112, 184
Territory Clause, 97
The Federalist Papers, 95
Third Amendment, 193, 194
Thirteenth Amendment, 238
three-fifths compromise, 62
three-fifths rule, 167
Thucydides, 26
Thucydides (Greek historican), 92
time limits for amendments, 234
Times, Places and Manner Clause, 116, 118
Times, Places, and Manner Clause, 127
  opposition to, 118
Times XE "Elections Clause" , Places, and Manner Clause (Elections Clause), 115
titles of nobility, 170
tobacco, 49
tonnage, 49
Tories, 3, 176
transportation, congressional power, 101
travel, right to, 53
treason, 81, 159, 162, 222

Treason Act of 1351, 194
Treason Clause, 109, 194
treaty
  distinguished from compact, 46
  whether self-executing, 145
Treaty Clause, 102, 107, 113, 141, 143
Treaty of Dover 1670, 144
Treaty of Paris 1783, 144
Treaty Power
  and Bill of Rights, 146
treaty, distinguished from compact, 143
Trump, Donald J., 222
Tucker, Thomas Tudor, 67
Twelfth Amendment, 75, 76, 121, 128, 238
Twentieth Amendment, 121, 239
Twenty-Fifth Amendment, 121, 239
Twenty-First Amendment, 239
Twenty-Fourth Amendment, 240
Twenty-Second Amendment, 126, 239
Twenty-Seventh Amendment, 164, 234, 239
Twenty-Sixth Amendment, 240
Twenty-Third Amendment, 240
U.S. Steel Corp. v. Multistate Tax Comm'n, 46
unalienable rights, 212
unamendable provisions, 234
unenumerated rights, 208
Uniformity Clause, 93, 166
uniformity rule, 102
United States v. Belmont, 143
United States v. Brown, 55
United States v. Butler, 96, 241
United States v. Curtiss-Wright, 241
United States v. Curtiss-Wright Export Corp, 38
United States v. Darby Lumber, 241
United States v. Pink, 143
United States v. South-Eastern Underwriters Ass'n, 241
Vattel, Emer de, 73, 132

Verba aliquid operari debent—
   debent intellegi ut aliquid
   operantur, 28
Verba intentioni non e contra
   debent inservire, 28
Vermont, i, 27, 34
veto, presidential, 133, 134, 135
Vice President, 59, 75, 129
   election, 72
   qualifications, 75, 131
   term of office, 126
   votes in case of tie, 76
Virginia, i, v, 2, 4, 5, 6, 18, 33, 37,
   43, 45, 49, 57, 60, 144, 156, 158,
   198, 204, 214, 216, 218, 219
Virginia Declaration of Rights, 2
war
   articles of, 108
   declaration of, 70
   defensive, 105
   division of powers, 47
   offensive, 105, 107

war power, defensive, 45
war power, offensive, 46
war power, state, 45
Warren, v
   Mercy Otis, v
Washington
   D.C., 6
Washington, George, 4, 216
Webster, Noah, 2, 13, 37, 114, 195
weights and measures, 69, 98
Weights and Measures Clause, 98,
   101
Whig, 7, 83, 144
Whigs, 3, 64
Wickard v. Filburn, 241
Wilson, James, 3, 18, 43, 144, 217
Winthrop, John, 42
women, 64
Worrell, John, 18
writ, definition, 195
Wythe, George, 4, 17
Yates, Robert, 4, 95

About the Author

Robert G. Natelson is one of the nation's top constitutional scholars. His published research has been cited repeatedly by U.S. Supreme Court justices and by state supreme courts. Formerly a professor of Constitutional Law and Constitutional History at the University of Montana, he is currently Senior Fellow in Constitutional Jurisprudence at the Independence Institute in Denver. His background also includes extensive experience in business, politics, print and broadcast journalism, and the practice of law.

A fervent outdoorsman, he and his wife Betty divide their time between Colorado and Montana.

www.ingramcontent.com/pod-product-compliance
Lightning Source LLC
Chambersburg PA
CBHW030103170426
43198CB00009B/469